CLOSING SYSCO

Industrial Decline in Atlantic Canada's Steel City

Lachlan MacKinnon

Closing Sysco presents a history of deindustrialization and working-class resistance in the Cape Breton steel industry between 1945 and 2001. The Sydney Steel Works is at the heart of this story, having existed in tandem with Cape Breton's larger coal operations since the early twentieth century. The book explores the multifaceted nature of deindustrialization; the internal politics of the steelworkers' union; the successful efforts to nationalize the mill in 1967; the years in transition under public ownership; and the confrontations over health, safety, and environmental degradation in the 1990s and 2000s. *Closing Sysco* moves beyond the moment of closure to trace the cultural, historical, and political ramifications of deindustrialization that continue to play out in post-industrial Cape Breton Island. A significant intervention into the international literature on deindustrialization, this study pushes scholarship beyond the bounds of political economy and cultural change to begin tackling issues of bodily health, environment, and historical memory in post-industrial places.

The experiences of the men and women who were displaced by the decline and closure of Sydney Steel are central to this book. Featuring interviews with former steelworkers, office employees, managers, politicians, and community activists, these one-on-one conversations reveal both the human cost of industrial closure and the lingering after-effects of deindustrialization.

(Studies in Atlantic Canada History)

LACHLAN MACKINNON is an assistant professor in the Department of Humanities at Cape Breton University.

STUDIES IN ATLANTIC CANADA HISTORY

Editors: John G. Reid and Peter L. Twohig

This monograph series focuses on the history of Atlantic Canada, inter-preting the scope of this field in a way that is deliberately inclusive and accommodating. As well as studies that deal wholly with any aspect of the history of the Atlantic region (or part thereof), the series extends to neighbouring geographical areas that are considered in conjunction with or in parallel with a portion of Atlantic Canada. Atlantic Canada's oceanic or global relationships are also included, and studies from any thematic or historiographical perspective are welcome.

BOOKS IN THE SERIES

Meaghan Elizabeth Beaton, *The Centennial Cure: Commemoration, Identity, and Cultural Capital in Nova Scotia during Canada's 1967 Centennial Celebrations*

Jeffers Lennox, *Homelands and Empires: Indigenous Spaces, Imperial Fictions, and Competition for Territory in Northeastern North America, 1690–1763*

Lachlan MacKinnon, *Closing Sysco: Industrial Decline in Atlantic Canada's Steel City*

Closing Sysco

*Industrial Decline in Atlantic
Canada's Steel City*

LACHLAN MACKINNON

UNIVERSITY OF TORONTO PRESS
Toronto   Buffalo   London

ISBN 978-1-4875-0591-2 (cloth)   ISBN 978-1-4875-3296-3 (EPUB)
ISBN 978-1-4875-2402-9 (paper)   ISBN 978-1-4875-3295-6 (PDF)

Studies in Atlantic Canada History

Library and Archives Canada Cataloguing in Publication

Title: Closing Sysco : industrial decline in Atlantic Canada's steel city / Lachlan
MacKinnon.
Names: MacKinnon, Lachlan, 1988– author.
Series: Studies in Atlantic Canada history.
Description: Series statement: Studies in Atlantic Canada history | Includes
bibliographical references and index.
Identifiers: Canadiana (print) 20190204044 | Canadiana (ebook) 20190204753 |
ISBN 9781487524029 (softcover) | ISBN 9781487505912 (hardcover) |
ISBN 9781487532956 (PDF) | ISBN 9781487532963 (EPUB)
Subjects: LCSH: Sydney Steel Corporation. | LCSH: Deindustrialization –
Nova Scotia – Sydney – History – 20th century. | LCSH: Deindustrialization –
Social aspects – Nova Scotia – Sydney. | LCSH: Plant shutdowns – Nova Scotia –
Sydney – History – 20th century. | LCSH: Steel industry and trade – Nova Scotia –
Sydney – History – 20th century. | LCSH: Steel industry and trade – Nova Scotia –
Sydney Employees – Social conditions – 20th century. |
LCSH: Sydney (N.S.) – Social conditions – 20th century.
Classification: LCC HD3616.C24 S936 2019 | DDC 338.9716/95—dc23

This book has been published with the help of a grant from the Federation for the
Humanities and Social Sciences, through the Awards to Scholarly Publications
Program using funds provided by the Social Sciences and Humanities Research
Council of Canada.

University of Toronto Press acknowledges the financial assistance to its publishing
program of the Canada Council for the Arts and the Ontario Arts Council, an
agency of the Government of Ontario.

Canada Council   **Conseil des Arts**
for the Arts   **du Canada**

ONTARIO ARTS COUNCIL
CONSEIL DES ARTS DE L'ONTARIO
an Ontario government agency
un organisme du gouvernement de l'Ontario

Funded by the   Financé par le
Government   gouvernement
of Canada   du Canada

Canada

For Jim McCarron.
Whose life, work, and memory inform these pages and
influence those who remain.

Jim McCarron. Photograph provided by Tommy McCarron.

Contents

Contents

Illustrations

Tables

Acknowledgments

Many people have helped to bring this book to publication. Steven High was an indispensable thesis adviser, mentor, and friend. Ron Rudin, Barbara Lorenzkowski, Craig Heron, and Cynthia Hammond each provided their time, expertise, and generous comments on the manuscript.

The McCarron family – Tommy, Gerry, Bobby, and Lorraine have all generously walked me through their memories. Thanks to each of you for your willingness to answer my endless questions about growing up as members of a steelmaking family in Sydney and working at the plant.

I am also eternally grateful to all of those who shared their stories. Dave Ervin, Elizabeth Beaton, Fred James, Bernie Britten, Mickey Campbell, Adrian Murphy, John Campbell, Fabian Smith, Joe Legge, Charles MacDonald, Manning MacDonald, John Hamm, Sheldon Andrews, George MacNeil, Bill McNeil, John Murphy, Dave Nalepa, Greg MacLeod, Teresa MacNeil, Scott Stewart, Gordie Gosse, Don MacGillivray, Joel MacLean, Alana MacNeil, Debbie Ouellette, and Juanita McKenzie all contributed to this manuscript through their accounts.

I also want to offer thanks to the staff at the Beaton Institute Archives at Cape Breton University for their help in identifying and retrieving documents, audio files, images, maps, and many other sources that are cited within these pages. Anne Marie MacNeil and Jane Arnold are especially appreciated for their extensive knowledge of the archival holdings, their constant care for material and requests, and their knowledge of Cape Breton. This project could not have happened without the resources of the Beaton Institute.

My appreciation goes out to all of my friends. Kris Archibald, Andy Parnaby, and Don Nerbas have likely heard each of these chapters in depth over copious amounts of coffee – thanks for always helping to talk it through.

A special thanks to Steven Wadden for his photography and his interest in the project – coming from the same generational space, it's interesting that we started asking many of the same questions from different angles.

To my father and mother, Richard MacKinnon and Joan Weeks, thank you for all the help and support during this project and many others.

I would also like to thank the Social Sciences and Humanities Research Council of Canada, the School for Graduate Studies, the Faculty of Arts and Science, and the Department of History at Concordia University, the Canada Research Chairs program, the Dan David Foundation, and Museum Nova Scotia for supporting this research.

Thank you, Sheralynne, for everything. And to Landon and Addison, for being you.

CLOSING SYSCO

Industrial Decline in Atlantic Canada's Steel City

Introduction

Cape Breton Island, a 10,311-square-kilometre rocky outcropping on the Atlantic coast – connected to mainland Nova Scotia only by a short causeway traversing the Strait of Canso – has commanded its share of historical attention. Its Indigenous history, colonial Louisbourg, and the industrial labour conflicts that erupted in the late nineteenth and early twentieth centuries have proven fertile ground for researchers from across Canada and beyond. The island's unique culture, influenced by centuries of interaction between Indigenous and settler communities, continues to shape conversations about class, identity, heritage, and memory.

The place of Cape Breton and its residents within the Canadian landscape of marketable tourist destinations has likewise prompted discussion and debate among historians and folklorists. But none of these things speak to my first-hand experiences growing up in Sydney, the island's largest city, in the aftermath of the mine and mill closures that rocked the local economy between 2000 and 2001. Nowhere, outside of the annual Celtic Colours music festival and summer visits to the Feis an Eilein square dance, did I experience the spontaneous fiddle music or Highland jigs that are associated with the island in Canadian popular culture. Nor do I recall the belching smokestacks of the city's steel mill, often described in oral history accounts, that coloured its air in the years before the plant was modernized in the late 1980s. The historical moment in which I grew up was defined wholly by what came before – be that an anti-modern Celticity or some ill-defined industrial "Golden Age" that I was only aware of in terms of its palpable absence.

Coming of age among the ephemera of steelmaking and coal mining, my generation was faced with the unspooling of some great fabric that, we were told, had stitched our communities together through the struggles of the coal miners, labour conflicts like that which saw

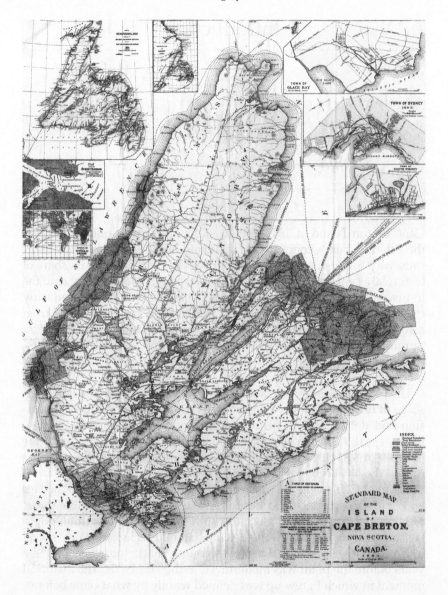

0.1 Cape Breton Island, 1903. Standard Map of the Island of Cape Breton, Nova Scotia, Canada, 1903. Map by Nation Publishing Company. Map 813. Beaton Institute, Cape Breton University.

William Davis murdered by "The Company" in 1925, and the hundreds of men whose lives were taken from them by underground explosions, rock falls, or accidents at the steel mill. My grandfather, like the grandfathers of many friends, was a coal miner in the New Waterford pits; my wife's family all worked for Sydney Steel and Dominion Steel and Coal Company before that. But to me as a teenager, those worlds seemed – in many ways – as distant as the Gaelic of my great-grandparents or the fiddle music and step dancing that existed somewhere else on the periphery of my cultural milieu.

My world, what Marx might have called the material conditions of post-industrial Cape Breton, was shaped by other forces. Out of a cohort of approximately 200 students, my graduating class from 2006 lost several to suicide or drug overdose – trends that have continued and worsened among the island's youth in the decades since. Poverty was there, too – though it was less visible among my largely middle-class circle of friends. In the shadow of mill and mine closures, the problems deepened. Child poverty in the city ballooned to a rate of approximately 33 per cent by 2014 – the worst in Atlantic Canada.[1] Unemployment hovered consistently between 14 and 20 per cent, and we were all keenly aware that our futures likely lay "out West," a familiar story for Maritimers who have long existed as a reserve labour pool for other regions.[2] Our notions of escape were only cemented as we watched the periodic arrival of Tar Ponds tour buses, filled with economic development staff or other professionals, who stepped out into Whitney Pier only briefly to gawk at the marred landscape and scattered working-class homes adjacent to the Sydney Steel site.[3] We, literally and figuratively, were living among the ruins of the industrial past and alongside the ruination that its collapse had produced.[4]

The same year that I graduated from high school, the National Film Board of Canada released a film detailing the prescription pill crisis that had taken hold in the nearby coal town of Glace Bay.[5] It might as well have been billed as a cautionary tale; it represented a warning for those who might stay of the depths to which a community can fall when its economic heart stills. The film, *Cottonland*, traces the emergence and contagion of oxycodone abuse – an opioid known as "Oxy," "hillbilly heroin," or "Ox" – that killed twenty-one people in Cape Breton during an eighteen-month period in the early 2000s.[6] The powerful painkiller, familiar in deindustrializing and post-industrial areas from Cape Breton to the hills of Appalachia, was prescribed to laid-off steelworkers or coal miners before trickling down to the street-level black market through their children or grandchildren.

Was it Steve Earle's post-industrial "OxyContin Blues" that held Cape Breton in its grip during these fraught years?[7] Or were we a group of immiserated and alienated proletariat-turned-lumpenproletariat, struggling with the class dimensions of our dispossession?[8] Perhaps we were experiencing the second part of the theorized "half-life" of the industrial world; it fell to my peers in this industrial interregnum to bear witness to the aftermath of a collapse that would continue to affect each of us long after mill gates were chained and locked or the mines sealed and flooded.[9] Each of these possible positionalities, famously cemented through former Prime Minister Stephen Harper's oft-cited assessment that Atlantic Canadians were broadly suffering from a "culture of defeat," have emerged from an unfolding process of global capitalism that had been termed "deindustrialization."[10] Recognizing the broad contours of this process is necessary for understanding the present conditions of Cape Breton Island and other deindustrialized locales around the world, and oral history – cutting to the heart of localized experiences of loss – reveal how these processes continue to influence the men and women who experienced it directly.

While the oral history accounts that inform my research give the analysis of deindustrialization in Sydney a strikingly local flavour – mediated through economic, cultural, environmental, and social frameworks – these stories converge with those found within post-industrial areas across Canada and around the world. Indeed, deindustrialization is not only a local process. It is part and parcel of the Schumpeterian "creative destruction" that has long been used to forestall criticism of stagnating blue-collar wages or geographical capital relocation. In cities like Sydney, the destructive nature of such processes is always more visible than the creative – doubly so for rural resource hubs or other single-industry towns. Correspondingly, there has emerged a great sense of cultural displacement and working-class *invisibility* that frequently results in political polarization. Since 2015, we have witnessed the collapse of neoliberal pragmatic politics as anti-establishment candidates on the left and the right now appeal directly to an abandoned working class that finds itself marginalized by an increasingly globalized world and forty years of "bipartisan" laissez-faire doctrine.

The popularity of Labour's Jeremy Corbyn in the United Kingdom and the appeal of left-Democrats like Bernie Sanders and Alexandria Ocasio-Cortez in the United States indicate that the solutions offered by so-called 'third way' politics are quickly becoming untenable.[11] The Thatcherite mantra "There is no alternative" has been viscerally rejected as a dispossessed electorate casts about for *any* other solution. Right-wing nationalism offers another possibility, made starkly clear in the consecutive elections of Viktor Orbán in Hungary, Jair Bolsonaro in Brazil, and – of course – Donald Trump in the United States. In an interesting break from Republican rhetoric, Trump has frequently castigated free trade in both word – throughout the 2016 campaign – and in action through the establishment of several new tariffs. Indeed, these sorties against the bastion of free trade orthodoxy are not entirely dissimilar from the type of rhetoric one might have heard marshalled by anti-deindustrialization activists during the 1980s – most notably in the signalled desire to move away from NAFTA and the erection of tariff barriers for international steel and aluminium. Likewise, the "Make America Great Again" sloganeering brings a host of racialized, gendered, and class-based hierarchies openly into the public sphere, but so, too, does it reveal the real perception that a moment of working-class achievement has been lost and is in need of recovery. As with any Golden Age, the historical moment described therein was fraught, exclusionary, and based on an array of other forms of privilege, but to dismiss its appeal as purely nostalgic and misguided would be a disservice to the working-class men and women who continue to suffer from its absence. In other words, there really was something about the postwar years – with their high rates of union density, wide availability of blue-collar work, and increasing possibilities for social mobility, that continues to command a great sense of longing for those who have experienced its loss.

We might think of deindustrialization both as a process and as an unfolding set of relationships that connect those who are directly affected and the affecting forces of the market, political sphere, and ecology. These relationships are by no means one-dimensional, unalterable, or inevitable, but are shaped through forms of resistance, struggle, acquiescence, and acceptance. In his history of Hamilton, Ontario, Craig Heron describes both resistance and protest, but some of his most poignant insights come from the exploration of "the much quieter heroism of families, neighbours, gangs of friends, and groups of workmates who used every resource available to them to fashion daily lives that would give them a modicum of security and at least a small amount of pleasure – lives that would lead to a profound sense of personal decency and respectability."[12] With this in mind, it is important to recognize that the economic and bodily violence that accompanies deindustrialization do not *wholly* characterize the lives of those who remain in post-industrial regions. The men and women who participated in the research project that formed the basis for this book, while deeply impacted by the operation and closure of the Sydney Steel Corporation, are also a reminder that life continues after disruption.

Visible in their accounts are the multiple ways in which human beings experience the coming apart of a societal form: in this instance, the disassembly of a geography known at one time as "industrial Cape Breton" and its reconstitution as something different. Such disruptions are, of course, not new. Industrial Cape Breton was itself the product of a purposeful and continuing colonial project that sought the disruption of Unama'ki and the displacement of its Mi'kmaq people. The processes by which these transformations occur are vast and imprecise, but there are several theories that help to unpack the changes that we bear witness to in such places. Pierre Bourdieu's conception of *habitus* is one way that we might think about the totalizing, world-making nature of working-class experiences of industrial employment. Habitus, in this sense, is the combination of habits, skills, dispositions, and ways-of-knowing that each of us unconsciously develops as the result of our specific social environment. It is not a formalized set of expected behaviours, but a conglomeration that emerges out of lived experience.[13]

Writing of his industrial hometown of Rotherham in the UK, Simon Charlesworth puts this more simply: "Our perception of the sense of the world, our spontaneous experience of its being meaningful, takes place through our acceptance of a whole range of what we know to be there, in its 'place,' as part of an immense network of interlaced practices."[14] While habitus is useful in understanding the embodied nature of industrial society, and indeed provides some insight into the scale of the changes that continue to affect these areas as they slouch towards "post-industrialism," Raymond Williams's notion of "structure of feeling" provides greater insight into the ways that such changes are internalized and affected by the thoughts and emotions of the men and women who are directly influenced.

Industrialization settled into Sydney in the nineteenth century and came to constitute much of how people in the city perceived their world. Others have explored how deindustrialization has resulted in significant cultural change, social and political erasure, and the gentrification of former working-class political institutions, but Williams remains instrumental in connecting class experiences to the transition between emergent, dominant, and residual cultural formations.[15] In deindustrializing areas, the breakdown of working-class identities and their contingent institutions produces an acute sense of trauma that is both personal and deeply collective. In other words, trauma is a significant by-product of the transition between dominant and residual cultural forms.[16] This book traces the multiple strands of this process as it has occurred in Sydney, roots it within the personal accounts of men and women who were directly affected and implicated, and examines the shape of an emergent, post-industrial Cape Breton Island. In this final instance, diverging from the gentrified – but no less vicious – forms of deindustrialization that occurred in larger "post-industrial" urban centres like Pittsburgh or Montreal, nothing has substantively taken the place of the mines and mills that marked our island.

It is also important to recognize how the decline of industry on Cape Breton Island has created room for alternative spaces of power to emerge. Steven High is careful in his analysis of what he calls "mill colonialism" in the resource frontier of northern Ontario; there, the working class that found employment within the mills was largely white and blue collar. The same is true of the steel mill and collieries of Cape Breton Island. Despite the proximity of Indigenous communities such as the Membertou First Nation, the industrial worksite was – to a large degree – racially exclusionary. With the decentring of these industries from the economic heart of island life, Membertou has emerged as one of Canada's most successful First Nations and its "economic miracle" is often positioned as an important example of state- and-community-led development.[17] In these ways, the collapse of industrial employment has opened the door to a more equitable social order. But in applauding those effects, we must not forget the "enormous personal cost to mainly white blue-collar workers, whose standard of living is in free fall in some areas and who find that their tastes, values, and politics are increasingly parodied by university-educated people."[18]

Before unpacking deindustrialization and post-industrial transformation on Cape Breton Island, it is first necessary to explore the "creative" half of the so-called "creative destruction" of industrial capitalism. Emerging as a secondary industry to the Cape Breton collieries, the Sydney Steel Works could have been the basis for a broad expansion in secondary and tertiary production. That this did not occur is perhaps unsurprising, considering the vicissitudes of Canadian political economy in a "peripheral" region, but the industrialization of Sydney between 1899 and 1944 set the stage for a large-scale, corporate-driven divestment during the postwar years.

Industrialization and Working-Class Sydney, 1899–1944

The Second Industrial Revolution of the late nineteenth and early twentieth centuries was predicated upon the expansion of coal and steel production. Technological advances, urbanization, working-class organization, and the mobility of industrial capital provoked huge changes within the social and economic order. It was within this landscape that

0.2 Building the Steelworks at Sydney, 1899. Patricia MacKinnon Collection.
Beaton Institute, Cape Breton University.

four large producers came to corner the Canadian market. These were
the Nova Scotia Steel Company (Scotia) in Trenton, Nova Scotia, the
Dominion Iron and Steel Company (Disco) in Sydney, the Steel Company of Canada (Stelco) in Hamilton, and the Algoma Steel Company
in Sault St Marie.[19] In Sydney, the founder of Disco, H.M. Whitney, had
previously established the Dominion Coal Company in 1893, and construction began on the Sydney Works in 1899 to take advantage of this
ready supply of raw materials.[20]

Sydney expanded quickly.[21] In a twenty-year span, between 1891
and 1911, its population more than septupled – growing from 2,427 to
17,723.[22] In addition to a smattering of Acadian, Irish, Mi'kmaq, Scottish, and other Cape Breton–born workers, the island's coal mines and
steel mill attracted workers from farther afield. Of the 6,246 immigrants

0.3 Blast furnace crew, Dominion Iron and Steel Company, Sydney, c. 1900.
Photograph by Kelly and Dodge. Reference number: 91–602–22563. Beaton
Institute, Cape Breton University.

in Cape Breton County in 1901, "54 percent were from Newfoundland,
25 percent from the British Isles, 11 percent from the United States
(some of whom were Blacks from the south), 2 percent from Italy, and
the remaining 8 percent from other countries."[23] Among these "others"
were Eastern Europeans – Ukrainians, Russians, and Polish – as well as
European Jews.[24] Many of these ethnic and cultural identities remain
visible in the social landscape of industrial Cape Breton.[25]

This growth was predicated upon the operations of the steelworks
at the centre of the town, which rested on nearly 450 hectares of land.
Residential expansion was frantic; by 1900, more than 400 structures
were completed to house the influx of workers. Former estates such as
Colby, Ashby, Brooklands, and Sherwood were divided and made into
the basis for new working- and middle-class neighbourhoods. As one

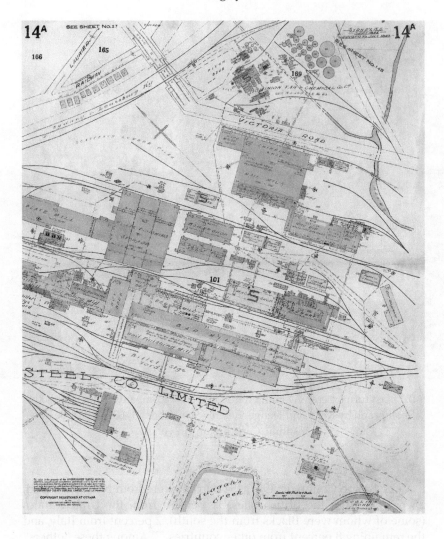

0.4 Sydney Works, 1914. Insurance Plan of Sydney (Cape Breton) Nova Scotia by Chas E. Goad, Civil Engineer, November 1907. Plan No. 96. Beaton Institute, Cape Breton University.

citizen reported, "Houses are going up in places where the streets are as yet on paper."[26] At shift change, the streets surrounding the plant would be full of men walking to and from work with lunch pails in hand. By New Year's Day in 1904, the government of Nova Scotia officially declared Sydney the newest city in the province.[27]

The class dimension of life in the steel city was visible from the beginning. Its contrasts were striking; while workers in Whitney Pier struggled to find viable housing – often packing tightly into small, smoky shacks in the streets closest to the plant, Disco management built grand homes on the waterfront. Arthur J. Moxham, the first general manager of the Sydney Works, had his home – "Rockaway" – transported to Sydney brick by brick from his prior estate in Pittsburgh.[28] The thirty-room mansion, colloquially known as "Moxham Castle" and replete with an indoor swimming pool, was starkly different from the crowded boarding houses near the coke ovens, where "beds were constantly being slept in as night workmen turned in as soon as the day workers got up."[29] While workers suffered through periodic outbreaks of smallpox, diphtheria, and dangerous conditions at the mill, Moxham and his wife entertained members of the city's elite at lavish parties where – as Moira Ross writes – "Mrs. Moxham always wore white and Miss Moxham always wore black."[30]

Despite this growth, Canadian steel firms faced structural challenges.[31] Nova Scotia producers began to trend towards consolidation in the first decades of the twentieth century. The Nova Scotia Steel Company in Trenton and Dominion Iron and Steel in Sydney soon found their ownership contested by extra-regional forces. In 1910, Disco was combined with the Dominion Coal Company by a consortium of Montreal and Toronto business interests. Scotia, meanwhile, came under the control of American investors in 1917.[32] Both companies were in serious trouble by the 1920s, when over-specialization and distance from markets required the curtailment of production.[33] Further consolidation was the result, as Scotia and Disco were merged under the control of the British Empire Steel Corporation (Besco) in 1921. Operations at a Scotia-owned mill in Sydney Mines were wound down, and the Cape Breton collieries were – at this point – largely under the control of the single company – Besco.[34]

The 1920s loom large in the collective memory of industrial Cape Breton. Poor management, a watered stock scandal, and corporate intransigence meant that Besco was beginning to feel the pinch of a protracted market downturn by the late 1910s. In an atmosphere of working-class resistance in Canada, which famously erupted in 1919, the company sought major concessions from its employees.[35] A failed

union recognition strike by the steelworkers in 1923 saw troops sta-
tioned at the plant and sporadic attacks on workers and their families
along Victoria Road in Whitney Pier. In 1925, company police murdered
striking miner William Davis. This event is still memorialized each year
on 11 June – "Davis Day" in Cape Breton – and local children have the
day off of school in the former coal towns.

Besco did not survive the decade. In 1928, it was placed under the
control of a new operating company, the Dominion Steel and Coal
Corporation (Dosco), which controlled the Cape Breton coal and steel
industries until the government takeovers of the 1960s. This period in
Cape Breton's economic history, ranging from the 1880s to the 1920s,
represents a pattern of industrial development that necessarily resulted
in protracted crisis. It would fundamentally change the island's role in
a centralized Canadian economy; after the 1920s, Cape Breton came to
occupy a functional position both as a ready supplier of labour and as a
reserve supplier for the Canadian energy and steel markets.[36]

This period has also been explored within a regional framework in
the context of historical out-migration from the Maritimes. Compounding the regional economic crisis, the 1920s represented a moment of
demographic disaster – with more than 147,000 people exiting the
region during the decade.[37] While Cape Breton Island avoided this general trend during its period of industrialization, the 1920s and 1930s
prompted an exodus of workers heading for "the Boston States" and
other points west.[38] Although the population in Sydney would continue to increase until reaching an apex of 33,617 in 1961, the context of
this growth within a broader environment of regional underdevelopment and out-migration cannot be ignored.

Organized labour also achieved several significant goals during the
Depression years, particularly within the Canadian steel industry. By
the mid-1930s, independent steel unions had emerged in Sydney, Trenton, Hamilton, and the Sault.[39] Although the Second World War proved
a boon for Canadian producers, the Sydney Works did not benefit to the
same extent as its competitors. As a result, the postwar years witnessed
marginal growth compared to the firm's direct competitors – setting the
stage for a protracted project of corporate disinvestment by the 1950s
and 1960s.

Oral Histories of Sydney Steel

Oral history helps to personalize the processes of deindustrialization.
The personal stories of people living in deindustrializing and post-
industrial areas provide insight into both individual experiences and

perceptions of the social world. As Christine Walley describes, "telling personal stories means not only looking inward but also turning the self outward and tracing the links and relationships that shape and define not only who we are as individuals but also the broader social worlds of which we are a part."[40] This research draws upon two primary repositories of oral history material relating to the deindustrialization of Sydney Steel. The first consists of audio and video interviews that I conducted with thirty-two informants between 2013 and 2016. Our conversations were structured as "life-history" interviews where participants had the opportunity to reflect upon their personal experiences, their connection with the history of deindustrialization, and their perceptions of the city during the nearly two decades after the closure of Sydney Steel.

The second collection was created in 1990 as part of the "Steel Project" at the Beaton Institute Archives at Cape Breton University. The Steel Project emerged under the direction of folklorist Elizabeth Beaton in 1987 as part of an SSHRC-funded project to document the history of integrated steelmaking in Sydney throughout a series of plant modernizations that occurred contemporaneously. This project oversaw the archiving of thousands of documents relating to the Cape Breton Development Corporation (DEVCO) and the Sydney Steel Corporation (Sysco), the production of a National Film Board of Canada documentary, *Making Steel*, and several scholarly publications. In addition to this, Beaton and her co-researchers conducted 163 audio interviews with current and former steelworkers, managers, and other employees at the Sydney steel plant – intending to "emphasize the centrality of the history of Sydney Steel and [to] provide a link between the past and the future of the workers and their community."[41]

Historically, this collection offers insight into a moment of economic disruption; as a result of the ongoing modernization, the Sysco workforce was being reduced by nearly half at the time that these interviews were undertaken. Alongside the spectre of mass layoffs, the stories presented therein reflect the ways that life stories are constructed in relation to conditions that are contemporary to the telling.[42] As a result, the comparative analysis that is afforded by the availability of two collections of oral history interviews, conducted twenty-five years apart, helps to reveal how experiences of deindustrialization are historically contingent.

Thankfully, oral histories no longer require a spirited defence against methodological scepticism – having escaped from what Paul Thompson refers to as "the stigma of amateurism."[43] The debates of the 1970s, which encompassed issues of historical subjectivity, historical memory, and the role of the historian, have given way to broader understand-ings of the interview process and the applicability of digital methods.[44] In my interviews, I relied upon the practical oral history methodolo-gies described by Alessandro Portelli in his 1979 article, "Sulla speci-ficità della storia orale." In this piece, reprinted in English in 1981, Portelli offers three main lessons: we must move beyond text-based transcriptions and begin to take language, tone, volume, and body language into account; we must apply narrative analysis to oral tes-timony and pay attention to narrative cues such as repetition or time spent on a particular subject; and we must keep in mind the question of "who speaks" in the interview process.[45] Video interviews provide one avenue for this type of analysis. Only five of my interviewees – when offered the choice between audio and video recording – were comfortable sitting for the camera.[46] In other instances, I took hand-written notes on a pad of paper during our discussions – making sure to consider *how* the story was being relayed as much as the content of the spoken words.

"Shared authority" is another methodological goal of many practis-ing oral historians. The notion, articulated initially by Michael Frisch and taken up by others, requires the deep consideration of authority wielding during both the interview process and in the analysis of his-torical experiences.[47] It requires the construction of long-term relation-ships based upon a mutual trust between interviewer and interviewee, as well as a willingness on the part of the historian to take participants' analytical frameworks seriously. Further, a shared authority necessi-tates a willingness to reject the notion of uninterrupted objectivity on behalf of the historian in favour of achieving a shared understanding of the past.[48] In practice, however, this is more difficult than it might first appear; each of my interviews was co-created, but it proved more chal-lenging to extend this collaboration beyond the scope of the recorded interview itself. This was particularly true of instances where infor-mants agreed to sit for only a single interview.

Where I fit within the story, as a lifelong resident of Sydney, was something that I had to carefully consider. Initially, I thought of myself as an insider. I lived in the city and my grandfather worked in the nearby collieries, after all. It soon became clear that these would not open as many doors as I had hoped. Cold-calling possible interview-ees was made more difficult by my having to respond in the negative to the frequent question: "Are you related to any of the MacKinnons that were on at the plant?" This slowly became easier, particularly as Gerry McCarron – my wife's uncle and a former Sydney steelworker – became more closely involved with the project.

Gerry and his brother Tommy were the first two people I interviewed. We came together in August 2013 at my in-laws' home, where we sat in the gazebo and talked about their connection to the plant. The McCarrons were a steelworking family. Jim, their father, worked on the plant between 1943 and 1992, as did his father and grandfather. Rewatching our first interview now, I am struck by the awkwardness of the encounter. While we discussed a number of issues relating to work at the plant and socializing among employees, our conversation also contains a number of pauses, false starts, and direct answers to narrowly framed questions. Until that point, I had not spent much time in conversation with either of the men; we did not share the type of close personal relationship that would make such an interview immediately comfortable. Although this was the only time that I sat with Tommy for a formal interview, Gerry would help to organize – and sit in on – several others.[49]

By the end of the project, it was not unusual for me to call Gerry with a quick question about the plant, the people who worked there, or any number of other things. Sometimes, when the answer was not immediately clear, he would reach out to other former employees before getting back to me. We met at his home in Sydney on another instance to go over some documents that he came across relating to the history of Sysco. I hope that I have also been able to offer something to the McCarrons. Whenever I came across the work records of their father, Jim, I copied them for the family. When Gerry needed information on the date of birth for a former Sysco employee being memorialized on the site of the former plant, our roles reversed and I was able to help him with the information. While this sort of personal relationship is impossible to build with every informant, it represents a meaningful effort at oral history as engaged scholarship, reflexive practice, and shared inquiry. In eight chapters, this book moves between the impact of deindustrialization on workers' bodies and the changes it prompts on the shop floor, community-based resistance tactics, and political economy.

The first chapter provides a macroeconomic and political overview of the actions of the Dominion Steel and Coal Corporation – the controlling company of the Sydney Works. In refusing to provide the necessary upgrades to mill and consolidating its holdings in Montreal and Toronto, the company's actions reveal an explicit corporate strategy of deindustrialization and divestment from Cape Breton. Chapter 2 shifts focus towards "the local," revealing how the labour achievements of the postwar period resulted in a perceived strengthening of working-class institutions and social positions. Here, we witness a turning away from the so-called "red phase" of Cape Breton workers' culture towards a set of more mainstream understandings of steelworkers – their place in the city and the importance of institutional unionism – that reflect contemporary concerns throughout Canadian society.

In the third chapter we examine "Black Friday" – 13 October 1967 – for what it tells us about how nationalization was seen as an acceptable response to deindustrialization by the provincial state. Black Friday, as it became known locally, was the day that Dosco announced the planned closure of the Sydney Works. A corresponding community protest movement, which included a massive "Parade of Concern," reveals the extent to which locals perceived the mill to be the economic and cultural heart of the city. Oral history testimony expresses a moment of profound disruption; the "moral economy" of industrial Cape Breton was directly challenged and traditional beliefs about industrial employment, methods of resistance, and working-class masculinities were exposed as far more precarious than had been previously imagined.

With the mill under public ownership, the next chapters explore Sysco's gradual decline and the resulting impact on steelworkers and other residents of the deindustrializing city. Shop-floor changes at Sydney Steel between 1968 and 1989 form the basis of chapter 4. Oral history accounts of steelworkers in the mill's departments help to articulate the transition from integrated steelmaking to the downsizing of the 1980s, culminating with the changeover to electric arc production. Workers' accounts provide insight into both individual methods of resistance to managerial control and the tensions that arose between the desire to maintain employment numbers and an administrative desire for "competitive efficiencies" visible throughout the Canadian steel industry. These experiences are framed within a broader discussion of Fordist and post-Fordist production in twentieth-century Canada. For its part, chapter 5 reveals the aftermath of industrial production as it is expressed within workers' bodies. By the 1980s, steelworkers were beginning to demand state recognition for the dangers associated with exposure to carcinogenic agents at work. As workers became more aware of these risks, recognizing the significant number of steelworkers afflicted with cancer and other illnesses, a small group of coke-oven workers began independently lobbying the provincial government for compensation. Their struggle and the resulting concessions on behalf of the province reveal the interconnections between bodily health, political activism, and shop-floor environmentalism.

Soon thereafter, other groups within the community became increasingly involved in discussions surrounding the environmental and health legacies that resulted from nearly 100 years of industrial production. Much of this discussion centred upon the Sydney "tar ponds" – a polluted watershed that flowed alongside the steel plant into the harbour. The historical question of how to remediate this site forms the basis for chapter 6. Included in this chapter is an exploration of a failed incineration plan between 1986 and 1996, environmental protest and cross-class solidarities within the community, and the experiences of two women who were relocated from their homes near the site of the former coke ovens in 1999 after arsenic and other contaminants were found leaching into their basements.

The provincial decision to close Sysco is the focus of chapter 7. Circumstances involving the plant had changed dramatically between 1967 and 2001 – after Premier John Hamm was elected in Nova Scotia on a platform that included the closure or sale of Sysco. A set of political and ideational influences are probed in this chapter; while Hamm views the decision as simply a reorientation of state interventionism, the popular convergence of neoliberal doctrine and regional economic development theory during the 1990s meant that market-based solutions had become hegemonic by 1999. This chapter also traces the intellectual history of the notion, still popular today, that an industrial mindset stands in the way of fostering so-called entrepreneurial culture in deindustrializing and post-industrial areas. The role of the local university in this process is also explored, as are the constraints placed upon the ability of workers and other community members to meaningfully challenge the closure decision.

Chapter 8 examines the representation and memory of Sydney Steel in the period following closure. The creation of "Open Hearth Park" on the site of the former plant, part of a $400 million federal/provincial remediation effort, reveals how industrial history corresponds with modern politics of place and identity. This includes discussion of steelworkers' current perceptions of the site and a public history exploration of the representational value of industrial heritage. More broadly, these discussions reflect the residual industrial structure of feeling that survives in Sydney. Although the steel plant no longer exists, the working-class cultures, understandings, and moral economies that it shaped continue to inform daily life on the island.

Deindustrialization stretches further than the immediate disruption caused by a factory, mill, or mine closure. It is rooted in the fabric of market capitalism, and its causes – both direct and indirect –are in place long before the final shift. It is a transformative process, simultaneously affecting political economy, place identity, environment, and even the bodies of workers, their families, and neighbours. It is not an inevitability, nor are the ways that it unfolds predetermined. From Black Friday to ecological activism during the 1990s, residents of the "steel city" of

Atlantic Canada were active in their response to the forces buffeting
their community. But memory and representation have a role to play,
as well. How people reflect upon these struggles, victories, and defeats
inform how working-class communities respond to present challenges.
For Sydney, as for post-industrial rural resource economies throughout
the world, the road forward must be based on an honest assessment of
the past.

Chapter One

Diversify or Die: Planned Obsolescence in the Dosco Years

There is nothing more depressing than idle works on a cold winter day.
– F.L. Estep, "Report to the Minister of Industry," 1944[1]

Mine, mill, and factory closures have disrupted the lives of millions of working-class men and women. The announcements of such closures are often recalled with near-photographic detail, representing a sort of "flashbulb memory" for those who experience these traumatic events first-hand. In 2016, one such announcement was launched into the public sphere as a "viral video" that soon became central to the ongoing US electoral campaigns. The video – soon amassing millions of views – depicts an uncomfortable-looking man revealing to gathered workers that Carrier Corp., based in Indiana, had intentions to move operations to Monterrey, Mexico. Donald Trump weighed into the fray on social media – promising the soon-to-be-displaced workers that, were he to be elected, their jobs would be safe. Playing the saviour, Trump positioned himself in stark relief to the imagery on the shaky video footage – giving voice to a deeply engrained anti-offshoring, anti-globalization sentiment familiar throughout much of the Rust Belt.[2] Leaders of the Carrier workers' union, members of the United Steelworkers of America (USWA), expressed their scepticism of Trump's newfound support for the working class – but another employee would later admit, "We all voted for him, we just thought he was going to protect our jobs."[3]

While the Carrier encounter could easily be dismissed as a one-off in a campaign season full of gaffes, missteps, and scandals, Trump's reaction to the announcement revealed some awareness of the deep discontent felt by Midwestern voters at compounding job losses in basic manufacturing. Indeed, Trump continued to eschew the type of language that has characterized much policy discussion surrounding deindustrializing areas of Canada and the United States since the 1980s. Foundationally, the neoclassical position on the decline of manufacturing employment has been to note the greater efficiencies that become possible as capital relocates from areas with higher rates of unionization and wages to other places where these variables do not exert the same pressure on the competitiveness of the firm. Joseph Schumpeter articulated the basics of this position as early as the 1940s, when he described capitalist creative destruction. "In dealing with capitalism, we are dealing with an evolutionary process," he writes:

> The opening up of new markets, foreign or domestic, and the organizational development from the craft shop and factory to such concerns as U.S. Steel illustrate the same process of industrial mutation – if I may use that biological term – that incessantly revolutionizes the economic structure *from within*, incessantly destroying the old one, incessantly creating a new one.[4]

Geographically and culturally situated, an analysis of these processes within rural resource communities reveals the undercurrents of regional political economy and working-class culture under conditions of corporate divestment. The destructive aspects, frequently compounding existing ethnic, racial, or cultural animus, can easily produce the sort of political anomie that conservative and nationalist movements have been successful in exploiting.

In Cape Breton, the slow churning of creative destruction continued in the aftermath of the Second World War and glided towards the events of the Sydney Steel Crisis in 1967. An exploration of Dosco operations between 1944 and 1966 belies the commonly held belief that corporate ineptitude during the postwar years was to blame for declining profits at Sydney Steel. Notably, many interviewees reflected upon the corporate hesitancy to provide modernization or other forms of investment to Cape Breton operations as an important misstep.[5] From a political economy perspective, it becomes clear that such decisions were *not* based on a misreading of market conditions, but that the withholding of modernization and product diversification from the steel plant at Sydney was part of a purposeful corporate strategy of deindustrialization and divestment through planned obsolescence.

Historians and economic geographers have revisited Harold Innis's staples thesis, arguing that it remains a useful framework for the development and underdevelopment of resource peripheries in Canada. As Mel Watkins has argued since the 1970s, staples theory articulates a geographic and spatial argument for the underdevelopment of rural resource frontiers.[6] While Innis famously applied his ideas to the cod fishery and fur trade, they have since been expanded upon to describe – in broad strokes – Canadian national economic development within a global system. As we shall see, the concept of a staples trap is particularly useful for understanding how peripheral regions, such as rural economies that are predicated upon resource extraction, are stuck dealing with underdevelopment and, eventually, decline.

The concept is based upon the idea that resource economies – small or large – become reliant upon primary industry and nearby service resources. This has been successfully applied in the analysis of the logging industry in British Columbia, where researchers have shown that capital tends to be oriented towards export. As a result, this has limited the range of opportunities in which local and regional capitalists are willing to invest; in addition to this, the need for significant early capitalization and fixed infrastructure provides sizeable barriers to entry within the resource market.[7] Likewise, the staples trap remains an appropriate theory to use in framing the Cape Breton experience, based – as it was – on the extraction of bituminous coal for the entirety of its industrial history. While steel did emerge as a secondary corollary to the coal industry, this was an aberration based upon the availability of raw materials and the particular economic circumstances in place briefly at the turn of the twentieth century. The island's steel industry never branched into the other types of tertiary production that would have been required for a sustainable, long-term manufacturing base to take shape.

This argument is not simply a rehashing of an old theory in application to yet another disparate region. Instead, exploring the decline of steel in Cape Breton as a corollary to a staples trap within the island's coal industry provides insight into some of the regional contradictions of the Canadian national economy and complicates the analysis put forward by Paul Kellogg in his recent book *Escape from the Staples Trap*. There, the author does not argue against the concept tout court, but challenges the idea that Canada might be considered to be situated within its own global form of the trap. Kellogg applies an internationalist perspective and argues that attempts to position Canada as a dependent economy in a global context, beset by the staples trap, are ultimately misguided. Noting the experience of nations in the Global South, he reflects, "The economies at the top of the [global] hierarchy benefit from, and aggressively work to sustain, the conditions that trap poor countries into dependency on staples – and Canada is very much ensconced at the top of this hierarchy ... not at the bottom."[8]

The political economy of Cape Breton, interrogated here between 1944 and 1966, attempts to reckon with the boundaries of the staples trap as an explanatory mechanism within Canada and among its regions. Certainly, such an analysis is possible; indeed, Kellogg demands that we begin to take seriously the complex relations between nations within Canada – with Indigenous and Québécois experiences highlighted explicitly.[9] The contours of Cape Breton nationalism have been explored extensively elsewhere, including its boundaries and exclusions, but the concept of a Cape Breton nation is not necessary to consider its place as a sub-region of Atlantic Canada that found itself marginalized and underdeveloped as the result of a staples trap.[10] In this case, a historical examination of Dosco's operations reveals how decisions to downgrade operations in Cape Breton were directly related to the island's place within a staples trap based upon the extraction of coal and the secondary production of steel.

The Postwar Recovery: 1944–1950

Dominion Steel and Coal Company was an economic giant. By the 1940s, it controlled approximately 85 per cent of Nova Scotia collieries in addition to the integrated steel mill at Sydney.[11] On Cape Breton Island, its collieries spanned from the Sydney coalfield to working seams on the western side of the island in Port Hood, Inverness, and Mabou. As the largest industrial employer in the Maritimes, the company wielded a great deal of economic and political power. Among its holdings were firms throughout Nova Scotia, New Brunswick, Quebec, Ontario, and Newfoundland.

The Royal Commission on Coal, which set about investigating the Canadian coal industry between 1945 and 1946, included a section on the Dosco coal holdings. Production from the Sydney coal field yielded more than 30 per cent of the total Canadian coal production at the time, and "although the field has been extensively mined during the past 120 years," the company noted, " its remaining reserves are very considerable ... the company foresees some 80 years of operations on developed reserves along, a further 100 years of operations being suggested in the estimate of other coal resources."[12] Despite the rosy outlook presented by Dosco, the Cape Breton miners were fearful about the future. They were staunch in their desire for greater mechanization and modernization, and – in their brief to the Royal Commission – the call for industrial nationalization. Though unfulfilled, this desire was rooted in a broad class-based understanding about the tendency of capital within the

Canadian economy to accumulate in the central provinces, especially when extracted from resource hinterlands like Cape Breton Island.[13]

The intersections between the island's industries were obvious. Strict supply-chain discipline through vertical integration was key to the Dosco business model. Cape Breton coal was baked into coke at the Sydney Works to feed the fires of the blast furnaces. Iron ore from Bell Island arrived at the piers for use in iron making.[14] Limestone was sourced from Dominion Limestone Limited in Aguathuna, Newfoundland.[15] Despite the proximity of these Maritimes-based resources, the company began to shift its investment westward in the years after the Second World War.

Under the wartime economy, the Canadian steel industry benefited from the provision of federal capital for modernization. The Sydney Works, however, did not benefit to the same extent as its direct competitors. The Maritimes, let alone Cape Breton Island, did not fit within C.D. Howe's vision of a postwar Canada that was to be characterized by centralized industrial manufacturing and close integration with the United States.[16] Some were quick to recognize these developments; in the summer of 1940, the general manager of the Sydney Works – Clem Anson – met with steel controller Hugh Scully about a proposal for upgrades to the mill. Anson would express anger and disbelief when Scully, just a few months later, denied ever having heard such a proposal.[17]

Company executives used the apparent weakness of their market position as a bargaining chip against employees in its regional collieries, steel works, and foundries. In advance of the national steel strike in 1946, Dosco ran a series of full-page advertisements in the *Sydney Post Record* to highlight the precarious circumstances at the Sydney Works – created, they argued, by the company's position on the geographical margins of the Canadian national economy.[18]

Struggling to recover from wartime shortfalls, the company still controlled ore mines in Bell Island, Newfoundland; railroad car shops, forge shops, a nut and bolt factory, and rolling mills at Trenton, Nova Scotia; limestone and dolomite quarries; wire mills in Sydney, Saint John, and Toronto; power-generating stations; and rolling mills in Montreal.[19] A report by the Arthur G. McKee & Company outlined some of the problems facing the company's regional holdings: significant modernization was required at the Sydney Works, the transportation fleet – which had been destroyed during the war – needed to be replaced, investment was necessary for the beneficiation of raw materials, and – unsurprisingly – labour power needed to be suppressed.[20]

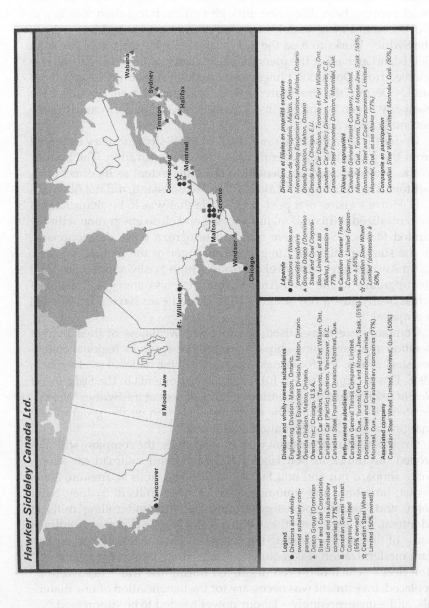

Hawker Siddeley Canada Ltd.

Wabana
Sydney
Trenton
Halifax
Contrecoeur
Montreal
Toronto
Malton
Windsor
Chicago
Ft. William
Moose Jaw
Vancouver

Legend

● Divisions and wholly-owned subsidiary companies.
 Divisions and wholly-owned subsidiaries
 Engineering Division, Malton, Ontario.
 Merchandising Equipment Division, Malton, Ontario.
 Orenda Division, Malton, Ontario.
 Orenda Inc., Chicago, U.S.A.
 Canadian Car Division, Toronto, and Fort William, Ont.
 Canadian Car (Pacific) Division, Vancouver, B.C.
 Canadian Steel Foundries Division, Montreal, Que.

▲ Dosco Group (Dominion Steel and Coal Corporation, Limited and its subsidiary companies) 77% owned.

■ Canadian General Transit Company, Limited (55% owned).
 Partly-owned subsidiaries
 Canadian General Transit Company, Limited.
 Montreal, Que., Toronto, Ont., and Moose Jaw, Sask. (55%)
 Dominion Steel and Coal Corporation, Limited.
 Montreal, Que., and its subsidiary companies (77%)

☆ Canadian Steel Wheel Limited (50% owned).
 Associated company
 Canadian Steel Wheel Limited, Montreal, Que. (50%)

Légende

● Divisions et filiales en propriété exclusive
 Divisions et filiales en propriété exclusive
 Division de technographie, Malton, Ontario
 Merchandising Equipment Division, Malton, Ontario
 Orenda Division, Malton, Ontario
 Orenda Inc., Chicago, E.U.
 Canadian Car Division, Toronto et Fort William, Ont.
 Canadian Car (Pacific) Division, Vancouver, C.B.
 Canadian Steel Foundries Division, Montréal, Qué.

▲ Groupe Dosco (Dominion Steel and Coal Corporation, Limited, et ses filiales), possession à 77%
 Filiales en copropriété
 Canadian General Transit Company, Limited (possession à 55%)
 Montréal, Qué., Toronto, Ont. et Moose Jaw, Sask. (55%)
 Dominion Steel and Coal Corporation, Limited
 Montréal, Qué., et ses filiales (77%)

■ Canadian General Transit Company, Limited (possession à 55%)
 Compagnie en participation
 Canadian Steel Wheel Limited, Montréal, Qué. (50%)

☆ Canadian Steel Wheel Limited (possession à 50%)

1.1 Hawker Siddeley Canada, 1965; Dosco properties are marked with triangles. Halifax Industries Fonds, Corporate Records 1990–215–001, File 4, Hawker Siddeley Annual Report, 1965, NSARM

Table 1.1 Profit Margins for Canadian Steel Firms, 1945–1950 (per cent)

Year	Algoma	Dofasco	Dosco	Stelco
1945	8.15	5.47	3.05	3.96
1946	3.88	9.66	2.04	2.28
1947	4.58	9.08	3.63	7.11
1948	7.66	7.45	6.97	8.99
1949	13.06	10.19	7.30	10.87
1950	10.41	9.11	6.31	13.57

Source: R.B. Elver, *Economic Character and Change in the Canadian Steel Industry since 1945* (Ottawa: Queen's Printer, 1969), 20.

These issues translated into a persistent popular narrative of hard times at the Sydney steel mill; they are recalled in several interviews describing the structural limitations of regional industry. Anson, interviewed by *Cape Breton's Magazine* in 1981, recalled:

We didn't have good raw materials to work with. Our iron ore was one of the very poorest iron ores to smelt in the world, a very dense hematite [...] And the same thing about the coal. You know, the Cape Breton coal is not a good metallurgical coal [...] Made very weak coke, Weak in strength. And the result was that when it got in the blast furnace it broke up before it had done its work. And you had to use more coke than you should have – consequently costing more money.[21]

John Campbell, a raw materials engineer and manager at Dosco, described the situation in similar terms during an interview in 2014:

JOHN: One of the disadvantages that we had here was that we were pretty distant from other heavy industries. A lot of the steel plants in the US and even in the Hamilton area would be relatively close to other heavy industries for repairs and maintenance and so on [...] And one of the problems Sydney got into in the early days, even pre-1950 [...] Wabana ore was very poor, by today's standards [...] It was high in phosphorous and high in silica [...] And the conclusion of research at that time that it was difficult, if not impossible, to make any great improvement – because of the structure of the iron ore [...] But the other problem was that the coal in Sydney was very high in sulphur, so even [if] you could cut the slag volume down, because you cut the slag volume down you couldn't remove the sulphur anymore. So that showed that Sydney coals were no longer really suitable for making coke, in that situation. So over the years [...] Dosco started to buy iron ore from Labrador [and

Brazil], but as time went on they went to pelletizing the iron ore [...] So because of that, it became optimum to buy other coals. So there were coals brought in from the US and even Western Canada to make coke [...] Suddenly the plant finds that all those advantages that they had, you know [...] they lost the main thing, which was the coal supply, and the iron ore supply.

LACHLAN: And, so is that what led to the decision in 1967? To close it?

JOHN: Part, I would say ... There was also a feeling ... that maybe the investment wasn't being made in the plant. To modernize or to expand.[22]

Both of these accounts are offered decades after the events of 1967, when it became clear that private industry would abandon Cape Breton coal and steel. For Anson, industrial decline in Cape Breton was predicated upon technological and metallurgical advances that outpaced the capabilities of local raw materials. From his perspective, the decision to develop mills in Quebec and Ontario was simply a natural response to the centralization of the Canadian economy and the nature of competitive capitalism. John Campbell remains reluctant to explain the exodus of private industry as inevitable, although he describes many of the same material limitations. Rather, he believes that Dosco was constrained by technological factors that might have been overcome had proper infrastructure investment been provided.

Campbell's position, articulated in a 2014 interview, was also argued by Cape Breton trade unionists as early as 1946. In that year, the steelworkers' union identified lack of investment as a key area of disagreement with corporate management. Charles Millard, the Canadian director of the United Steelworkers, accused Dosco of purposefully allowing operations at the Sydney Works to atrophy. He believed that management was acting either deliberately or carelessly in their inattention to the requirements of industrial engineering and maintenance at the mill. Recognizing that the voices of its workers may have little effect on the corporation's decisions, Millard called upon either the provincial government of Nova Scotia or the government of Canada to "place a competent administrator in charge of the Sydney operations" should the firm "fail to meet its responsibility to the Steelworkers [sic] and the people of Nova Scotia and Canada."[23] Although Dosco provided minor additions to the Sydney Works during the late 1940s and early 1950s, these were consistently outstripped by its contributions to the newer mills in the central provinces.[24]

The miners soon echoed these concerns. In 1948, representatives of District 26 of the United Mineworkers penned a memorandum to C.D. Howe. There, they demanded an investigation into "the reasons why

[Dosco] is not expanding its primary steel operations in Nova Scotia and is failing to establish secondary steel industries based on export trade." The miners' union was prescient in their fears; they describe a possible future where, without expansion, Dosco falls further and further behind its competitors. They beseech the Canadian government to never allow the Nova Scotia steel industry to "pass into foreign hands," and express the firm belief that the island's steel and coal industries "should be operated as a public utility."[25] In light of later events, the lack of investment at this key juncture presented an important obstacle for the later competitiveness of Cape Breton's industrial operations.

At the operations level, Howe grew increasingly sceptical of Dosco President Arthur Cross. In contrast to the close friendship that blossomed between Howe and James Dunn of Algoma Steel, Dosco officials were often shut out of industrial planning discussions altogether. As historian Duncan McDowell writes, "Dosco's lethargic response to wartime incentives irritated Howe to such a point that he had unofficially directed Steel Control to 'use that company to the minimum extent possible even if we have to buy the steel in the United States.'"[26] Some aspects of federal regulatory controls remained after the war; an accelerated depreciation program was intended to stimulate expansion in national steel production.[27] Examined holistically, it was a combination of economic geography, the maturity of Canadian market capitalism, and the decisions of the federal regulatory state that left Dosco in crisis as it entered the 1950s. State and business interests continued to promote steel production, though in ways that flattened and ignored regional differences.[28]

In Sydney, steelworkers and their families suffered the immediate impacts of these changes. Nearly half of Nova Scotia's 20,000 unemployed workers were located in Cape Breton in 1947. Many of these men and women held out hopes for the entrance of Newfoundland into Confederation, as newly discovered ore deposits were viewed as an answer to the challenges of raw materials. Renewed US commitment to the St Lawrence Seaway project, however, would make it easier to transport Labrador ore to central markets by the end of the 1950s, to the great benefit of the central Canadian steel producers. As a result, the political argument for modernization at Sydney began to shift away from highlighting its geographical proximity to raw materials and towards the mill's position within a sound national industrial strategy.[29] This would resound after the mid-1950s within a political environment more attuned to the economic realities of Canadian regionalism.

Losing Ground in the Boom Years, 1950–1957

The ability of international steel firms to realize economies of scale during the 1950s was a key metric of increased productivity and profitability. Reconstruction in West Germany witnessed the development of several new integrated mills in the Ruhr, which overtook the smaller British steelworks in productive capacity by 1959.[30] The countries of the European Coal and Steel Community each significantly expanded steel production during the decade.[31] Although Japan was weakened in the immediate aftermath of the war, the geopolitical atmosphere of the 1950s prompted the US to support the redevelopment of that country's industrial capabilities – including the production of raw steel. As a result, the country more than doubled its steel output between 1955 and 1960.[32] Each of the major Canadian firms also expanded, although the concentration of output within the industry slightly declined during this same period as a result of comparative growth by small producers.[33]

Tariff policy further impacted the Canadian steel industry and fostered a closer economic relationship with the United States. Both countries reduced tariffs according to the agreements reached under the General Agreement on Tariffs and Trade (GATT) at Geneva, Switzerland (1947), Annecy, France (1949), and Torquay, England (1950–1), creating a sort of "*de facto* bilateralism."[34] In 1955, just three major tariffs remained: the General Tariff, the Most Favoured Nation Tariff, and the British Preferential Tariff. These were applied to a variety of products, including bars and rods, plate, sheet, band and strip, angles and shapes.[35] Rates were simplified to a 5, 10, and 20 per cent structure after 1958, and specific products were no longer singled out for protection.[36]

Exchange rates likewise reduced import barriers. The Canadian dollar began trading higher than the US dollar in 1952 – a circumstance that remained until 1961 when it returned below parity.[37] Despite healthy demand for consumer goods and a corresponding increase in basic industry and manufacturing throughout North America, Dosco's ability to reach markets was a perennial constraint. The company shipped coal and steel products to purchasers in the Maritimes, Quebec, and Ontario, but high transportation costs meant that central Canadian steel firms could often outcompete within these markets. The American market remained restricted through trade policy; as late as 1966, USWA researchers Harry Waisglass and Andrew Hogan called for a Canada–US common market for steel to allow for prosperous trade between Atlantic Canada and New England.[38] Lacking a stable domestic market,

Table 1.2 Annual Ingot Capacity of Major Canadian Steel Firms, 1950–1960 (thousands of tons and percentage of total)

Year	1950	1955	1960
Stelco	1,247 (35.8)	2,150 (42.9)	2,500 (37)
Algoma	866 (24.9)	1,120 (22.4)	1,600 (23.7)
Dofasco	378 (10.9)	785 (15.7)	1,165 (17.3)
Dosco	877 (25.2)	733 (14.7)	1,050 (15.6)

Source: Elver, *Economic Character and Change in the Canadian Steel Industry since 1945*, 23.
Note: Remaining percentages are divided among small producers.

the Sydney Works was more reliant on world exports than were any of its direct competitors.

Despite the capabilities of the Sydney plant, the product line was not comparable with that in place at either Stelco or Algoma. Steel ingots and casting remained the largest product, followed by pig iron, blooms and billets, rails and track material, rods and bars, wire, and nails. The Sydney Works was not capable of producing sheet and strip or skelp and plate.[39] Even the increased steel orders that resulted from hostilities in Korea could not offset the relative decline of the firm.[40] The ingot capacity at Canadian integrated mills increased between 1950 and 1959, but each of the other firms eclipsed Dosco's growth. This includes Dominion Foundries and Steel Company (Dofasco), which opened its first blast furnace in August 1951 and began operations as a fully integrated mill.

Lionel Forsyth, who took over as president of Dosco in 1949, did not hesitate to use promises of modernization to try and suppress resistance from the steelworkers' union. On 2 October 1951, he addressed the Maritime Provinces Board of Trade at the Isle Royale Hotel in downtown Sydney. The future of industry in the Maritimes, he told the audience, would be cemented through a massive modernization project. Investment included $18 million in additions to the Sydney plant, $7.4 million for the Wabana ore mines, and smaller upgrades at Trenton and the Halifax Shipyards. Almost immediately, Forsyth moved on to discuss his concern over union activity. In pressing for cost-of-living wage increases, rank-and-file members had recently engaged in a number of work stoppages. He cautioned:

Such conduct has within it the seeds of a harvest which may well set at naught our plans for the future of the industry [...] At the risk of undue repetition may I mention again our program for capital expenditures in the Maritime Provinces and the impressive total of the funds which we are committed to provide to complete that program. Such a project creates a heavy burden of responsibility for those who have conceived it [...] It places an even heavier burden upon any individual or any group who by failing to do his or their share toward its realization may interfere with, impede, or defeat it. Nothing [...] could cause me greater disappointment than to be obliged for any reason to curtail this program or delay its execution.[41]

The company, aware of the desire for modernization within the USWA, used such threats as part of a carrot-and-stick strategy to promote internal discord both within the union and on the shop floor.

A recession in the final quarters of 1953 and early 1954 briefly stalled the Canadian economy and put Forsyth in the unenviable position of detailing a stagnant profit rate to shareholders.[42] He explained that the company had posted net earnings of $3,867,714.97 for the year 1953 – lower by $330,160.73 than the previous year.[43] Despite its threats, Dosco invested in several upgrades and additions to its holdings in Atlantic Canada during the early years of the decade. These included rail-finishing mills and a blooming mill at the Sydney plant, as well as a new open-hearth furnace; the Wabana mines, Trenton Works, and the Halifax Shipyards also benefited. Shareholders hoped that these investments would offset the slumping market position and increase the quality of available raw materials. The new rolling mills, in fact, cemented the Sydney works as one of the most efficient rail producers in North America – though it could still not produce flat rolled product.[44]

Although Dosco posted higher-than average net profits in 1956 and 1957, it was not able to achieve comparable profit margins to its competitors.[45] With the company facing declining relevancy in the Canadian market, Forsyth passed away in 1957 at his home in Montreal – leaving C.B. Lang, the former Dosco chairman of the board, to accept a new position as company president.[46] In his first address to shareholders, Lang described the terms of a two-year contract that had been negotiated with the steelworkers' union, a slight increase in the company's finances, and ongoing mechanization efforts – supported in part through a $5.3 million loan from the federal government.[47] Just two months after this address, representatives of A.V. Roe Canada Ltd officially expressed interest in acquiring ownership of the firm.

The corporate history of A.V. Roe Canada is complicated. Its earliest predecessor was A.V. Roe and Company, an aircraft manufacturer founded by Alliot Verdon Roe in Manchester, England, in 1910. The company designed, produced, and tested aircraft throughout the

Table 1.3 Profit Margins for Canadian Steel Firms, 1951–1957 (per cent)

Year	Algoma	Dofasco	Dosco	Stelco
1951	14.13	5.63	6.31	9.18
1952	6.83	6.08	6.72	7.85
1953	9.36	6.36	5.67	7.89
1954	6.91	6.30	5.46	7.27
1955	11.76	9.04	4.71	10.01
1956	14.35	9.40	3.59	10.53
1957	11.94	8.96	6.57	9.35

Source: Elver, *Economic Character and Change in the Canadian Steel Industry since 1945*, 20.

First World War and during the interwar period. In 1935, another UK-based aeronautics firm – the Hawker Siddeley Group – purchased A.V. Roe and Company as a subsidiary. By the Second World War, Hawker Siddeley was one of the largest aircraft producers in Britain. Its designs included the Hawker Hurricane and the Supermarine Spitfire, both of which were used extensively during the Battle of Britain. In 1944, Hawker Siddeley entered into negotiations with C.D. Howe to purchase the Victory Aircraft factory in Malton, Ontario. When this purchase was finalized on 11 November 1945, Hawker Siddeley created A.V. Roe Canada as a subsidiary of A.V. Roe and Company.

A.V. Roe Canada's overtures to Dosco were part of a broader strategy of expansion and diversification within the Hawker Siddeley Group. Chairman Thomas Sopwith, speaking to the twenty-second general meeting in London on 8 January 1958, described a company in the midst of a major restructuring. Just two years prior, Hawker Siddeley Group assets were divided in proportion of approximately 85 per cent aviation and 15 per cent industrial holdings. By the time of the attempted Dosco takeover, these numbers had radically shifted – with industrial assets representing 70 per cent of total holdings. In Sopwith's view, this diversification was necessary in a rapidly changing global economic landscape. "I think you will agree," he told the gathered shareholders, "that with such an industrial spread we should be able to weather any storm which may arise."[48]

It is perhaps unsurprising that a firm as large as Hawker Siddeley was suddenly interested in the steel industry – after all, the global steel market had experienced remarkable growth through much of the 1950s. Indeed, the attempted Dosco purchase was not Hawker Siddeley's first foray into the Canadian steel industry. In 1956, A.V. Roe and several partnered European conglomerates attempted to gain control of

Algoma following the death of its owner James Dunn. Although they failed to gain a controlling interest, the cohort purchased nearly a half-million Algoma common shares at a price tag of nearly $60 million. It was only months after this attempted acquisition that Crawford Gordon, the president of A.V. Roe, approached representatives from Dosco.[49]

According to the terms outlined by Gordon, the Dosco companies would continue to exist alongside A.V. Roe's other Canadian holdings. These were further divided between aeronautical and industrial divisions. The aeronautical division included lesser subsidiaries such as Avro Aircraft, Orenda Engines, and Canadian Steel Improvement, while the industrial division held, among others, Canadian Car and Canadian Steel Foundries.[50] In correspondence, Gordon adopted a conciliatory tone:

> The importance of Dosco to the Maritime Provinces and to Canada is fully realized by Avro and the Hawker Siddeley Group. It would be the position of Avro to strengthen and maintain the separate identity and autonomy of Dosco within the framework of Avro's Canadian group [...] You may wish, for the early information of Dosco security holders and to put an end to rumours [...] to communicate the contents of this letter to them pending [...] the formal offer.[51]

The rumours to which Gordon refers had been circulating for nearly six months, with various company officials speaking off the record about possible bids by A.V. Roe, Pheonix-Rheinrohr, and Mannesmann International. As news of the deal was leaked, Dosco stock prices climbed to approximately $30 per share, although some community members publicly speculated about the possibility of forthcoming industrial closures or the liquidation of redundant assets.[52]

The proposed terms of the purchase would see A.V. Roe immediately gain control of at least 52 per cent of Dosco common shares – a controlling interest.[53] The board of directors was surprised to receive such an offer, and several members argued resolutely against accepting the deal. Roy Jodrey, the founder of Minas Basin Pulp and Power, led the opposition with support from regional capitalist Frank Sobey.[54]

The opposition of the two men culminated with a letter to shareholders recommending against the offer. "The price being offered is too low," they wrote. "Your Board of Directors is in a position to report the highest earning for any first six-month period in the history of the Company." The $80 million spent on modernization, argued the directors, had already resulted in a stronger, more competitive industrial firm.

They also enumerated some of the company's most recent upgrades: a new 120-acre site in Etobicoke purchased for the expansion of Graham Nail and Wire Products and the Canadian Steel Corporation, a plant in Toronto, a new Canadian Bridge Company facility, and a plant for Truscon Steel in Montreal. Investment in Cape Breton included funding for another blast furnace at the Sydney works. They appealed:

> Acceptance of the Avro offer will mean that you, as a Dosco shareholder now playing an independent part in one of Canada's oldest and largest industries, will become one of a vast number of minority shareholders in a post-war holding company (itself a subsidiary) whose future plans for Dosco are still to be disclosed.[55]

While Jodrey continued to campaign against the sale, A.V. Roe Canada assumed control over nearly 76 per cent of Dosco common shares on Wednesday, 9 October 1957. The Sydney Works, just as in the Besco days, was now under the control of a foreign conglomerate based in the UK. Shareholders hoped that new management could escape the comparative decline that had plagued Dosco since the war years.[56] In spite of some infrastructure investment, the Sydney Works remained significantly behind its competitors in terms of both technological development and modernization.[57] Although former employees often identify the Hawker Siddeley takeover as the beginning of the end, the acquisition appears to have initially been intended to play a role within the company's diversification and expansion strategy. As circumstances facing A.V. Roe changed in the late 1950s, this strategy very quickly transitioned into a policy of explicit deindustrialization and liquidation.

"Death by Natural Causes?": From A.V. Roe to Hawker Siddeley Canada, 1957–1966

With the October takeover complete, Cape Breton was positioned in the midst of what William MacNutt termed the "Atlantic Revolution."[58] Technological advances contributed to a developing consumer market. Television and telephones brought Atlantic Canadians into closer contact with their neighbours across the country. Regional economic development became an important plank in federal and provincial platforms, and the election of Robert Stanfield as premier in 1956 signalled a commitment to economic growth in Nova Scotia predicated upon state intervention and regionalism.[59] At the Sydney steel plant, employment fluctuated – peaking at an all-time high in 1952 – although ultimately shedding 1,043 jobs between 1951 and 1960.

Table 1.4 Sydney Works, Average Employment, 1950–1960

Year	Number of hourly rated workers
1951	5,439
1952	5,952
1953	5,674
1954	4,494
1955	4,486
1956	4,732
1957	4,976
1958	4,335
1959	4,040
1960	4,396

Source: Sydney Works Force, Employment Office, 1950–1967, Dominion
Steel and Coal Company Papers, MG 14, 26, Box 7, File 1, BI.

The federal election in June 1957 swept the Liberals from power and
established John Diefenbaker as prime minister with a minority government. Conservative MP George Nowlan, who maintained close ties
with the newly appointed cabinet, had been staunch in his support for
Jodrey's resistance to the Dosco sale, citing fears of decline in Maritime
coal and steel.[60] Although the Conservatives did not interfere directly,
these political developments were of concern to A.V. Roe Canada's
directors. In 1957, all but one member of the board were committed
Liberal Party loyalists. Their fears were compounded by the fact that
the company's most lucrative contracts were awarded by the federal
government, including orders for the CF-105 – the "Avro Arrow."

The original $200,000 CF-105 design contract was awarded to A.V.
Roe in May 1953, and hundreds of millions of dollars were allocated to
the project before the end of the decade. The roll-out of the first CF-105
occurred in 1957, and several test flights took place over the following
months. The next year, Diefenbaker was elected again – this time with a
majority government – and he was now in a position to scrap the project altogether.[61] Although the reasons for the decision remain contested,
the Canadian government decided to follow US proposals for a missile-
based air defence system and cancel the Arrow.[62] This was announced
to the public in 1959 and the company immediately laid off 14,528 Avro
and Orenda employees. With its aeronautical division decimated, A.V.
Roe was in crisis by the final months of 1959.[63]

The Dosco division could not help to offset this disaster, as Maritime coal and steel were also facing hardship. In 1959, R.B. Elver of
the Mineral Resources Division authored his report to the Royal Commission on Coal on the competitive position of Dosco. Although he

describes problems with raw materials, Elver echoes the position of Cape Breton trade unionists from previous years – asserting that the primary reason for the Sydney Works' inability to remain competitive was lack of appropriate levels of infrastructure investment and product diversification. He warned that the diversification of the product line at the Sydney plant should be a top priority to stave off the threat of downsizing; likewise, he highlighted the importance of reducing the relative cost of raw materials as a secondary consideration. If such steps were not taken by Dosco in a timely manner, it was likely – he revealed to the Commission – that the company "will stagnate and even decline, in absolute as well as in relative terms."[64] As an important consumer of Cape Breton coal, the Sydney plant occupied an important position in the island's industrial landscape in any consideration of the future.

In addition to the problems besetting the mill, Dosco collieries in Cape Breton were facing their own issues. Coal reserves, it was revealed, were becoming less and less economically recoverable. Miners were travelling farther underground to recover their tonnages, and Ivan Rand – the head of the Royal Commission – predicted the closure of at least four major collieries by 1970. Despite these issues, Rand recommended further subsidy.[65]

Another study, this time by Arthur D. Little Inc., revealed further challenges relating to product diversification. The inability of the Sydney mill to produce flat-rolled product had become a major problem; these comprised 50 per cent of the rolled steel market in 1960. The company recognized this by 1957, when planning began for a new mill with flat-rolling capabilities to be established at Contrecoeur, Quebec. In the view of management, the addition of these mills to operations at Sydney was not an option; freight rates meant that shipping from Sydney over a ten-year period would accrue an approximate cost differential of $40 million.[66] This decision signalled a major intention to move away from the Sydney steel operations. It was clear that twenty years of steelworkers' calls for the diversification of the product line at the Sydney Works – to "diversify or die" – was about to go largely unheeded by Dosco, A.V. Roe, and the Hawker Siddeley Group.[67] Importantly, it was not simple folly that saw such advice fall on deaf ears, but rather that diversification and expansion did not fit within the framework that Dosco had chosen for itself. Rather, the firm set upon a different path – expansion and investment in central Canada and slow extrication from the Maritimes.

These issues were compounded by national and international developments. The opening of the St Lawrence Seaway proved a boon for

Table 1.5 Installation of New Steel Facilities, 1950–1960

Type of equipment	Canada and US	Europe and Japan
Blooming mills	37	40
Hot strip mills	16	31
Structural mills	1	6
Plate mills	4	30
Merchant and light mills	15	28
Rod mills	7	14

Source: Arthur D. Little Inc., *The Future of Steel-Making*, 34.

mills in Hamilton and the Soo, as it offered a ready supply of iron ore from the Ungava region of the Labrador-Quebec border, but this further diminished the geographical reasoning for production at Sydney.[68] Competition from modernized European and Japanese producers remained fierce; in 1958, British steelmakers spent $280 million on upgrades to achieve an even greater productive capacity.[69] In the US, the Iron and Steel Rate Disparities Investigation in 1963–4 found that "lower Japanese [steel] production costs were an almost insurmountable barrier to American sales in that country."[70]

Sir Roy Dobson, the new chairman of the Hawker Siddeley Group, found himself the darling of the Canadian media. Standing at five-foot-six, as Marjorie Earl of *Maclean's* revealed, he commanded "a firm fighting stance … a pair of brilliant eyes literally light his ruddy face with laughter whenever laughter is called for. But at other times [he] pounds out his displeasure at bungling, inefficiency, and red tape."[71] This reputation resulted in Dobson's continued support among shareholders as he outlined the company's flagging position in December 1960. Singled out for particular umbrage was Dosco, which had posted only a $495,192 net profit between July and December 1960. This indicated a decline from the previous twelve-month period, wherein the company had amassed nearly $3.5 million. According to the Dosco financial reports, "There has been no general increase in selling prices, thereby offsetting our increased costs, mainly labour, which have continued to rise. Basically wage costs […] handicap Canadian producers against those of every country except the United States."[72] Net income decreased again in 1961, to $1.1 million, before an uptick the next year to nearly $2.3 million – the result of a declining Canadian dollar and increased steel exports. By 1962, rails from Sydney were shipping to countries such as the UK, Colombia, Mexico, South Africa, and Venezuela in an attempt to make up lost ground through expanding international exports.[73]

The problems facing A.V. Roe worsened. Since the cancellation of the Arrow, several of the company's top executives – including Crawford Gordon – had resigned. The rail division was increasingly uneconomical as the result of car and air transport, and a failed attempt to acquire American shipbuilding contracts resulted in protracted losses.[74] The company reported nearly $3.6 million in losses during 1961.[75] Dobson turned to a corporate hatchet man to stem the bleeding. T.J. Emmert, who crafted his executive résumé at Ford and Massey Ferguson, was brought in as president and CEO of A.V. Roe Canada Ltd and parachuted into a directorship at Dosco.[76] His immediate task was to create a shell company, Hawker Siddeley Canada Ltd, and to oversee the complete divestment from Nova Scotia coal and steel.

The staples trap was approaching its terminal crisis by this point. A wide-ranging failure to create final demand linkages under Dosco meant that when nearby raw materials were exhausted there would be little need for continued investment in Cape Breton. The supply chain of the Sydney Works, the initial basis for the location of the facility, was increasingly threatened by problems with raw materials and capacity throughout the Cape Breton coal industry and the Wabana ore mines. These issues were compounded by the financial problems facing A.V. Roe after the infamous collapse of its aviation division.

The creation of Hawker Siddeley Canada Ltd was officially announced at the annual shareholders meeting of A.V. Roe in Toronto on 30 April 1962 and the company's holdings were placed under five new divisions.[77] The new steel division included the integrated works at Sydney, rolling and wire mills at Montreal and Etobicoke, a power plant near Sydney, the limestone quarry in Newfoundland, and the $20 million rod and bar mill at Contrecoeur – which became fully operational in 1964. The Wabana mines, Halifax shipyard, Cape Breton collieries, and fabrication mills at Trenton were placed under the auspices of "Dosco Industries." Other A.V. Roe holdings were reorganized under the Transportation Equipment Division, Orenda Division, and Engineering Division.[78]

Financial reports reveal a short-term plan for the move away from vertical integration. Hawker Siddeley Canada continued to fund the expansion of flat-rolling capabilities at Contrecoeur and continuous billet casting in Montreal while demanding subsidization from the Nova Scotia government for any upgrades at Sydney. Although construction began on a $12 million coal pier at the Sydney Works in 1965, this project was almost entirely funded through a grant from the Atlantic Development Board (ADB). Steel production was briefly interrupted

that same year, as the two antiquated blast furnaces in Sydney were
in such poor condition that they could not continue to operate without substantial investment and time-consuming repairs. The company
responded by relining both furnaces – a temporary fix – but refused to
replace either. This was the minimum amount necessary to maintain
even a basic level of production.[79]

Despite an upward trend for net sales within Hawker Siddeley Canada, the parent company blamed the industrial division for a shortfall
in expected profits. "Income from operations for 1965 was apprecia-
bly below that of 1964," reads another annual report. "The decline was
wholly attributable to operating results of our largest partly-owned
subsidiary (77%), Dominion Steel and Coal Corporation."[80] With this,
the liquidation of assets began in earnest; the Seaboard Power Station
in Cape Breton was sold to Nova Scotia Power for $2,553,465.[81] Two of
the Bell Island ore mines closed between 1959 and 1962, and on 19 April
1966 Dosco announced that Wabana No. 3, the longest continuously
operating iron ore mine in the country, was to shut down by June.[82]

The steelworkers' union recognized these actions as the final stages of
the corporate exit strategy that they had warned about for decades. New
wire drawing machines had been added to the Sydney Works during
the 1950s, but in March 1966 the company revealed that these were to
be transported out of Sydney to facilities at Etobicoke, Ontario. Sydney
steelworker and USWA District 2 President James Nicholson opined that
Dosco was "stripping the mill" of useful equipment. He writes:

> One can quite honestly assume that, after a comparatively short period
> with the additional high costs [associated with stripping the mill] and
> inefficiency arguments added to their arsenal of reasons why finished
> steel should not be processed in Sydney, the Company may well want to
> close this mill.[83]

Union researchers supported these points in a presentation to the ADB
at the end of the month:

> Our concern is not a new one. For a very considerable period of time, [the
> USWA has] warned of impending disaster for the Sydney Steel operations
> if diversification was not carried out. Our admonitions seem, for all
> practical purposes to have fallen on deaf ears
> [...]
> What should be the ultimate fate of the Sydney Steel Plant? That is the
> critical question [...] We can be sure that the future for steel will not be

decided by the Steelworkers or by the people of Cape Breton, nor should it be expected that the decision should rest exclusively on the basis of their particular economic interests, or solely on the considerations of their welfare. At the same time, however, the decision should not be based exclusively on the ambitions of private business to maximize its profits, or on the self-interest [sic] decisions of private capital which are rationalized by the counterfeit principles of a free enterprise system which has proved to be neither free nor enterprising.[84]

By the end of 1966, Dosco revealed plans to divest from its holdings in the Cape Breton coal field entirely, and the federal government announced that these operations would be taken over by the newly formed Cape Breton Development Corporation (Devco).

Considering this framework of a years-long process of corporate withdrawal, it is hardly surprising that Dosco announced the closure of the Sydney Works on 13 October 1967. For residents in Sydney, however, the decision could not have come as more of a surprise. Shock is the primary sentiment expressed through written narratives, oral history accounts, and cultural productions of the event from the decades after 1967. While the provincial government quickly announced plans to take control of the Sydney mill, Hawker Siddeley Canada continued to shutter and sell Dosco assets as part of what they called the "elimination of non-competitive costs."[85]

Operations in central Canada, including the mills at Contrecoeur, were sold to Sidérugie du Québec (Sidbec) – a provincial crown corporation formed in 1964 by the Quebec government. In the midst of the Quiet Revolution, the Sidbec nationalization occurred alongside a renewed conceptualization of the provincial state under Jean Lesage. It corresponded with the overarching trend toward modernization and organization of the public service, the secularization of education and health care, and the creation of several state-run enterprises.[86] Between 1960 and 1966, Quebec created several public corporations; these included: Société Générale de Financement, the Société Québécoise d'Exploration Minière, and the Caisse de Dépôt et Placement du Québec. In 1963, the province also nationalized private power corporations to add to Hydro-Québec.[87] Through its industrial acquisitions, "Sidbec" officially became "Sidbec-Dosco" in 1968.[88]

Meanwhile, the remainder of Dosco's holdings in Atlantic Canada were transferred to another Hawker Siddeley Group subsidiary, Hawker Industries Ltd. These included the Trenton Works, Halifax

Shipyards, Canadian Bridge Divisions, Dosco Overseas Engineering, and all colliery assets outside of Cape Breton.[89] The company that had controlled Cape Breton coal and steel since its incorporation in 1928 was, by this time, so fragmented and fractured as to be unrecognizable. After more than two decades of planned obsolescence, the era of private ownership at the Sydney Works drew to a close.

Chapter Two

Radical Reds and Responsible Unionism: Building a "Working-Class Town"

The most difficult thing to get hold of, in studying any past period, is this felt sense of the quality of life at a particular place and time: a sense of the ways in which the particular activities combined into a way of thinking and living.
                                                                   – Raymond Williams, 1961[1]

The long downgrading of Dosco's Cape Breton coal and steel operations could be presented as part of a declensionist reading of regional industry under Canadian capitalism. Workers' accounts of the postwar period, however, provide a challenge at the boundaries of such a historical reading. Rather than viewing the years between 1945 and 1967 as an unmitigated slide towards industrial closure, marked by underinvestment and decline, former employees often recall the better wages and working conditions that were made possible through trade unionism, the emergence of popular and consumer culture, and the urban expansion of the city. While the historical and sociological representation of these positive recollections have sometimes been castigated as "smokestack nostalgia," the work of Steven High and David Lewis reminds us that "there is also a danger in middle class academic audiences assuming that the warm memories of working people are *nothing but* nostalgia."[2]

There is tension between this reading of regional political economy and the direct, lived experiences of residents and former steelworkers in Sydney. In one sense, corporate divestment from industrial Cape Breton was recognized; certainly, the response of the steelworkers' union to the removal of equipment and the lack of continued investment reveals that this was perceived as a serious possibility. On the other hand, Dosco employees and other community members perceived a strengthening of their local institutions and class identities – the ascendance of an "industrial structure of feeling." As opposed to the aforementioned *habitus*, which consists of the embodied and lived nature of life under capitalism, Raymond Williams's "structure of feeling" is rooted in the intricacies of human emotion of perception.[3] The Black Friday announcement of an impending closure at the Sydney steel plant was shocking not only because it challenged the economic base of the city – after all, such challenges were well understood during the postwar period – but because it struck at the heart of an entire, fully developed set of local understandings that had formed around the nucleus of an industrial, working-class culture.

Culture has long been imagined as the lens through which "structures of feeling" might be better understood and analysed. When Williams first articulated the concept in 1954, he argued that literature and art were the primary modes through which "the effect of the totality, the dominant structure of feeling, [can be] expressed and embodied."[4] The closest he comes to offering a working definition for the theory is a paragraph from his 1961 book *The Long Revolution*. He writes:

> [A structure of feeling] is as firm and definite as "structure" suggests, yet it operates in the most delicate and least tangible parts of our activity. In one sense, this structure of feeling is the culture of a period: it is the particular living result of all the elements in the general organization. [...] I do not mean that the structure of feeling, any more than the social character, is possessed in the same way by the many individuals in the community. But I think that it is a very deep and very wide procession, in all actual communities, precisely because it is on it that communication depends.[5]

This is not simply the reduction of *the social* to fixed forms, or to a Hegelian spirit of the times – nor should it be read as short-hand for "prevailing ideology" or homogeneous class outlook.[6] Rather, it represents the relationships that exist between materialist structuring forces and the agency or perceptions of the individual. Further, multiple cultural forms can exist alongside one another within the same space at the same time. Recognizing this, cultural critics need to examine "residual" and "emergent" cultural forms – as they "are significant both in themselves and in what they reveal about the characteristics of the 'dominant.'"[7]

An industrial structure of feeling began to take shape in the coal and steel towns of Cape Breton alongside industrialization. As an emergent form, it shaped itself as folk practices and traditions converged with the new experiences of the island's industrial workers to articulate new themes.[8] Common experiences of the industrial environment combined with older folk practices, resulting in a strong tradition of industrial folklore and folk song writing.[9] During Cape Breton's infamous labours of the 1920s, dozens of working-class poets and songwriters contributed to the construction of local, working-class identities based upon shared experiences of work and class struggle. These radical worker-poets existed at the crux of a cultural crisis. While poets such as Dawn Fraser and Dannie Boutilier were known generally as committed "reds," this would not have been true of the majority of Cape Breton's industrial workers. Thus, the new cultural forms that they helped to engender were not entirely "radical," but – as David Frank and Donald MacGillivray have argued – they did help to "strengthen and maintain the 'rebel' outlook and populist critique of industrial capitalism" that would remain integral to workers' culture in Cape Breton for decades.[10]

Of course, these developments did not occur within a vacuum. The set of economic relationships that emboldened white, working-class poets to express their emergent culture was, itself, positioned within a settler-colonial landscape constructed through the physical displacement of the Mi'kmaq and the exclusion of Indigenous communities from the wealth generated by the island's industrial resources. However, Indigenous voices were not absent from this process; Cape Breton poet Rita Joe, born in Whycocomagh in 1932, famously expressed her experience of cultural and linguistic erasure in her 1978 poem "I Lost My Talk."[11] There, she reflects upon the enforced forgetting that occurred at the Shubenacadie residential school, which she attended at the age of twelve. Her poetry and the work of other Mi'kmaq cultural producers reveal the intricacies of the cultural forces at play; from an intersectional perspective, the work-poetry of the Sydney steel mill and the Cape Breton coal mines emerged from a set of forces imagined as normative by the non-Indigenous population. Thus, the work-poetry of this emergent industrial structure of feeling must also be read as part of a broader complicity, both by working-class settlers and the capitalists who held them in their employ, with the unfolding structures of industrial settler-colonialism.

Work-poetry is one of the finest examples of this nascent industrial structure of feeling, and Cape Breton provides a variety of instances. John "Slim" McInnis is one of the best-known worker-poets who found employment at the Sydney Works. He wrote poetry for much of his life, his oeuvre spanning from 1940 to 1988. McInnis's earliest poem, "From Breadlines to Battlefields," was published in 1940 as part of a concerted critique of the war effort and provided a direct call for class-based solidarity from the island's industrial workforce. He writes:

> What right, we ask, have this useless class
> To demand we engage a foe
> They helped maintain with the selfish aim
> Of saving the "status quo"?
>
> Why should we band in a far off land
> And wealth for another wrest,
> If here at home we have only known
> The fate of the dispossessed?[12]

The rebel outlook is clearly visible here, although McInnis's poetry soon began to express the hope that industrial unionism could achieve better circumstances for workers without necessitating revolution. The following is from his 1946 "The Steel Strike":

> But at last there came an end to the pain
> And my heart no more could feel,
> Then the talks were stalled and the union called
> For a national strike in steel.
>
> So we're struck at last and all we ask
> Is a forty-hour week
> So our brave young sons who fought the Huns
> Can find the work they seek
>
> And a slight increase will give release
> From the worry we have long known
> And a chance to pay for the right to stay
> In the hovel we call our home.[13]

By the 1950s, local cultural productions lacked the bitterness and the explicit calls for class war that so obviously emboldened their predecessors. The *Dishpan Parade* program on CJCB radio asked local composers to contribute songs and poems. Nell Campbell of Glace Bay, whose husband Joseph worked in the Dosco collieries, submitted "Plain Ol' Miner Boy" as a description of working-class life:

> I'm a plain ol' miner boy, a tough hard-workin' miner boy,
> I have a few on Saturday night and I sleep all day on Sunday

I lead a very simple life, but I love my kids and I love my wife
I'll be goin' down that ol mine shaft when the whistle blows on Monday.[14]

This poem expresses a different sort of experience than do those of labour strife in earlier decades. In her verses, the life of a Cape Breton working-class family remains difficult – but it is a far cry from the poverty, starvation, and state-sanctioned violence of the interwar years. Her representation fits with the understanding of historians of the working class, who have identified an increasing awareness among many people in North America that material conditions had, in fact, improved dramatically in comparison to the years before the Second World War."[15] For steelworkers in Sydney, this prevailing sentiment cannot be divorced from their achievement of union recognition in 1937 and the material gains of Canadian steelworkers in the years following the Second World War.

This line of inquiry does not begin with the assumption that economic pressures and the resulting class struggle *determined* the contours of an industrial structure of feeling in Sydney. It is not purely rooted in classical historical materialism, but rather in the prevailing sense – articulated by Williams – that the base productive mode is itself dynamic and internally contradictory. Far from producing stable categories of "superstructural" institutions, this instability produces contradictions throughout capitalist societies.[16] It is for this reason that the understandings of life in Sydney during the postwar period that are articulated through oral histories and visible through cultural productions are so obviously contrasting with the visible indicators of economic crisis. Through an understanding of these contradictions, we come to recognize that the production of this sort of cognitive dissonance was the result of the co-morbidity of two predominant variables: Dosco's ongoing disinvestment in Cape Breton coal and steel and the concurrent material gains achieved by the steelworkers' union, United Steelworkers of America, Local 1064.

The Decline of Union Militancy, 1946–1949

Stories of union militancy formed the backbone of the "working-class town" of Sydney, especially among steelworking families. Gordie Gosse, a third-generation steelworker in Sydney, remembers growing up in Whitney Pier and hearing countless tales of work at the plant from both father and grandfather. Gosse was hired by Sysco in 1974 and worked in the mill until he was laid off in 1992. Following his time at the mill, Gosse acted as the director of the Whitney Pier

2.1 Steel plant during the 1923 strike. Photographer unknown, reference
number: 89-517-18712, Beaton Institute, Cape Breton University.

Boys and Girls Club; he also served as the provincial MLA for Sydney
and Whitney Pier between 2003 and 2015. Growing up in the Pier,
he remembers "Bloody Sunday" being a frequent recollection of the
older steelworkers. He related:

> I remember my grandfather talking about Bloody Sunday [in 1923]
> when they came to Whitney Pier with troops ... and beat [the striking
> steelworkers] up and ran them over and everything [...] They had brought
> in the army, my grandfather said, and the provincial police at that time. And
> they were on horses. And people were coming home from church [...] And
> the army and provincial police beat them up and everything [...] And they
> had Gatling guns at the General Office, set up on the roof! [...] Oh [things]
> were a lot better [by the 1950s]. My father said, and my grandfather ... They
> could retire then, with a small pension, and get on with their lives – you
> know?[17]

Bloody Sunday was a significant event during the 1923 steelworkers'
strike. On 28 June, workers walked out of the mill and set up pickets, preventing strikebreakers from entering the plant. Soldiers arrived
from Halifax two days later and provincial police reached Sydney on
1 July . That evening, sixteen mounted police charged through striking
miners at one of the gates of the mill. They continued up Victoria Road,

the main street in working-class Whitney Pier, and assaulted several pedestrians in a show of strength against the strikers. Men, women, and children all recalled being chased off of the street, and several were knocked down, struck, or injured.[18]

Although the 1923 strike was ultimately broken, the state violence enacted upon the steelworkers in Sydney has remained a lasting part of their occupational memory. That such stories were passed down to later generations of workers is unsurprising; indeed, it is perhaps unremarkable, then, that the postwar period would be imbued with a sense of nostalgia. This is especially the case when postwar steelworkers would have contrasted their own experiences with the stories that they heard of the violence and upheaval of earlier struggles. These changes mirrored shifts in labour relations occurring nationally and internationally.

In the Canadian context, labour relations grew increasingly bureaucratic and institutional during the 1940s. Between 1941 and 1943, more than 425,000 workers were involved in strikes related to wages, working conditions, or shop-floor issues across the country. This includes a national steel strike of more than 13,000 steelworkers in 1943, wherein Steel Workers Organizing Committee (SWOC) unionists sought to equalize wage rates across the entire industry.[19] Members of the National War Labour Board pressured the federal government to develop a collective bargaining policy, in response to which the King government passed its signature order-in-council PC 1003 on 20 March 1944.[20] This legislation compelled employers within federal and war-related industries to bargain with unions, participate in conciliation, and engage in grievance arbitration.[21]

The analytical contours of this "capital-labour compromise" remain contested; Marxist and feminist scholars have broadly challenged the notion that PC 1003 represented a major victory for Canadian labour on the grounds that it simply reified traditional systems of power.[22] Peter McInnis reflects that "historians have either assessed this moment as one of intense conflict that secured a measure of legitimacy for organized labour or, alternatively, as a time when workers and their leadership entered into a Faustian bargain that limited unions' effectiveness in succeeding generations."[23]

In Sydney, the steelworkers' union achieved recognition earlier than did their colleagues across the country. The Independent Steelworkers' Union of Nova Scotia met as early as 1935 and gained a SWOC charter as Lodge 1064 the following year under the CIO. Nova Scotia Premier Angus L. MacDonald signed the Nova Scotia Trade Union Act in 1937, which forced Dosco to recognize the new union; this was done in the hopes of avoiding a plant-wide recognition strike.[24] The timing of these

Table 2.1 Milestones in the History of Local 1064, 1900–1946

1904	First plant-wide strike
1923	Canadian military and provincial police arrive in Sydney to defeat steelworkers' attempts to gain union recognition
1935	Independent Steelworkers' Union of Nova Scotia formed in opposition to the plant workers' council
1936	Steelworkers are granted a charter as Lodge 1064 of the Pittsburgh-based Steel Workers Organizing Committee (SWOC)
1937	Passage of the Nova Scotia Trade Union Act by the provincial legislature; Dosco recognizes the steelworkers' union
1942	Sydney Lodge 1064 votes to affiliate with the United Steelworkers of America and officially becomes USWA Local 1064

decisions matched developments on the American side of the border; on 3 March, the *New York Times* reported that CIO President John L. Lewis and Myron C. Taylor, the chairman of the board for US Steel, had reached an agreement for SWOC recognition from the country's largest steel producer.[25] In 1942, SWOC Lodge 1064 officially became Local 1064 of the United Steelworkers of America. Despite these early victories, as Craig Heron and Robert Storey remind us, "Canadian steel companies fought back, and the struggle for collective representation became bitter and pronounced."[26]

Despite the changing landscape of labour relations, Canadian workers soon turned to their traditional method of achieving gains from recalcitrant employers: strike action. Between May 1946 and November 1947, more than 180,000 workers engaged in strikes across the country. This includes the 1946 Canadian steel strike, which involved workers from Stelco, Algoma, and Dosco.

Much of the scholarly interest in this strike wave has focused on the charged conflict at Stelco. The industry leader in Hamilton was positioned as a bellwether for the Canadian steel industry and – similarly to Sydney – management had attempted to avoid unionization through the creation of a workers' council. Stelco was forced to recognize USWA Local 1005 and a contract was agreed upon in February 1945.[27] Hamilton was also an epicentre for workers' resistance in other sectors; employees at Westinghouse, the *Spectator*, and the National Knitting Mills all engaged in strike action before the year's end.[28] Dofasco steelworkers were conspicuously absent from this agitation; unlike its competitors, that company was successful at stamping out unionism through a campaign of corporate welfare and targeted intimidation during the 1920s and 1930s.[29]

2.2 The Sydney Steel Union (SWOC) executive of 1942. Front row, left to right: Charles Mallard, Canadian director, SWOC; George MacEachern, president; Bill MacQueen, corresponding representative; Forman Waye, district organizer; James Nicholson, financial secretary; Jack Flannery, California district, SWOC. Second row, extreme left: Kenzie MacNeil, vice-president. Third row, left to right: Bernard MacDonald, secretary; Palmer Robertson, journal agent; George MacNeil, treasurer. Top left: Member of Parliament Clarie Gillis. Steel Union Executive Members, 1942. Reference number: 77-845-979. Beaton Institute, Cape Breton University.

During the 1946 national strike in steel, union organizers at Stelco, Algoma, and Dosco each formulated their demands based upon the fundamental tenets of fairness and security. This did not extend to challenging the right of employers to control production; rather, steelworkers and their representatives sought internal systems of bureaucracy that would regulate hiring and provide economic security from the arbitrary exertion of power by foremen or supervisors.[30] Despite the common goals of industrial unionism, better wage rates, and the forty-hour week, steelworkers at Dosco were more hesitant than those at Stelco or Algoma to resolve in favour of the proposed contract. The tabled offer left the matter of a 5¢ wage differential in Sydney undecided and did not cement the forty-hour week.[31] Although members of Local 1064 ultimately voted by a margin of five to one in favour of the contract, this was far narrower than the vote at other firms – implying, perhaps, stronger support for militancy within Sydney's rank and file.[32]

The response of Local 1064 to the new contract was fractured; a significant number of workers voiced displeasure over the compromise offered by National Director Charles Millard – who already had a reputation as an anti-communist and anti-radical. Not all of this opposition was rooted in the radical left – indeed, non-communist oppositionists also felt that they were being undercut by what they perceived as an abdication to management.[33] Communist leader Tim Buck visited Sydney in the aftermath of the strike to congratulate steelworkers on their gains, later reflecting, "I argued it was a tremendous *achievement* because recognition of the *legal* necessity for collective bargaining, placing it *on the level of the law* [...] was, perhaps, one of the most revolutionary advances that the trade union movement had made."[34]

Among management, Arthur Cross was also unhappy with the outcome of the confrontation. Refusing to reopen the Sydney Works, the company sought assurance from the federal government that any redress of the "Sydney differential" would be provided through subsidy – not from the company's profits. Some 1064 members viewed this as further grandstanding not dissimilar from Dosco's earlier claims of financial exigency. One poem published pseudonymously in the Sydney independent labour weekly, *Steelworker and Miner*, reveals:

> No brother, Dosco carries on
> Entirely for Cape Breton's good
> It daily loses cash upon
> It's job of giving you your food
> Or so it says.[35]

For its part, the National War Labour Board found that "the weight of evidence supports the Union's contention that a gross inequality existed in the wage rates of the production workers at Sydney," and revealed a prorated wage scale ranging from a full 5¢ per hour increase for those employees earning less than 61¢ per hour, to a ½ ¢ increase for employees between 80–89.5¢ per hour.[36] Donald Gordon, chairman of the Wartime Prices and Trade Board, soon announced that the federal government would subsidize Dosco to offset these increases.[37] With this, the company finally agreed to restart steel production.

Despite a broad turn away from the radical left throughout the Canadian labour movement, radical voices remained within the rank and file.[38] Several letters to *Steelworker and Miner* in Sydney excoriated Millard and local 1064 president Ed Corbett for the perceived failure to achieve the forty-hour work week.[39] By 1948, with communists officially excluded from the executive, one editorial reflected:

> The workers, now being securely shackled, the big talks starts all over again. Our information is that National Director C.H. Millard is calling on the locals to take part in a nation-wide campaign for a forty-hour week. And so the cycle starts again – militant statements to the press, militant demands, tub thumping at its phoniest between negotiations, and then, in the crisis, the let-down.[40]

This left-opposition within Local 1064 suffered a major defeat in 1949, when a strike by the Communist-led Canadian Seamen's Union (CSU) brought radical and conservative trade unionists into direct conflict.[41] Harry David, president of the CSU, announced the strike on 31 March 1949; steelworkers in Sydney initially supported this action, as did Corbett and the union executive. Members were ready to support CSU pickets at the Dosco piers and ignore orders to unload cargo brought in by non-union crews.[42] Then, suddenly, the executive reversed its decision and announced that Local 1064 would not honour CSU pickets. In his autobiography, former 1064 president and labour activist George MacEachern writes:

> When Eddie Corbett [...] was called to Ottawa, he was supporting the seamen's strike. When he came back from Ottawa, he was in a terrible nervous state. They had to get a doctor for him. They had to put a policeman out on the lawn. I don't know what they did to him in Ottawa, but he was terrified when he came home. He wasn't bribed, because he wasn't any better off when he came back than he was going. But whatever pressures they put on him, whatever they told him [...] I never asked him.[43]

In 1990, former steelworker Walter Pickles recalled the situation during an interview with Michael Earle:

MICHAEL: Well, there were some pretty controversial things that went on when [Corbett] was president. That business with the Canadian Seamen's Union and so on … ?
WALTER: Oh yes, a lot of those things, yeah. And he told us a lot of stories about being in Montreal and places like that and being followed, shadowed, and knowing that their phone was tapped and … government keeping track of things going on too, you know? [...] Oh yeah, he went on at great lengths to tell us different stories about that.
MICHAEL: But who'd be doing that though?
WALTER: Oh, God. Who knows the intrigue that goes on between unions and rival political factions, and governments, you know.[44]

Although other workers expressed disbelief that Corbett could have been intimidated, this common explanatory narrative presents the executive's abandonment of radical politics as the result of unnamed "off-island" actors and agitators – including within the national USWA.[45]

A Working-Class Structure of Feeling in the 1950s

The decisive turn towards so-called "responsible unionism" occurred alongside what Ira Katznelson describes as "the long moment when liberalism thickened and became both more legitimate (swallowing some of its former conservative and socialist competitors) and more vulnerable."[46] While Cold War political tensions played a role in this process, including anti-democratic red-baiting within the USWA, material gains achieved through contract negotiations helped to shore up support among the local rank and file.

Between 15 November 1941 and 15 October 1946, the basic wage rate at the Sydney Works increased from 43.5¢ to 59.5¢ per hour – outpacing increases in cost of living during the same period.[47] Members benefited from another 6 per cent wage increase following the 1946 strike and an additional 11.5¢ in 1948, which was based on the pattern set by Local 1005 at Stelco.[48] Although the forty-hour week was not achieved in 1949, members of Local 1064 voted to approve a contract that offered a 10¢ increase and the forty-four-hour week; this was in spite of popular criticisms of the "penalty clauses," which punished strike action during the terms of the contract.[49] With these gains, the years immediately following the Second World War are recalled fondly. As Sydney steelworker Wally MacKinnon told historian Michael Earle:

2.3 Sydney, from St Rita's Hospital, c. 1950. Reference number: 81-818-5898. Beaton Institute, Cape Breton University.

That was really the crunch in 1946 […] From then on, the union played a major part in the industry and in the community. Local 1064 played a magnificent role, in my opinion. It produced great leaders. And it's a sad commentary on the fact that many men who led the union are forgotten. They're still my heroes. They're still men who made a major contribution to the welfare not only of steelworkers, but of steelworkers' families, grandchildren and great-grandchildren. You know vacations with pay, the right to have free time, to have some sort of quality of life, came out of Local 1064 […] It was a bright, bright period in the history of this region.[50]

During the 1950s, USWA negotiators continued to seek wage concessions. In 1950, Local 1005 in Hamilton reached a deal whereby steelworkers were offered the forty-hour week and a wage increase.[51] Dosco refused to abide by this pattern, offering a smaller wage increase and a scaled transition to the forty-hour week over a period of two years.[52] The Sydney steelworkers were once again unable to achieve parity in 1952, when those in Hamilton had negotiated for a $1.43½ base labour rate per hour and the introduction of the Co-operative Wage Study (CWS) to help regulate job rates throughout the industry.[53] Local 1064 did achieve short-lived parity in 1954, when Dosco agreed to the implementation of the CWS system, but broke from the pattern again in 1956 when they were held to only an 8¢ increase over a two-year period.[54] The pay rate in Sydney would remain approximately 6¢ behind the wage commanded by steelworkers in Ontario for the remainder of the decade.

Historian Ron Crawley, who has written an excellent labour history of Local 1064, argues that the gains made by the Sydney steelworkers during the late 1940s and 1950s pale in comparison to what would have been possible had the membership decided to take a more radical approach. Noting the declining share of productivity achieved by workers during the decade, Crawley reflects, "Overall, the moderate and accommodationist approach by the [1064] leadership produced modest results in improving the material benefits to workers when one considers the possibilities that presented themselves to the union."[55] Nonetheless, the accommodationist approach *did* provide significant tangible benefits for employees at the Sydney Works, and the repeated re-election of moderate leaders reflects widespread support among a majority of the rank and file.

As with any oral history accounts, workers' recollections of the 1950s in Sydney must be contextualized within the life histories of each speaker and the circumstances surrounding each story's transmission. Among the informants who were interviewed between 2013 and 2015, Bernie Britten, Mickey Campbell, John Campbell, and Fabian Smith each worked at the plant prior to 1960.[56] While the specificities of wage gains during the decade are not explicitly discussed, all four men reflect upon the interconnections between work in the steel mill, familial relationships, and the fabric of the community. John, who began on the plant as a summer student in 1950, describes:

I grew up in a steelmaking family with dad and uncles and, you know, steel was a topic of conversation when anybody dropped in […] The steel plant was a dominant part of the fabric of the community in 1950. A lot of people worked there and a lot of people depended on it.[57]

Bernie started working in the chemical lab at the Dosco mill in 1951 at the age of eighteen. He says:

2.4 Local 1064 contract negotiations, 1950. Front: M.E. Corbett, Walter Coadic, Alphonso Murray, Clarence Mac Innis, Charles Millard, E.P. Pledge, James Nicholson. Back: Eamon Park, Martin Merner, Bob McNaughton, Ben O'Neil, Dan Mac Kay, unidentified, Cleve Kidd, Ted Joliffe. [Photographer unknown, Reference 76-78, Beaton Institute, Cape Breton University.]

That was 1951. The people were coming back from the war were now well-established. And finished university, that kind of thing. So things were booming […] In the Dosco days, I was quite far removed from the seats of power but Mr. Anson was the general manager at a time. He was a very powerful individual and he didn't take too much baloney from people in Montreal as far as we could tell. And he ran a good ship. Always made money, as far as we know. Which of course changed after Hawker Siddeley took over and that … wasn't the best of times, with them.[58]

Mickey also speaks of a boom in the postwar years, and recalls – correctly – that it was in 1952 that the mill employed the most workers of any time in its operational history.[59] All agree that Sydney in the 1950s was a quintessential steel town – a "going concern" where a significant amount of employment in the city relied upon the continued operations of the steelworks.

Their memories, relayed more than sixty years after the fact and thirteen years after the final closure of the mill, reveal an "in-between moment" in the historical memory of the plant that stretches from the end of the Second World War to the uncertainty of the 1960s. Within this period, the achievements of unionism were being felt without the violence of the earlier labour wars while the worst anxieties of deindustrialization were yet to be made manifest. These retirees recognize and describe an epoch when Sydney steelworkers fundamentally belonged to the time and place.[60] Jackie Clarke writes that deindustrialization operates to render industrial workers *invisible* through "various forms of marginalization, occlusion, and disqualification from the mainstream political and media discourses which play an important role in shaping public understanding of the social world."[61] Contrarily, it was in the postwar decade that a working-class structure of feeling – albeit one de-radicalized from its pre-war iterations – was most visible and strongly felt.

Returning to the analysis of cultural representations of working-class life in Sydney during the 1950s further underscores this point. At this point, local songs and poems began expressing a dramatic and optimistic sense of modernity not found within the protest song tradition of earlier decades.[62] It should be noted, however, that the community of working-class cultural producers also expanded beyond the factory floor. The early works of miner-poet Dawn Fraser and steelworker Slim McInnis were published in the pages of local labour newspapers or through word of mouth, while the availability of mass media after the 1940s provided avenues for other popular representations of life in the steel city.[63]

While Nell Campbell's "Plain Ol' Miner Boy" described life in the Cape Breton coal towns, several other entries to the CJCB competition detailed life in and around the Sydney Works. Aileen Stephen penned "Dumping the Slag" for CJCB – a song that has since entered into popular memory in Sydney. The verses detail a newcomer to the city becoming acclimatized to the night-time noises of steel production:

> The first night in Sydney heard an awful bang,
> The windows rattled and the rafters rang!
> Jumped three feet and was half out of bed,
> Papa grabbed me by the ankle and calmly said:

> They're dumping the slag over at the steel plant,
> Dumping the slag in the middle of the night,
> They're dumping the slag over at the steel plant,
> Come back to bed, Momma, everything's alright![64]

Industrial sounds, at first alien to the narrator, slowly become symbols of normalcy and comfort. In the final verse, the narrator returns to her country town only to find herself unable to sleep without the noise of the plant. The notion that industrial noise was central to the sensory-scape of Sydney is also something that arises in accounts of the post-industrial city. Syd Slaven, who was raised in the city and also worked at the plant, writes:

> When I was a boy I would lay in bed on open window summer nights listening to the symphony of night music that pervaded our community [...] A loud clang signified the dropping of a sling of rails at the rail-finishing mill. On a clear night the softer sound of rails being loaded into a ship's hole could be heard from the distant International Piers. The zing of the hot saw cutting a glowing rail at the rail mill had a unique sound of its own [...] Now, outside of the siren of an emergency response vehicle, the nights of Sydney are, please excuse the metaphor, as silent as a cemetery.[65]

Another unattributed entry describes how fair wages at the Sydney Works impact the entire city:

> What is it keeps the steelman on his mettle night and day,
> It's the income ...
> What is it pays his pension when he's getting old and gray,
> It's the income ...
> What's it keeps the living standard of Cape Breton up to par
> ...
> It's the income.[66]

"Spring in Sydney," focuses on the natural world, contrasting the expected change of seasons with the ever-present sooty air in the neighbourhoods surrounding the plant:

> Went for a walk around the town,
> Wore a grey hat and now it's brown
> The soot and smoke sure get me down,
> It's Spring in Sydney darlin'[67]

These cultural artefacts reflect the culmination of a more mainstream working-class structure of feeling than was visible in earlier radical expressions. The steel plant and its employees, in each of these entries, are central to the sense of place within the city. The structure of feeling is not entirely divorced from the earlier radical phase, but it is more directly informed by the political circumstances of the postwar compromise in Canada and the local achievements of the steelworkers and their union. These newer representations could not be more distinct, for instance, from the vision of the city articulated by H.M. Bartholomew in 1923:

> Steel is the backbone of Sydney. The long rows of ugly chimneys belching forth torrents of smoke and fire bear witness to the fact (of which the papers are so proud) that Sydney is a town of steel [...] Under this small forest of chimneys toil the slaves of steel – chained, by grim necessity, to the chariot of a brutal, relentless corporation.[68]

Again, we might return to Williams's metaphor of language to understanding the fuzzy processes by which structures of feeling are transformed. He writes, "No generation speaks quite the same language as its predecessor [...] It is a general change, rather than a set of deliberate choices, yet choices can be deduced from it, as well as effects."[69]

By the time of the A.V. Roe takeover in 1957, the declining power of left-opposition within the USWA and Local 1064 more specifically had resulted in the entrenchment of moderate and conservative leadership. In Sydney, this transition found purchase among the rank and file as a result of both Cold War anti-communism and the material achievements of the postwar period. The leadership of 1064 had become an important part of the community; Ed Corbett, for example, held positions on the Canso causeway committee and the hospital commission – and was even invited to sit on the conservative Board of Trade, although he graciously declined the offer.[70] For a brief moment, expressed through the recollections of former employees and contemporary cultural creations, Sydney steelworkers were able to reflect upon their past achievements and look forward to a promising future. This sense of belonging would be challenged as deindustrialization became more visible in the early 1960s.

A Return to Militancy? Responding to Deindustrialization, 1957–1967

The announcement of new facilities at Contrecoeur by Dosco management along with a stated desire to suppress local labour costs in Sydney by increasing efficiency had the effect of mobilizing support among rank-and-file steelworkers for a re-evaluation of the accommodationist approach.[71] On the shop floor, some workers began to openly lobby for the union to challenge some aspects of Dosco's work control. In 1961, Dosco greatly contributed to this dissatisfaction by hiring a team of Taylorist efficiency experts. The Alexander Proudfoot Company, unaffectionately nicknamed "the cutworms" by steelworkers, was contracted to conduct an on-site efficiency review of all operations at the Sydney Works.[72] Otis Cossit, a linesman at the plant, recalls:

They were just a bunch of hoodlums from up around Chicago, I believe, is where that outfit came from. They all came dressed like Dick Tracy. They all looked alike. They reminded you of some of these religious sects that you see going around like a flock of herring.[73]

Another steelworker, Walter Clarke, describes the activities of the efficiency experts:

Everybody was up in arms about it because ... you had to write down what you done on this job and how long it took you to do this and how long it took you to do that [...] All the while they were there, they had trouble [...] One less man, that was the name of their game – to cut down on manpower and get more production [...] Sometimes he used to have a stopwatch there – how long did it take you to do this? And you'd have to write it down.[74]

Popular discontent with these measures resulted in increasing local support for direct action and militant tactics during the early 1960s. The "cutworms," combined with growing uncertainty surrounding the unfolding Hawker Siddeley deal, prompted steelworkers in Sydney to walk off the job at least forty-six times between 1961 and 1964.[75] The largest of these walkouts occurred between the fall and winter of 1961–2, when the efficiency teams arrived on-site.[76] On 10 October 1961, nearly 500 employees walked off the job in a protest over proposed scheduling changes; workers interviewed by the *Cape Breton Post* also expressed dissatisfaction over managerial strategy.[77] Large walkouts also occurred in January and March, when wildcat strikes by workers in the rod and bar mills prompted employees in other departments to join in sympathy.[78] Union officials and members of the USWA International Executive Board quickly condemned these expressions of class militancy.[79]

The walkouts at the Sydney Works also correspond with a period of growing radicalism within the Canadian labour movement. This culminated in the "wildcat wave" of 1965–6, when between 359 and 575 wildcat strikes took place across the country.[80] Shifting demographics have been posited as one reason for this, with males under the age of twenty-five occupying a larger percentage of the labour market and facing more precarious employment than their older colleagues.[81] Analyses of strikes by USWA 6500 (Sudbury) and USWA 1005 (Hamilton) offer further credence to the theory that a combination of youthfulness and masculine posturing contributed to the strike wave during the summer of 1966. As Ian Milligan argues, "At both [Hamilton and Sudbury], young men were the sparks that ignited large conflagrations, confounding union leaders, government agents, and managers alike."[82]

Demographic changes bear less explanatory weight in consideration of the increasingly radical rank and file at Sydney. During the Stelco walkout in 1966, one older steelworker blamed the newer, younger workers for instigating the strike action.[83] In 1962, the walkout wave at the Sydney Works was primarily instigated by older, more experienced workers. Of the approximately 255 workers in the Sydney rod and bar mill, where the two largest walkouts began, even the employees who held the least seniority had been at the plant for more than a decade.[84] After another brief work stoppage on 30 August 1963, management identified seven workers as the possible cause. Only one of these men had been hired within the previous year, while each of the others had started at the plant between 1940 and 1953.[85] By 1964, the average worker within the rod and bar department had twenty years of plant experience.[86]

This shift was also visible in the election results of Local 1064. In 1962, radical leader Jim Ryan was elected as local union president. Ryan, who defeated the moderate Martin Merner, favoured a more militant style of trade unionism.[87] National leadership was concerned; Ryan was a reputed communist, which was soon brought to the direct attention of Canadian Director William Mahoney. Roy Flood, another member of 1064, wrote to Mahoney to describe a perceived breakdown of leadership within the Sydney local. He describes a confrontation between himself and Ryan:

> [Mr. Ryan] berated what he referred to as my ideology and among other things called me a "wiseacre" and a "smart Alec." Here I might say that I suspect the outburst was prompted by past experience when on numerous occasions I took issue with Mr. Ryan and some of his cohorts who were noted for their loud-mouthed negativism. You are no doubt aware that Mr. Ryan is suspected of having communist leanings. Certain it is that he fought every effort of the previous President.[88]

2.5 Local 1064 Steelworkers' Hall, Prince Street, Sydney, 1963. Photograph by the Steel Project, Reference 90-1790-21222b, Beaton Institute, Cape Breton University.

Mahoney responded positively to another member of the 1064 executive, Ben O'Neill, noting that "[Flood] sounds like a type who might be quite useful in the local union."[89]

If young workers in Ontario and Quebec rallied against their employers and union executives based upon a forward-looking enthusiasm for "new unionism" and "the just society," employees at the Sydney Works responded to a different set of pressures.[90] While the workforce at Stelco expanded by 62 per cent between 1960 and 1966, employment at the Sydney plant was reduced by 28 per cent during the same years.[91] This reduction was most palpable during the period in which the majority of walkouts occurred, with 887 workers laid off between September 1961 and March 1962.[92] Unlike Stelco's "rebel youth," who perhaps took the gains of the postwar years for granted, steelworkers in Sydney were confronted with a slow unraveling of their place on the shop floor and, ultimately – within the community that they had helped to build.

Chapter Three

It Brought Us Joy, It Brought Us Tears: Black Friday and the Parade of Concern

We Stand United, One and All
The Maritimes must never fall
So let's all get behind the wheel
To save our coal and save our steel

– Charlie MacKinnon, 1967

On Thursday afternoon, 12 October 1967, a group of Dosco executives arrived in Ottawa to meet with federal officials. T.J. Emmert was there, along with Sir Arnold Hall – president of the Hawker Siddeley Group, and Chip Drury, president of Dosco. The three men met for nearly two hours with representatives of the federal government – Allan J. MacEachen, Jean-Luc Pépin, and Charles M. "Bud" Drury, the minister of industry.[1] Charles and Chip Drury were scions of Montreal businessman Victor M. Drury, who had gained prominence through his involvement with the Royal Securities Corporation in the early twentieth century.[2] Although each of the men remained tight-lipped after the meeting, refusing to answer questions, news of their assembly prompted rumours on the shop floor at Sydney.

Steelworkers openly wondered whether Dosco was about to announce a new product line or whether officials planned to expand or reduce investment in the aging plant. Shop talk was frequently rife with considerations of what direction the company would take, and this was no exception. Former steelworker and union representative Charles MacDonald would later laugh as he recalled, "Some people always said, you know, if you didn't hear a good rumour by ten o'clock it's time to start one."[3] In October of 1967, the big news at Sydney Steel was that the findings of the *Sydney Steelmaking Study* had been made public just a week prior. The study, commissioned by the Voluntary Economic Planning Board, described competitive challenges arising from technological advancements in steelmaking. Although the report assured that production in Sydney would be maintained, this did not stymie fears of reductions at the plant.[4]

The next morning, Dosco's board of directors gathered at corporate headquarters in Ville Sainte Pierre, Montreal. In the spacious offices, Emmert outlined a recommendation that the company "disengage itself from the operations carried out at the Sydney Steel Plant at Sydney, Nova Scotia." The board unanimously passed the resolution, although Frank Sobey abstained from the vote.[5] It was the possibility of this decision that the executives had communicated privately to representatives of the federal government the previous afternoon. Emmert and Hall immediately set out for the Montreal airport, where they boarded a private aircraft for a scheduled 4:30 p.m. meeting in Halifax with Nova Scotia Premier George Isaac Smith.[6] According to the *Brandon Sun* newspaper, "the two company officials were stern-faced and silent when they entered the meeting [...] They left with similar expressions, still refusing to comment."[7]

Three hours later, Emmert's assistant issued a press release that outpaced even the most pessimistic shop-floor conjecture. The decision was made. The Sydney Works was to close. Further, the release explained, "If the money was available to completely modernize the mill, its geographical location relative to markets and the resulting freight charges on its products would still prevent Sydney from being truly competitive."[8] In human costs, 3,225 steelworkers – more than 25 per cent of the city's workforce – would be unemployed within months. Switchboards at newspaper offices and radio stations throughout the Maritimes lit with activity as the news spread to Sydney and beyond. Martin Merner, again the Local 1064 president after defeating the incumbent Jim Ryan, heard the news while returning from the USWA national offices in Toronto. Arriving in Sydney, he found himself before television cameras attempting to calm a city already in the grip of panic.[9]

Black Friday, as 13 October became known in Sydney, was a profoundly traumatic event for those who were directly impacted. Representatives from the business community immediately denounced the decision; the shops and stores that had sprouted in the streets surrounding the plant since the early decades of the twentieth century were suddenly facing the complete destruction of their customer base.[10] Employees of the Sydney Works recall the great sense of disruption wrought by the sudden announcement.

Adrian Murphy was in his early twenties when he had his first shift in the mill's general yard on 28 April 1964. He worked the night of Black Friday:

I was down in the docks, down in the rail boat, and it was over a dirty, rotten, cold night. On the 4:00 to 12:00. And it was rainy and miserable, it was. Somebody said, "They're closing the plant." And all, well, like I said what would I have been then – 24 or [2]5, whatever I was, not very old. "Thank Christ, let me out of here," I said. I came up, my father – he had, well, he was on 1940, so he had 27 years on – he had tears coming down his cheeks. And rightly so, he had about 7 or 8 kids going to school. So rightly so. He was in big trouble. And then they had the big Parade of Concern. And then they got together and turned it around.[11]

Fabian Smith, who worked in the General Office, was married with three children. He clearly remembers the feeling of shock, and describes going downtown in the aftermath:

It was a Friday night. And Bill Jessome was on [...] to read the news. And he had a lead in. He said, "We have a very important announcement about the steel plant." And at that time, I think it was Brazil. We were looking for a rail order, anyway. And I said, "Oh jeez, we must have got that rail order. And I had my coat on, I was sitting on the arm of the chair, and we, my wife and I were going to the Vogue for a movie. And she said, "Are you coming," and I said "No, no, let's wait for that announcement. Anyway, he came on. And he read ... And if you have ever been hit in the stomach – hard – that's what it felt like. And I mean, she was in shock. We had four kids, you know? Well, three kids at the time [...] She says, "What are we going to do?" I said, "We're going to a movie. And we went ... Charlotte Street was wall-to-wall people. The whole length of Charlotte Street. [...] Just people. And it was almost like you were looking at zombies because, you know, everybody's shaking their heads. "How could this possibly be?" You know? [...] And Monday morning at work was total silence.[12]

Mickey Campbell remembers seeing the Dosco press release posted inside the Coke Ovens Department:

I seen guys there that didn't believe it. Yeah, there was a notice put up in every office in the plant [...] that they were going to close. So one guy read it, and he was going to tear it off the wall. And I told him if he did that I'd report him [pauses] I said there's other fellas that'll want to see it. Sure enough, they didn't believe it. Thought it was put there for a joke or something. It was right out of the blue.[13]

In these accounts, the perceived finality of the decision and its potential impact on the families of the plant's workers are highlighted. The interpenetration between workplace and industrial community is clearly visible; indeed, the workplace and the city itself are perceived to be irrevocably connected – a framing device that is not uncommon among displaced workers in deindustrializing locales.[14] Fabian specifically explores the impact of the decision in the city's streets, while Adrian immediately compares his youthful obliviousness with his father's sober understanding of the closure from inside the mill's gates. In many accounts of this event, the moment of disaster – while deeply important – is quickly superseded by a lengthier description of the community-based response. This is also visible in Adrian's recollection, where he turns – almost instantaneously – to the community reaction and the ultimately successful effort to save the mill.

Shock soon turned to anger. The *Cape Breton Post* featured a "Street Reaction" column; of the ten men interviewed, six immediately called for resistance. Gus MacDonald, the operator of a local service station, was clear: "We can't allow this to happen. The steel industry is the mainstay of our economy. Let's fight to keep it. Unity is necessary."[15] The editorial cartoon summed up the situation with an image of two stereotypical capitalists, replete with top hats and coats marked "Hawker Siddeley," strolling away from Cape Breton Island as it sinks beneath the waves of the Atlantic. The local response brings to mind a series of questions posed, decades later and in a different deindustrializing city, by American labour activist and scholar Staughton Lynd:

> Why may a corporation unilaterally decide to destroy the livelihood of an entire community? Why should it be allowed to come into a community, dirty its air, foul its water, make use of the energies of its young people for generations, and then throw the place away like an orange peel and walk off?[16]

Through November, the public and members of the political class worked in tandem to formulate a suitable response to the existential threat facing the city.

Taking Political Action: Deindustrialization and Regional Economic Development

The man tasked with organizing the provincial response to the Steel Crisis, G.I. Smith, held an extensive pedigree in Nova Scotia politics. Elected as an MLA for Colchester County in 1949, Smith's first cabinet experience came under Premier Robert Stanfield when the Progressive

Conservative (PC) party was elected in 1956. Stanfield viewed state-driven industrial diversification as an appropriate response to regional underdevelopment and disparity. In 1957, this focus led to the creation of Industrial Estates Limited (IEL) – a provincial crown corporation headed by Dosco board member and regional businessman Frank Sobey. IEL's mandate was to attract extra-regional investment to the province.[17] Following the popularity of these efforts, the government rechristened the Department of the Provincial Treasurer as the Department of Finance and Economics in 1962. Stanfield appointed G.I. Smith as minister of this new department.[18]

In his role as minister, Smith was an "enthusiastic advocate of planned regional development [...] [he] described the European planning experiences as a middle way, offering advantages over laissez-faire policies on the one hand and wholesale social ownership on the other."[19] These positions were informed by a trip that Smith had taken to Britain and France in 1962, where he witnessed first-hand the successes of the Marshall Plan development strategy.[20] Consequently, he supported the establishment of the provincial Voluntary Economic Planning Board later that year. This board was intended to operate alongside IEL to mobilize business and labour in the service of a workable economic plan for Nova Scotia.[21]

Between 1962 and 1967 these methods of economic intervention appeared to have found some success. IEL brought extra-regional companies into the province, directly supporting more than sixty firms by 1968 and adding nearly $40 million to the province's books.[22] Despite this, the relative increase in regional prosperity was unable to reduce the disparity that remained between the Atlantic Provinces and the rest of Canada.[23] When Smith took the reigns of the provincial government in 1967, he found himself thrust into a heady atmosphere wherein targeted state intervention and economic support for private industry was viewed, in some quarters, as a panacea.

Nova Scotia went to the polls in May of 1967. The incumbent PCs routed the Liberals and wiped out the provincial NDP contingent. Stanfield's economic reforms were at the heart of the campaign, and his personal popularity helped to drive the party to victory.[24] Meanwhile, the federal Tories were deeply split between duelling factions. By the summer, Stanfield was under pressure from party loyalists to submit his candidacy for the September leadership convention. On 9 September 1967, he was elected leader of the federal party and – after resigning his provincial post two days later – G.I. Smith officially became the eighteenth premier of Nova Scotia.[25]

Smith was premier for just over a month when the steel crisis erupted.[26] He immediately contacted Allan J. MacEachen to schedule a meeting to explore the province's options in response to the Black Friday announcement. The two men met late into the night at the Isle Royale Hotel in downtown Sydney, along with several other provincial and federal cabinet ministers, to discuss the possibility of some form of nationalization of the plant. In a handwritten note by Smith, dated 16 October, the premier outlines possible government actions under the "Industry Closing Act." This includes the option of calling an inquiry and forcing Dosco to open its financial records for inspection by the province.[27] That Monday, MacEachen revealed that a takeover of the Sydney plant by the recently formed Cape Breton Development Corporation (Devco) was under serious consideration.[28]

In raising the spectre of federal intervention, MacEachen was referring to the solution recently enacted in the Cape Breton coal industry. By the mid-1960s, the Sydney coal field alone employed more than five thousand miners.[29] In 1966, the company announced plans to phase out these operations. The federal government commissioned J.R. Donald to draft a report on the state of the industry, which recommended that the state help to facilitate the transition away from an industrial coal mining economy in Cape Breton.[30] Devco, a federal crown corporation with a mandate to "phase out Cape Breton's collieries, while establishing new industries on the Island to take the place of coal-mining," was the result of this decision[31] The Cape Breton coal field was nationalized under the control of Devco in 1966.

MacEachen's colleagues in the leadership of the federal Liberal Party were more hesitant to commit to this strategy. As with the creation of Devco, any consideration of nationalization was to be framed solely in terms of popular welfare – such interventions were never intended to exist as economic alternatives to private capital.[32] It was for this reason that Jean-Luc Pépin condemned the "instant solution" of nationalization in the House of Commons. According to Pépin, if such a strategy were followed in Sydney, it would be difficult to deny the same consideration for deindustrializing communities in northern Ontario or northwestern Quebec. Prime Minister Lester Pearson later wrote to Smith:

As indicated, [we are] prepared to assist financially in certain immediate steps […] to meet this situation. The primary responsibility […] remains with the Provincial Government. The Federal Government will continue to assist the industrial development and economic growth of the region as a whole.[33]

3.1 G.I. Smith (left) at the announcement of measures, 17 October 1967. Steel and
Steelworkers, Reference 83-11-8311, Beaton Institute, Cape Breton University.

In a move designed to buy time, Smith announced that the province
would underwrite Dosco's debt up to $4 million if the company would
maintain existing production until April 1968 without implementing a
mass layoff.[34]

Smith launched into a series of meetings with company officials, visiting with Dosco executives on several occasions in Sydney, Halifax,
Montreal, and Toronto.[35] The premier's intentions are clearly visible in
the draft copy of a letter sent to Emmert on 24 October. In marginalia,
Smith scrawled:

> The immediate objective of the Province is to maintain the Sydney Works
> as a going concern until such time as we have an opportunity to examine
> every way by which the Sydney Works may be continued as a going
> concern.

In a redacted paragraph, he continues, "These concepts are advanced
in the light of your understanding that our objective is to assure the

continued operations at the Sydney works for an indefinite period." Instead, this phrasing is replaced with:

> Our immediate purpose is to assure that nothing would be done in the immediate future to render the continued operation of the Sydney works an impracticability or an impossibility. These means [sic], of course, that operations as a going concern must be continued until such time as we have had an adequate opportunity to consider and make arrangements for possible alternatives.[36]

By the end of October, Dosco agreed to allow provincial auditors to examine its finances. The province pressed for access to these files in the hopes that a private buyer for the Sydney plant could be found.[37] Although there were several meetings with representatives from both Algoma and Stelco, neither company expressed interest in arranging a purchase agreement.[38]

Despite Smith's desire to maintain production in Sydney, the premier never intended for the plant to operate indefinitely under provincial control. This position, also favoured by Allen MacEachen, is visible in government approaches to regional economic development. Federal organizations, such as Devco, were not expected to operate solely as industrial firms, but to facilitate the orderly transition to an economy based upon other combinations of private capital.[39]

A major break occurred on 15 November – just four days before a planned major protest – the Parade of Concern. Following an afternoon conference with Emmert, the premier revealed that an agreement in principle had been reached. This would see the ownership of the plant pass into the hands of the provincial government by the end of December 1967; Smith hoped to call a special session of the legislature to approve the sale and establish a provincial crown corporation to operate the plant.[40]

That weekend, as residents of Sydney crowded the downtown in protest, Smith and his cabinet finalized the agreement. The deal was inked on 22 November. The province would pay approximately $25 million for all remaining stock and infrastructure and assume full control of the facility.[41] Although operations would continue for more than thirty years, the decision was initially designed to protect against immediate social and economic collapse while an alternative to public control could be found.[42] On New Year's Day 1968, the Province of Nova Scotia assumed control of operations through the newly formed Sydney Steel Corporation (Sysco), and a new era for steelmaking in Sydney began.[43]

The immediate state response to the Black Friday announcement distinguishes the shape of deindustrialization on Cape Breton Island from those forms that were experienced in other parts of the world. In the United States, laissez-faire notions of free-market stability prompted inaction in the face of crisis by the federal government. As Judith Stein reminds us, "the incentives to which all companies must respond are constructed by states."[44] In failing to recognize and act upon this reality, the state ultimately doomed many American steel facilities. Operating within a period of market liberalization, US steel producers were faced with assuming increased costs relating to modernization and upgrading while – contemporaneously – international competitors were receiving subsidy and other forms of support from their respective governments.[45] Inaction on behalf of the US government effectively doomed many cities and towns built around basic manufacturing, creating a situation ripe for offshoring and other forms of capital mobilization.[46]

Deindustrialization is a profoundly transnational process, and policy responses have varied greatly. In the United Kingdom, in contrast to the American experience, discussions surrounding deindustrialization have more often focused on the active role of the Thatcherite state in prompting industrial decline in favour of finance capital during the 1980s.[47] In this context, deindustrialization is frequently understood as an explicit consequence of particular forms of direct state action. In addition to this, different forms of state action also influence one another across borders; recall, for example, Smith's conceptualization of postwar economic planning in Europe as a model for the Atlantic Canadian development state.

Likewise, workers' challenges to deindustrialization took on different forms as they unfolded across provincial boundaries. Drawing upon a nascent "new nationalism," Ontario workers were able to figuratively wrap themselves in the Canadian flag to oppose a series of proposed industrial closures around the Golden Horseshoe during the 1970s. Famously, this includes protests that erupted at the news of a proposed closure at British-owned Dunlop Tire in 1970. The optics of a large multinational corporation leaving Canadians out of work with only a few weeks' notice prompted immediate calls for a legislative response on behalf of workers.[48] This tactic pressured federal and provincial governments to develop policies that would shield workers against the disastrous impact of sudden workplace closures.[49]

State responses to the 1967 Sydney Steel Crisis were not as heavily influenced by this selfsame sense of Canadian nationalism, although an emergent protest movement did draw heavily upon established notions of Cape Breton Island nationalism. Residents of Sydney and the surrounding coal towns, steeped in the lore of the labour wars, had become accustomed to the idea that foreign-owned conglomerates could not be trusted to operate in the best interests of the island. Dating back to the General Mining Association in the nineteenth century or the struggles against Besco in the 1920s, there remained an ingrained perception that Cape Breton workers needed to vigilantly defend local solidarities against the machinations of absentee owners.

Cape Breton nationalism did not inform the political response to the crisis in quite the same way. Instead, with obvious comparisons to the later political response to deindustrialization in the Canadian auto sector, Nova Scotia legislators recognized the political opportunity that presented itself. Protecting workers' interests would ensure political support from within the affected regions, but so, too, was state intervention understood as a beneficial policy formulation.[50] Steeped as he was in the politics of Stanfieldian interventionism, Smith did not hesitate to apply the levers of government to combat the effects of structural disparity.

The impact of regionalist modes of thinking on the processes of deindustrialization has also been explored in other contexts. Andrew Perchard and Jim Phillips argue that a regionalist "moral economy" in the Scottish coal field directly informed local resistance to workplace closures.[51] The concept of moral economy is defined at its basest level as a form of "popular consensus as to what [are] proper or improper [business] practices"; community outrage and direct action are the expected responses to any transgression.[52] Certainly, economic security was central to an existing moral economy in Sydney. The perception that Dosco was in violation of these mores is clearly visible.[53] The immediacy of the planned shutdown, with massive layoffs scheduled for the following month, was considered particularly galling, as was the perception that the company lied about maintaining production just a few weeks earlier.[54]

In this context, local members of the political class also felt betrayed by the perceived transgression. During a special session of the Nova Scotia legislature on 6 December 1967, the moral dimensions of Dosco's announcement were discussed. The following encounter between MLA G.H. Fitzgerald and Arthur Pattillo, senior council to Dosco, refers both to the proposed closure and to the company's plan to raid an employee contribution fund for unemployment or layoff insurance:

> FITZGERALD: Now we come to the question of legal and moral obligation. Do you think that there is any moral obligation, on the part of Dosco, to

refund to the employees or transfer the account, to whatever succeeds
you, for the purposes for which the fund was set up?

PATTILLO: And that question I can't propose to answer – morals are
objective things. As I see our society today, they are changing overnight.
What my morals may be tomorrow, I wouldn't like to say. [Laughter].[55]

Although politicians used the language of moral outrage to castigate
the architects of Black Friday – residents of Sydney – the steelworkers'
union, and the local business class expressed their rage in the streets.
This blossomed into a moment of community protest and upheaval
that continues to anchor historical memory of the event.

A Community Problem: The Parade of Concern and Cape Breton Identity

Despite the quickness with which Smith and other politicians reacted
to news of the proposed closure, their political response is generally
downplayed in popular recollections of Black Friday in Cape Breton.
Rather, a dominant historical narrative has taken shape wherein united
resistance, grassroots protest, and the Parade of Concern were successful in singlehandedly forcing the state to take action. Local organizers stressed the importance of the mill to the entire island – appealing
to a shared identity as Cape Bretoners to inform their actions. Others appealed to alternative identities; labour leaders, for example,
described the event as a bellwether for the Maritimes or Atlantic Canada as a whole, while politicians focused on the place of the Sydney
Works in the industrial economy of Nova Scotia.

Two days after Black Friday, with the city still reeling from the news,
priests and ministers took to their pulpits to decry the announcement.
Anglican Rev. J.W. Young of Saint Alban's Church in Whitney Pier told
his congregation that the plant must remain open at all costs. He went
further than the politicians in his call for ownership of the steel plant to
exist fully under the control of Cape Breton workers. George Topshee,
a Catholic priest and the director of the St Francis Xavier University
Extension Department urged parishioners to demand some form of
nationalization.[56] Another Catholic priest, Andrew Hogan, would later
publish a Teach-In for those seeking information on the steel crisis. He
writes:

I am sometimes asked if I was building a new steel plant today and was
trying to make the best profit would I put it in Sydney. My answer of
course is no. But there is a basic steel plant there already sustaining a large

community. It has made profit in the Post War period (not comparable to its competitors but a profit nonethe less [sic]) right up to and including 1966. It can be done again with modernization, good management, and the cooperation of the Union and employees.[57]

That evening, religious leaders met in Whitney Pier with nearly six hundred concerned steelworkers and other residents to discuss an organized and united response.

The days following were punctuated with meetings, youth protests outside the gates of the plant, and a protest of three hundred Xavier College students in the city's downtown.[58] Children in local elementary schools organized a letter-writing campaign to Prime Minister Lester Pearson; Helena, a grade five student from Constantine School, writes, "I want you to know how many jobs will be lost and how many people will go hungry. So you think about it!"[59] District 26 of the UMWA officially declared their support for the steelworkers. District president and local labour leader William "Bull" Marsh offered solidarity to the members of Local 1064: "We know the threat of closure and the effect it has on the morale and the outlook of the workers and their families [...] whatever the steel union wants us to do, they need only let us know."[60] In each of these examples, the perceptions and opinions of white working- and middle-class men are foregrounded. Women's thoughts on the crisis, when they were included in the media, were firmly anchored in the concerns of the home. Helen Muise, a woman interviewed in the *Post* on 18 October 1967, was asked about the closure only in terms of her family's future, the household budget, and mortgage payments.[61]

Local 1064 and the national office of the United Steelworkers' of America were involved in the crisis from the beginning. It was union officials who first spoke publicly not only of nationalizing the plant, but also of going further to expropriate Dosco holdings and regulate the national steel market. Merner supported calls for nationalization, but stopped short of supporting expropriation. William Mahoney, the Canadian director, issued a recommendation that "not only in Sydney, but the outlets for Sydney steel in Nova Scotia and Quebec be placed under immediate public control [...] recompense to Hawker-Siddeley must be tied to acceptance of steel deliveries, not paid over in advance or without strings attached."[62] This message appealed to residents in Sydney, some of whom had called for Hawker Siddeley to be "banned" from Canada as punishment for their actions.

Politically, expropriation was never an option that was seriously considered. In addition to mid-century fears regarding socialism, this solution did not fit within the regional development paradigm favoured by both Smith and Stanfield. Had expropriation occurred, the provincial government would almost certainly have needed to commit to a long-term plan of operations. Nonetheless, the option was popular enough in Sydney that Smith felt he had to address it in the legislature. On 1 December, the premier outlined the case against expropriation. The Dosco finishing mills at Contrecoeur, Quebec, were the major purchaser of product from the Sydney Works; therefore, to expropriate the mill would remove its largest source of demand.[63] The more radical calls for action declined as the province moved ahead with its purchase agreement.

The union almost immediately began working alongside a citizen's steering committee to plan the parade. This included representatives from Sydney's religious communities, union leaders, journalists, lawyers, and private citizens. Fr. William Roach later recalled, "The idea, right off the bat, was to take it away from the Steelworkers' Union [...] because we had them. [...] It wasn't like trying to put them down. [...] What we needed was broad community support."[64] The group soon settled upon 19 November as the date for the parade, and it was expected that huge numbers of Cape Bretoners would come out to show their support for the steel plant and its employees.

The city bustled with activity that morning. By noon, buses were arriving in the downtown to bring citizens from the nearby coal towns. In New Waterford, transportation was organized for all high school students and residents were encouraged not to go to Sydney without a full carload of protesters.[65] The march officially began at 12:30 p.m., starting outside of the plant and heading towards the city's horse racetrack. Roach later described concerns over the proposed route:

> We never had a crowd like that before, so we had no experience [...] We were hoping for no trouble. And people had told us there might be trouble. Because there was anger [...] And we intentionally, and this was no accident, we put that starting point [...] over at the beginning of the steel plant. Rather than Victoria Park [in the city's north end]. So we wouldn't have to come through the business district. And we went right down Inglis Street, out [...] And then we got to the Sports Centre [...] There was no parking – it was just the inside of a big field.[66]

Upon reaching the sports grounds, the marchers filed into the interior of the harness racing track. They continued to arrive for more than an hour, exceeding the capacity of the park.[67] After an opening prayer by archbishop W.W. Davis, Roach addressed the crowd:

3.2 Parade of Concern, 19 November 1967. Photograph by Abbass Studios. Reference number: B-8072.11. Beaton Institute, Cape Breton University.

The Sydney Steel Crisis is not an isolated thing. It is part of a much bigger problem. When we start talking about the future of Cape Breton, we must talk about more things than steel [...] We have to speed up our approach to new secondary industries [...] First of all, we must see to it that the Sydney steel industry continues. We must see to it that Cape Breton gets an industrial development program on a massive scale [...] The machinery for action is already there, the government of Canada and of Nova Scotia have already enacted legislation creating such bodies as the Atlantic Development Board, the new Cape Breton Development Corporation, the ARDA program, Industrial Estates Limited, and many others. There is nothing new or startling in this approach to regional industrial development [...] There are hundreds of precedents for government encouragement of industrial development ranging all the way from the building of the Canadian Pacific Railway in the last century, to the financing of Expo '67 this year.[68]

Identifying several examples of state intervention, he positioned nationalization as the most sensible course of action. "It is not revolutionary," he assured those gathered, to ask that government step in to take control of the situation.

The next speaker, Andy Andreas from the Canadian Labour Congress, placed the demands of the parade within a regional and national context:

It is not only a question of Sydney, it is not only a matter of Cape Breton Island, what is at stake here is the future of this part of Canada and, by inference, for Canada as a whole. Because we cannot tolerate for a moment a situation where the Maritimes are relegated to a state of economic stagnation and depopulation. If this is to be part of Canada, if Canada is to be a united nation, then we cannot afford the closure of Dosco, we cannot afford the destruction of Sydney.[69]

Andreas was followed by Allen MacEachen, who again committed his own efforts and those of the federal government.

The final speaker of the day was the premier, who highlighted the special resolve of all Cape Bretoners – singling out the steelworkers and Local 1064 for their contributions. He described the crisis as a matter of provincial and national concern, revealed that he had been in constant communication with members of the federal government since 13 October, and redoubled his promise: "I said that anything within the ability of the province to do would be done. And this I say again."[70]

The speeches during the Parade of Concern also reveal the different collectivities invoked by groups within the campaign. Local residents drew upon an imagined, shared island identity in their calls to action; the exodus of Dosco was perceived, in this narrative, as another stage in the history of exploitation by off-island capital. Cape Breton's existence at the margins of a national economy that grew to "devour its children" perhaps inspired a more insular response than those which would later erupt in the nationalist protests of central Canada.[71] For residents, whether the decision had been made in Montreal or London was immaterial – its impact would be the same in either case. Other speakers considered the issue in different ways. Government officials viewed the steel crisis as a provincial and regional issue. Roach obviously recognized these distinctions; in his speech, he cleverly avoided foreign examples of nationalization, such as the Attlee government's nationalization program within the UK, focusing instead on actions already taken by provincial and federal governments within Canada.

The next day, the headline of the *Post* declared the parade "a huge success." Although the day was overcast and cool, the final estimated number of participants were somewhere between twenty and thirty thousand.[72] One cultural production, Charlie MacKinnon's song "Let's Save Our Industry," retains a great deal of popular cachet in Sydney.[73] The song was initially broadcast live on CJCB radio. It was written the night before, reportedly at the urging of Martin Merner.[74] MacKinnon's daughter later recalled:

He was so wrapped up in the moment [...] that when he tried to stop, his hands and his knuckles and his fingers were almost freezing from the cold. And it was an effort to play that guitar. But the people just wanted more and more, and they were carrying on the song and consequently he had to keep going.[75]

In oral history interviews, respondents often referred to the song, or even began to hum or sing the chorus to illustrate popular sentiment at the time: "Let's save our industry (x3), The industry we need."

> It brought us joy and brought us tears
> It's been here more than sixty years
> It built our homes and stilled our fears
> And made this island what it is.
>
> We need the help of Ottawa
> We are also part of Canada
> They can subsidize Ontario
> Expo and the seaway, too!

Three days after the parade, the agreement that was first organized by Emmert and Smith on 15 November was officially signed. The province committed to assuming control of the Sydney Works. The perception of these events that is presented through oral history, however, is that the parade had a direct causative relationship with the decision to nationalize the plant. This was also visible in oral accounts from the 1980s. Leon Colford, who worked as a welder at the plant throughout the 1960s, recalled in a 1990 interview:

LEON: October of '67: Black Friday [...] We put on quite a demonstration, well organized, and the whole of Cape Breton Island turned out for that. We were successful in maintaining a Steel Plant in Sydney.
MICHAEL: Yes. Do you think it was the pressure the people put on in the political demonstrations and so on like that, that made the provincial government do something about it?
LEON: Definitely, definitely.[76]

The two events are interconnected to such an extent in the collective memory of the community that their meanings are sometimes transposed. When asked about "Black Friday," another former employee responds:

Black Friday. The day of the parade. I was working that day. I think I sneaked home [to attend the parade] because I felt kind of embarrassed.[77]

Storytellers frequently order accounts of the past to correspond with the conditions of the present. Alistair Thomson calls this process "composure": the composition of memory occurs through two predominant processes. The first deals with the mechanisms by which memories are selected, stored, and related. Only some of our experiences are stored permanently in our memories, and among these that are stored there are a variety of ways that they might be expressed, articulated, or communicated.[78] In a related process, narrative "composure" is used to explain the present in a satisfactory way – to provide a comfortable explanation for one's life and present set of circumstances. The narrative conflation of Black Friday and the Parade of Concern within oral accounts reveal these aspects of composure; it provides a comfortable and empowering sense of successful, community-based activism. It allows Cape Bretoners to have single-handedly saved their own steel mill.

Stories lauding the success of community fightback efforts are understandable. They allow for the restoration of personal and collective dignity after trauma.[79] After all, a narrative in which residents' protests were of secondary concern to political preferences does not restore the perceived power of the community after it was disrupted on Black Friday. We, as oral historians, must pay close attention to how "community" is considered in such recollections.[80] There are also exclusions visible in these accounts.

Despite the popular trope of unity and cross-class solidarity, there were residents in industrial Cape Breton who did not support the continued operation of the Sydney steel plant. A letter, posted from North Sydney on 1 November, arrived at the office of G.I. Smith. Without a return address and signed as "a disgruntled Cape Bretoner," the letter outlines the local case against saving the Sydney mill:

> Other than Sydney proper (Pop. 34,000) the steel crisis DOES NOT effect [sic] the surrounding districts [...] There is too much propaganda by a half dozen or more selfish interests. Who do not give a damn about the perpetual TAX PAYER [...] Cape Bretoners have become some sort of professional criers or mourners. ALWAYS making a mountain out of molehills. I was born here and do love the island, but the inhabitants are or have become a lot of PROFESSIONAL BEGGARS.[81]

Opposition to the Save Our Steel sentiment – when mentioned in interviews – is often attributed either to undefined residents of "the mainland" or to members of "the government." As the above letter reveals, there was some minor local opposition to the nationalization of the

3.3 Catholic nuns at the Parade of Concern, Sydney. Photograph by Abbass Studios. Reference number: B-8073.9. Beaton Institute, Cape Breton University.

plant. This opposition was never mentioned in interviews about Black Friday, and I have not identified any locals who had publicly argued against the decision in 1967. The reason for "disgruntled Cape Bretoner's" anonymity is likely the fear of recriminations. Certainly, social ostracism would have been a real concern – but physical safety in the emotional aftermath of the proposed closure might also have been a worry. After a closure announcement in Kenosha, Wisconsin, in 1988, for instance, locals opposed to the plant's continued operations had their homes fired upon, death threats were sent to local politicians, and violence nearly erupted at a town meeting.[82]

Women are also narrowly positioned in narratives about Black Friday and the parade. Notably, they are often left out of discussions relating to the immediate impact of the closure, but are drawn into the narrative to describe the "community" orientation of the protest. This occurrence is also visible elsewhere; as Lucy Taksa explores in the Australian context, community memory in working-class cities can sometimes serve to reify existing gendered systems of control and exclude women retroactively from moments of collective action and resistance.[83]

Media coverage reflects this truth. The *Post* interviewed several women for their thoughts on the crisis. In contrast to the interviews conducted with men, who were asked about the possibility of nationalization, their thoughts on Smith's capabilities, and the impact on local businesses, the women were asked to comment on domestic affairs.[84] In one article featuring women's responses, children, the household budget, and the possible negative impacts of uprooting large families are main subjects of concern.[85] Although the Sydney Works did employ women in the offices, the impact of looming layoffs is explored solely in reference to an assumed male breadwinner ideal. These gendered accounts reflect a predominantly masculine, work-ing-class place identity. Such identities are not frozen or static, but are constantly shifting as the result of different imaginings of place that exist among distinct groups.[86] Despite the presentation of men and women's roles in response to the crisis, historians must problem-atize the types of essentialism that present industrial closure and the protests that such moments engender as events that predominantly affect white, working-class men.[87]

There are also settler-colonial exclusions present within popular reimaginings of the community response. While women's voices are sometimes included in narratives of resistance, if only in gendered ref-erences to the home sphere, the reactions of Mi'kmaq residents in the nearby community of Membertou are entirely absent – though, admit-tedly, no Mi'kmaq residents were identified who recalled participating in the protest. This is reflective of what Steven High has termed "mill colonialism" in northern Ontario, wherein "aboriginal people were employed at the margins of these extractive industries and relatively few found employment in the mines or mills themselves."[88]

Although members of the Mi'kmaq First Nation only infrequently found employment at the steel mill, the experience of Indigenous peoples in the city are closely interconnected with the development of industry in Cape Breton. In 1882, two and a half acres of land was formally reserved as the "King's Road Reserve" for the Sydney Mi'kmaq population. This reservation grew as the city developed; European and American immigrants seeking work at the plant in the 1910s created demand for Mi'kmaq wares and residents some-times accepted small jobs.[89] After a series of legal complaints by lawyer and King's Road landowner J.H. Gillies, the federal govern-ment resolved to move the reservation. One proposed location for a new reserve was within walking distance of the Coke Ovens, but the Mi'kmaq rejected this plan. In 1926, the Department of Indian Affairs relocated the King's Road Reservation to a 65-acre lot away from the harbour.[90]

Despite the proximity of Membertou to the plant and its working-class neighbourhoods, only a single article in the *Post*, dated 20 Novem-ber 1967, refers to a "Group of Indians" in attendance at the Parade. This article celebrates the "diversity" found within the march:

Some sights were particularly significant. The number of women there, a nun who carried a sign "People Matter"; a group of Indians in traditional dress; a child being pushed in a baby carriage; a girl in a wheelchair; and above all the spirit of optimism.[91]

Groups found on the peripheries of a white, masculine industrial place identity can be enlisted into community resistance when that sense of place is explicitly under attack. The absence of these groups in more recent accounts of Black Friday and the Parade of Concern, however, reflect that the place identity being recalled can sometimes leave gender and racial hierarchies intact and unchallenged.

Conclusion

The Sydney Steel Crisis of 1967 is remembered as a community of Cape Bretoners rallying under the united banner of "Save Our Steel" to combat the predatory destruction of international capital. Canadian nationalism, when visible at all, is far less prominent than in other anti-shutdown campaigns – although Cape Breton nationalism is more visible. At first glance, the successful combination of community protest and state efforts to nationalize the mill appears to run counter to what has been termed the "High thesis": that Canadian workers relied upon strong unionism and a developed nationalist sentiment to combat the destructive aspects of so-called "creative destruction."[92] Without the opportunity to employ such tactics, American fightback campaigns in places like Youngstown, Ohio, were met with abject failure. In Sydney, the community response emerged at a time when the provincial government was more amenable to targeted interventionist models of regional economic development. Were this not the case, and barring the appropriation of nationalist rhetoric that would later enliven closure campaigns in Ontario, it is hard to imagine that circumstances in Sydney would have differed substantially from those in deindustrializing "Rust Belt" cities.

On 1 January 1968, employees officially began working under their new employer – the Sydney Steel Corporation. Although Dosco would continue managerial operations at the plant until April, its new directors sought to disentangle the mill from the company's influence as quickly as possible.[93] Sysco's new board of directors began exploring options for a private sale, while the new Chairman of the Board and President R.B. Cameron sought to expand production to prove the facility viable. Operations remained largely unchanged on the first day under new

management, but the coming weeks and years witnessed modernization attempts, new production techniques, and countless managerial
changes. The departure of private industry from Sydney represented
the end of an era, but on that January morning the city awoke with the
perception that a major battle had been won – the future, for once, was
hopeful.

Chapter Four

Decades in Transition: Modernization and Mechanization on the Shop Floor

From 1967 to 1989 ... If you wanted to say that the steel company owed the worker something, indeed they did. That's my own personal opinion. The workers were out of this world when they brought that plant back in 1967 [...] But it's like you say, the cutting still never stopped. It was always, "You must cut, you must cut." That's a nasty word in the union and it's a nasty word with supervisors. As a supervisor I don't like to see cutbacks. You're making it very hard for me to maintain my production when you're continually wanting to cut people.

– Garfield Ross, Finishing Mill Supervisor, 1990[1]

Fresh from the effort to keep the plant open, workers optimistically turned their attention towards increasing production and ensuring the continued viability of the operation. In addition to Sysco, major steel producers in Canada now included Dominion Foundries and Steel Limited (Dofasco), Algoma, and the Steel Company of Canada (Stelco).[2] At Sysco, decades of underinvestment meant that equipment and operations would have to be overhauled for the plant to remain viable. The province was not immediately willing to provide the necessary capitalization, as they intended to find a private buyer for the plant. The mill's blast furnaces, long maintained only at the minimum necessary level, were showing signs of age and running into frequent problems. As one consultancy report describes, there was "no solution to the problems involved other than by means of sizable capital outlays for modernization."[3]

New management tackled these problems head-on. Robert Burns "R.B." Cameron, a Pictou County businessman and president of Deuterium Canada, was appointed as CEO of the new crown corporation. Just months after the Sysco takeover, Cameron hired Derek Haysom – a

4.1 Aerial view, Sysco, c. 1970. Photograph by the Nova Scotia Information
Service, Reference 90-678-20110, Beaton Institute, Cape Breton University.

South African engineer – as his right-hand man and executive vice-
president of Sydney Steel.[4] Haysom became president of Sysco in 1970.
These men had a mandate to reorganize the to ensure short-term profitability. Although shop-floor changes were not immediately apparent in
the days after the provincial takeover, the years between 1968 and 1989
would witness a slow transition from Fordist to post-Fordist strategies
of production.

Meet the New Boss: Making Steel at Sysco, 1968–1970

The stages of steelmaking at Sysco under integrated steel production
help to reveal the intricacies of shop-floor relations. Pre-production
took place in the Coke Ovens Department, where two large coke oven
batteries were used in pre-production. Under Dosco, coal from the
Cape Breton mines was transported to the steel plant by rail and held

in large stockpiles, fed through a pulverizing machine and baked in the coke ovens along with oil and water to form the brittle, porous substance known as "coke."[5]

In the steelmaking process, the first steps occurred in the Blast Furnace Department. There, iron, coke, and limestone were fed into the large cylindrical tower – "eight buckets to a charge," in the words of Clarence Butler, "three ore, two limestone, and three coke."[6] Once these ingredients were added, hot air was blown through the bottom of the furnace. The burning coke consumes the oxygen from the ore, and the melting limestone forms a by-product known as "slag." The slag floats to the top of the iron and absorbs some of the impurities from the iron ore.

John Campbell – a former plant engineer – recalls these processes with great clarity:

> The blast furnace was the heart and soul of the steelmaking process ... The metallic iron drips down ... and collects in the bottom of the furnace. Slag, which is also molten, is much lower density so it floats on top of the iron. So periodically, you punch a hole in the bottom of the blast furnace, drain the iron out, and watch until the slag comes and then divert the slag into another area ... and it becomes the big pile of slag that we see over at the steel plant [site] today.[7]

Not only is slag still visible around the landscape of the former plant, but it has also been used in the construction of dozens of houses throughout Ashby and Whitney Pier. In this sense, these by-products of steelmaking remain a physical presence in the homes of many Sydney residents.[8]

Workers produced hot metal from two blast furnaces and ran on a three-shift system round the clock.[9] The first ran from 8:00 a.m. to 4:00 p.m., the second shift was 4:00 p.m. to 12:00 a.m., and the last shift was 12:00 a.m. to 8:00 a.m. Life in the city operated around these rhythms. People visiting might comment that "rush hour" began at strange times; it was not unusual for the streets to fill with traffic between 11 p.m. and 1 a.m., as workers changed shift. On each blast furnace, a stove tender, furnace blower, keeper, slagman, first keeper helper, craneman, and second keeper helper worked to maintain production.[10] These men were tasked with producing the supply of metallic iron, which would be transported to the next stage of the steelmaking process at the Open Hearth Department.

Adrian Murphy started working in the general yard, where labourers were assigned to different sections of the plant on a per-day basis.

"You didn't know where you were going, you didn't know how to dress, if you went in with an overcoat on they'd send you to the open hearth furnace, if you had a light coat on they'd send you out on the high piers or somewhere like that where you'd freeze to death."[11] After gaining some experience, Adrian was sent full-time into the Open Hearth Department – where his father also worked.

He arrived to find a 938-ft.-long building enclosing a 700-ton hot metal mixer and five large furnaces. Each was approximately 92 ft. long and 25 ft. wide, and there was also an additional 10-tonne electric furnace used for small tonnages of specialty steels.[12] There, pig iron from the blast furnace was combined with scrap metal, limestone, and alloys before being periodically exposed to superheated air. This air supports the combustion of an oil flame, which supplies direct heat to melt the charged material.[13] Adrian recalls his work:

> You put in your stone for the bottom, then you put in – depending on what you were making – if it was a rail ... everything had to be right. You had to have cleans, the fosse had to be good, the iron coming up couldn't be dirty – high in iron and fosse – but the fosse had to be down about 15, and you had to have the sulphur set. So then you put in scrap. Certain percentage of scrap depending on your supply of iron. If the iron was good you'd put in 100,000 of scrap and then the rest was iron and you'd make steel easy that way. If you had a really good supply of iron, and good clean iron, it was great, she was rolling right along.[14]

Crane operators transferred the hot metal into steel ladles, which poured into ingot moulds. Adrian worked as a crane operator in the late 1960s. "We started off on what they called the metal crane ... and they'd bring up 50 tonnes of molten iron, and all the guys were working on the bottom ... and you had to stick-handle, you had to be like Bobby Orr ... You wouldn't dare go over anybody's head or near anybody's head."[15] The temperature of each ingot was standardized in soaking pits before workers would forward the material on to the rolling mills.

The Sysco rolling mills were organized into the roll shops, the heavy mills, and the light mills. Within these were the blooming or "breakdown" mill, the billet mill, the rail mill and the rail-finishing mill. At this time, Sysco also included a rod and bar mill and a nail mill.[16] Ingots created at the open hearth were subjected to the first stage of rolling, which would transform the ingots into semi-finished steel products such as blooms or billets. These could be sold as semi-finished steel, which comprised a majority of Sysco sales in the late

1960s, or directed into the light mills to continue the process of creating finished steel products.[17]

The strict hierarchy of rolling mill jobs mirrored the processes of steelmaking, according to machinist Owen Bonnell. "When you first went in the shop, you worked on the billet rolls for the billet mill."[18] These included jobs such as billet pusher, catcher, and helper; these men were responsible for overseeing the shaping of the metal.[19] Dave Ervin began working at the "mechanical screw" machine in the rolling mills on 9 July 1968. He recalls working on the final roller, which placed grooves in rebar: "as soon as they would get it in the roller, I'd jam down the lever on the mechanical screw and it would run through. And I remember being in the lunch shack and some of the guys were taking off their shirts and showing where the bars had gone through their sides or singed their sides."[20]

Other finished steel products, such as nails, wire, or steel rail, required shaped billets. As John Campbell explains,

a rod mill would make a rod that was, well, various sizes, but something that was the diameter of a pencil or a pen. And that, in turn, could be taken to the wire mill and that rod would be drawn down to successive steps to get wire of a certain size ... and there would be specific composition for that kind of product. That would be taken into a nail machine, to make roofing nails or, ordinary nails, all kinds of specialized nails and so on.[21]

At the time of the provincial takeover, Sysco's production capabilities were divided between 22 per cent rails and rail accessories, such as tie plates and reinforcing bars, 70 per cent semi-finished steel, such as ingots, billets, or blooms, and 8 per cent rods, nails, wire, and other finished steel.[22] Not only would the plant's production line fail to diversify further after nationalization, within only a few years productive areas of the mill would experience significant cuts and downsizing.

Total production numbers were the measure upon which R.B. Cameron staked his claim to success. Speaking to the Empire Club in Toronto on 30 April 1970, he boasted: "In 1967, production had shrunk to less than 618,000 tons. In our first year of operation, we produced 870,000 ingot tons [...] in 1968, Sydney Steel Corporation had an operating profit of nearly three millions dollars [...] and in 1969, we broke the million-ton mark."[23] Fabian Smith had a different perspective on the claimed million tonnes:

That phantom million tons of steel ... we were digging up rails that were so darn rusty you could hardly see the marks on them, you know. But he

4.2 The 1,000,000th ton presentation, Open Hearth, Sysco, 1969. Pictured from
the left: Sysco Chairman R.B. Cameron, Premier G.I. Smith, 1064 President
Martin Merner, and company President D.R. Haysom. Photographer
unknown, Reference 90-1377-20809, Beaton Institute, Cape Breton University.

wanted that as his legacy … I mean, we did roll a lot of steel. But it wasn't
a million tons. And we all got a billet with our names on them, engraved
[…] We were drawing out inventory that never existed![24]

The rank and file, while largely supportive of this goal, were more
than willing to fight to protect their own interests. On 10 March 1969,
steelworkers in Sydney showed that they were not cowed by the events
of Black Friday. The majority of the 1,200 day-shift employees walked
out over the contracting-out of plant work. Martin Merner appealed
to the steelworkers to return to work, as he had in the wildcat wave of
the early 1960s. To a chorus of jeers, he addressed the striking workers, "regardless of the boos, return to your jobs immediately."[25] Steelworkers went back to the plant the following day, and one unidentified

employee told the *Cape Breton Post*: "Our point was well demonstrated, I think we should go back to work and let our executive work it out with management."[26]

In August, the province announced the impending closure of the wire and nail mill. Implicit within this decision was the concurrent closure of the rod mill – as rods were the semi-finished steel from which nails were produced.[27] Non-competitive production costs was the reason given, although management assured the *Post* that "the absorption of the mills' personnel into other functions of the steel plant can be carried out in a manner whereby the abilities of the [more than 100] individuals concerned are taken into consideration."[28] This decision was hardly based on sound economic reasoning. Historian Joan Bishop describes, "First, the province and management knew from the time [Sysco] was taken over that it suffered a cost disadvantage [...] Second, it was unsound to analyze each part of Sysco's operations separately [...] Finally, management had argued that modernization of the nail mill was not justified because the Maritime market was too small to absorb the output. Again, the province knew at the time of the takeover that this was true of Sysco's entire production line."[29] The wire and nail mill closed on 31 October, and although these jobs were reabsorbed, this represented the first major reduction of Sysco's product line after the provincial takeover.[30]

Another wildcat strike occurred just two days before the scheduled closure. Nearly two hundred maintenance workers left their jobs when eleven carpenters refused to abide by an imposed schedule change.[31] Employees from the mechanical and blast furnace departments soon joined in the work action, and management feared that these protests would soon spread to the entire plant.[32] Representatives from Local 1064 met with management the following day, and this time Winston Ruck – the local vice-president – once again asked all striking workers to return for their next scheduled shift. The steelworkers respected Ruck, who would go on to become the first black president of Local 1064. He was known as a more radical unionist, and had earned his reputation during his opposition to conservative union leaders in the intra-union conflicts of the 1950s. He was also known to conflict with the South African–born Derek Haysom, whose attitudes on race created tension between the two men. Employees once again returned to the mill and production drew closer to Cameron's goal – the much-discussed million tonnes of steel.[33]

It is worthwhile to note that production at Sydney Steel during this period can be considered Fordist in nature. Broadly speaking, Fordist systems of production can be understood as a combination

4.3 Winston Ruck, United Steelworkers of America presentation, 1970.
Photograph by Abbass Studios Ltd, Reference C-3310, Beaton Institute,
Cape Breton University.

of *Taylorism* on the shop floor, *Wagnerism* in the industrial relations sphere, and *Keynesianism* in the labour market.[34] The 1962 Proudfoot time-work study reveals the Taylorist characteristic of production, wherein strict managerial control was wielded over the work processes at the mill. The second characteristic, Wagnerism is distinguished by a set of established labour rights that includes the institutionalization of trade unionism, the establishment of penalty clauses for contract violations, and the enforcement of clear bargaining guidelines.[35] The Co-operative Wage Study (CWS), which was introduced in the Canadian steel industry, is one example of Wagnerism in industrial relations.[36] Under this system, jobs were ranked according to twelve factor requirements, which included categories such as training and experience. Each factor was associated with a particular number of points, which would be compiled to achieve a level of classification for the worker under consideration.[37] The final characteristic of the Fordist managerial paradigm, Keynesianism deals with the orientation of the labour market. The province's decision to actively intervene in the market by nationalizing the Sydney Works and the establishment of a state-driven regional economic development model are fundamentally Keynesian in nature.[38]

Skill and work control are also central aspects of the Fordist paradigm. In examining these factors, we must pay close attention to the subjective assessments of work that are described by steelworkers on the shop floor.[39] Such notions are complex, as Harry Braverman writes:

> For the worker, the concept of skill is traditionally bound up with craft mastery – that is to say, the combination of knowledge of materials and processes with the practiced manual dexterities required to carry on a specific branch of production. The breakup of craft skills and the reconstruction of production as a collective or social process have destroyed this traditional concept of skill and opened up only one way for mastery over labor processes to develop: in and through scientific, technical, and engineering knowledge.[40]

This definition of skill has been critiqued; Craig Heron, for instance, notes that the perception of uniform deskilling in the Canadian steel industry during the twentieth century has been overstated. He writes, "The assumption that mechanization inevitably means deskilling is too glib" as workers consistently develop new skills and aptitudes alongside mechanization and modernization of work typologies.[41]

Indeed, for Sydney's steelworkers, there has long been an understanding that the concept of *skilled work* is not solely defined by job

classifications and collective agreements – but the ways that occupational knowledge is enacted on the shop floor. Heron describes
a 1903 newspaper article from Sydney wherein blast furnace workers expressed frustration regarding the importation of professionally
trained, skilled chemists. They felt that these men lacked the practical
experience of the Sydney Works shop floor that defines truly skilled
work.[42] This concept has remained in evidence through oral history
accounts of work at Sysco throughout its history. Charles Anderson
describes an interaction in the Open Hearth Department:

> We had a fellow right out of college ... he was a chemist, and he went
> in and told the fellow that the heat was wrong. The old fellow called his
> friend and he said, "Don't you tell me how to make steel." He says, "I'm
> telling you, that's not right" [...] The fellow says, "Okay, we'll listen to
> you." We'll make it the way you want it." So the old gentleman did. He
> went over to the furnace, and he's firing this in and firing that in. "Is that
> what you want? That's what you got. You come back in four hours time
> and we'll have it poured for you" [...] They poured the heat, and when
> they went to roll it, it was way off specifications. It wasn't right at all![43]

Adrian Murphy also refers to this type of specialized skilled knowledge. He says:

> The only thing we found after the government took over, there was an
> awful lot of, I don't know what you'd call it, people were parachuted in
> here and there and they kind of didn't know. They didn't know how to
> run the thing. And they didn't have faith in the men ... even if you had
> the metallurgical ... you don't have the moxie of how this is run. And
> all of the sudden, you come over and there's a guy mounting on the
> furnace for the last twenty-five years, and you decide to say "Oh no Joe,
> we're going to do it this way." Well it won't work this way on this furnace.[44]

Through this type of testimony, it might be useful to imagine skill in
terms of its psychological value among those who consider themselves
capable and skilled workers within an internalized narrative, rather
than as an individual attribute of labour power within production.

Organized along Fordist lines, workers at Sysco habitually voiced
displeasure through traditional mechanisms of labour power – strikes,
walkouts, and grievances. By the 1970s, though, Sydney steelworkers
and their union began confronting some of the contradictions wrought
by deindustrialization throughout North America. Tension started to
emerge between the desire to maintain production at the mill – avoiding

the type of disaster that nearly befell the community on Black Friday – and an increasing awareness that the forms of modernization that would be necessary to achieve this goal would likely result in significant workforce reductions. In addition, early attempts at restructuring represented another threat to employees through the expansion of managerial control and the reduction of product lines. Resistance to some of these actions was less formal. On-the-job misbehaviour, such as drinking or playing pranks, can be considered both as forms of resistance and as expressions of work identity.[45] This is important to keep in mind as we examine the changing work processes at the plant, the importation of new technological and productive capabilities, and the significant cuts to employment that occurred after 1989.

Managerial Missteps: Planning for Modernization in the 1970s

Sydney Steel posted more than $35 million in profit during its first three years of operations. This was the combined result of the frantic pace of production, local tax breaks, and the subsidized price of Devco coal. In February 1970, G.I. Smith announced a much-anticipated $84 million in upgrades to the mill. He assured provincial taxpayers that public funds would not be required; rather, between Sysco's profits and predicted growth, Smith believed that the company could fund its own modernization. This was intended to unfold in two phases: the first would include new vacuum degassing facilities and an upgraded rail mill, while the second would involve the installation of two brand-new basic oxygen furnaces (BOF) to replace the aging open hearth.[46] The BOF process was the heart of this redevelopment. With these furnaces, the time required for the conversion of iron to steel could be significantly reduced.[47] Although Smith was voted out of office in the fall of 1970, the incoming Liberal premier – Gerald Regan – reiterated support for this plan.[48]

Cracks began to show within two years; in the fall of 1972, Regan revealed that $35 million of Sysco profits had already been allocated to other budget items associated with operating the mill. This meant that between 1971 and 1973 – rather than posting any further profits – the company had actually borrowed more than $11 million.[49] This ballooned into $12.7 million in losses by May 1973. Any further modernization would require extensive borrowing – which would, in turn, necessitate backing by federal and provincial loan guarantees.[50] Complicating this further was the depreciation of existing facilities. The No. 1 blast furnace suffered a major breakdown in 1972 that required a $50 million replacement in addition to the $84 million already committed, bringing the full cost of the planned upgrades to approximately $144 million – now to be assumed by Sysco in the form of debt.[51]

In the midst of Phase I of the modernization, management suddenly pivoted to another set of organizational principles. Haysom announced in June 1972 that the BOF upgrades had been scrapped. Instead, bewilderingly, Sysco would adopt a brand new, untested technology to increase productivity in the Open Hearth Department. R.P. Nicholson, the development officer at Sydney Steel, describes this decision:

> Original plans had called for a conventional BOF shop [...] Early in 1970 [...] a new steelmaking technique was brought to SYSCO's attention. Called the Oxygen Bottom Metallurgy process (OBM), it differed from the BOF in that the oxygen was delivered through the bottom of the vessel directly into the bath [...] SYSCO was sufficiently impressed with the potential of the new process to initiate research to test the system [...] and subsequently, to change plans, substituting OBM for BOF.
>
> While initial engineering work was being done [...] SYSCO was experimenting further. The German tuyeres were placed in the bottom of the open hearth furnace and the effects were astounding. Production time was drastically reduced, oxygen efficiency was increased, and furnace yields went up [...] Dubbed the 'Submerged Injection Process' (SIP) the technique [...] has recently been acclaimed in steelmaking journals and financial papers as the "saviour of the open hearth."
>
> When the open hearths are fully modified [...] one furnace will theoretically be able to produce as much as the five former ones. SYSCO will effectively triple its production capacity for only a fraction of the capital cost required for an equivalent BOF.[52]

The SIP was billed as providing more than $12 million in savings over the BOF model – an attractive option for the indebted mill. Nicholson does not mention, however, that Sysco President Haysom and Vice-President William Wells held the North American patent for this new technology.[53]

This decision, a crossroads in the early history of Sysco, is remarkable for its lack of oversight. Other historians have also noted the oddness of this decision, with Joan Bishop remarking, "It is striking that a marginal operation like SYSCO felt qualified to break new ground in steel-making technology. The decision to abandon the proven [BOF] technology was based on a short period of experimentation."[54] For its part, the province abdicated any responsibility to provide oversight into this process or to vet the newly proposed techniques. Management was left to disburse modernization funds as-necessary.

Steelworkers remember these events as a boondoggle; Harry Collins recalled the immediate failure of a process that had been billed as the solution to Sysco's financial woes:

> Everything would burn up, it would drive everyone crazy ... we were at that a good six or nine months [...] [Haysom] said it worked in other places, in Germany and others, but it certainly didn't work for us. It was the worst damn thing there ever was![55]

Not only did SIP not work in the Sysco open hearth, but its adoption meant that other portions of the planned modernization were now untenable and that the money that had been directed towards its implementation had been entirely wasted.

Drawing further condemnation from steelworkers were attempts to streamline production. The Sysco nail mill was sold to Sivaco Wire and Nail Company and moved to Dartmouth in 1971, and on 12 July 1972, Haysom announced that the bar mill would also be sold.[56] Nearly 2,700 of the plant's 3,411 employees walked out two days later in protest. Winston Ruck – now president of Local 1064 – demanded that Premier Regan reverse this decision.[57] The province promised to keep these departments open for at least ninety days while other options were explored.[58]

The bar mill remained, but the steelworkers' union soon found itself embroiled in another conflict. Contract negotiations were going badly. On 20 September 1972, Local 1064 called the first legal plant-wide strike since 1946.[59] The bungling of the plant's modernization was the major issue. Ruck told the *Post*, "Too much money is wasted on a plant administration, over-loaded with individuals describable as anything but steelmen [...] Ridding the plant of these incompetents is almost as important as the wage questions."[60] The community soon got involved. On 13 October – five years to the day after Black Friday – citizens marched in another protest, this time calling on the government to fast-track modernization in the best interests of the city.[61] Although steelworkers voted to approve a new contract on 23 October – after more than a month on strike – issues surrounding the beleaguered modernization went unresolved.[62]

Sysco, a promising and hopeful undertaking in 1968, was embedded in crisis by 1974. BOF funds had been squandered, the product line was quickly diminishing, and the company showed no signs of achieving profitability. Backed by loan guarantees, Sydney Steel was now more than $150 million in debt. The Canadian government quietly embarked upon a new study, working closely with Stelco management, to examine the viability of a new finished steel mill to be located elsewhere in Cape Breton.[63] The CANSTEL proposal considered the establishment of a mill in Gabarus – just over 40 km from Sydney – through a series of tariff and tax breaks to entice private investment.[64] The provincial Regan administration, sensing an opportunity to escape responsibility for the ballooning Sysco debt while maintaining jobs on the Island, supported the idea. CANSTEEL, a provincial crown corporation, was created in 1975 to further explore this option.[65]

A series of confidential reports reveal the various options that were considered: the first explores an immediate cessation of all activities at the Sysco plant, the second details a slow shutdown coming to a conclusion by 1984, while the third option would leave the majority of the Sysco mill in operation until 1983.[66] Any hope that CANSTEL or CANSTEEL would be implemented was dashed in late 1976, when a significant downturn in world steel markets effectively destroyed any possibility that private firms would be interested in such a scheme. As a result, Sysco was no closer to modernization – though Regan insisted that the provincial Liberal Party was still committed to supporting steelmaking in Sydney.[67]

Tom Kent, a Liberal Party stalwart and former adviser to Lester Pearson, was appointed as president of Sydney Steel in August 1977. Management hoped that Kent's federal connections would prove an asset, and he immediately announced intentions for a wholesale reorganization of operations.[68] Despite receiving $20.4 million from the federal government in December for business planning and a capital works program, the promised turnaround failed to materialize.[69] By 1979, with Sysco losses now approaching $1 million per week, the Nova Scotia Department of Development starkly warned:

> Sysco is, in effect, bankrupt [...] A primary government objective should be to transfer ownership and management of Sysco to non-government hands [and] all thought of building Sysco into a major steel plant [...] should be abandoned.[70]

Another recommendation, which would have been met with considerable protest had it been made public, was for Sydney Steel to reduce the workforce to approximately 950 personnel by 1982 as a cost-saving measure[71]

While these specific hardships were local in nature, they correspond with a broader set of challenges facing basic manufacturing in the mid-twentieth century. Through the 1970s, firms in Canada, the US, and Europe suffered from the impact of low-cost, high-quality steel from Japan, South Korea, and Brazil.[72] Even without the compounding effects of the 1973 oil crisis, it is likely that global demand for steel would have slackened anyway in response to a production glut. Technological changes also affected the types of products that were desired; Trevor Bain writes, "As economies matured, the relative position of heavy steel-intensive industries, such as ship-building and railroads, gave way to growth industries such as space technology, telecommunications, and biotechnology."[73] This was good news for specialized, boutique steelmakers and finishers, but did not bode well for the large, integrated plants that relied heavily upon the ability to produce more tonnes of steel more efficiently.

Save Sysco: Lean Production and Labour Flexibility in the 1980s

The highest levels of management downplayed the full impact of the steel slump, although Kent resigned in August 1979 and R.B. Cameron was reappointed as interim chairman of the board. In December, Cameron announced that production had increased by 15 per cent and the monthly operating loss had been halved.[74] This time, the problems facing Sysco would not be stemmed by increases in production. The mill's debt load was approaching $300 million when Cameron announced a series of layoffs in July 1980. In terms of total employment, the workforce at Sysco would have been reduced from just over 3,000 workers to approximately 2,150.[75]

The community responded with anger; letters to the editor called for a renewed Save Sysco campaign.[76] One employee directed his ire at R.B. Cameron:

> Let's ask ourselves a few questions. Who closed the rolling mill? Who closed the wire and nail mill? Who tried to close the bar mill? Who has shut down the bar mill? Who put the plant on strike in 1972? Who hired D.W.C. Haysom? Who scrapped plans for a BOF when the money was allowed for it and wasted money instead on the SIP process? [...] Who has decided to lay off over 900 workers? [...] May I suggest that everyone in this area knows who made those decisions.[77]

Cameron, a blustery man with a penchant for cigars, was an unsympathetic character for many in Sydney. Living in a Spanish-styled villa on Kings Road, just yards from where Arthur Moxham had built his mansion in the early 1900s, he was easily vilified. Many blamed him for the decision. At a two-hour community rally on 19 August, one young woman stood and addressed the crowd:

I'm not anyone important. Just a steelworkers' wife [...] My man wants to
work, not raise a family on $147 a week unemployment [...] Why [should
we leave]? Why should we have to raise our kids somewhere where they'll
never know their grandparents or their aunts and uncles?[78]

Others drew historical comparisons; "I lived through Black Friday and
I'll live through this. They can't close her, they can't get rid of us all."[79]
The provincial government, now under PC Premier John Buchanan,
responded by replacing Cameron with two new officials, John McCar-
thy as president and Michael Cochrane as chairman. These men doubled down on the layoffs, asserting that they were necessary for the
firm to become competitive.[80]

A federal and provincial cost-sharing agreement ignited the community's hopes that modernization would finally be achieved in June
1981, when $96.25 million was announced for the revitalization and
stabilization of the Sydney plant. Phase I now involved costly repairs
to one of the blast furnaces and at the aging coke ovens.[81] This decision
conforms largely to the Sysco business plan that had been developed
in 1980 between management, the Nova Scotia Department of Development, and the federal Department of Regional Economic Expansion (DREE). Designed to "secure basic operations, reduce operating
costs, and improve productivity," Phase II outlined the implementation
of BOF steelmaking and the use of an idle continuous caster that had
been added in 1975. This strategy recognized the need for economic
diversification. Modernization should be developed towards "forward
integration into additional finished products" – but the plan ultimately
concluded that, should this occur, it would be too far into the future to
make any specific recommendations.[82]

Although these reforms were initially welcomed by many steelworkers, they also reflect changes in the structural management of the plant
and a broader movement towards post-Fordist strategies of production. As was the case at other firms in Canada, the United States, and
Europe, steelworkers were asked to accept lean production, flexibility
in job classification, and even protracted job losses in order to remain
competitive in the new globalized economy. If the Fordist model comprised Taylorism, Wagnerism, and Keynesianism, then post-Fordism is
characterized by direct challenges to each of these pillars. The concept
of "flexible accumulation" is central to this process; as David Harvey
describes, this relied upon instilling "flexibility with respect to the
labour process, labour markets, products, and patterns of consump-
tion ... [and] above all greatly intensified rates of commercial, technological and organizational innovation."[83] The language of one 1979

Sysco managerial information systems study reveals the early shape of this transition. The report recommends greater attention to time study, characteristic of Fordism, but also highlights the importance of improving performance based on predicted market needs and retraining a team of on-site craftsmen to take on new interdepartmental planning responsibilities.[84]

The renewed federal and provincial commitment to modernization caused the leadership of Local 1064 to believe that greater bargaining leverage was also a possibility. This was a significant miscalculation. Unlike in previous decades, the mechanization of processes throughout the Canadian steel industry were not intended to increase production but to increase "efficiency" by allowing for more steel to be produced by fewer workers.[85] As a result, with $700,000 separating the positions of management and the steelworkers' union, an agreement over wages could not be reached and another strike was called in April 1982. More than two thousand steelworkers walked off the job, leaving a skeleton crew of only a few hundred to bank the furnaces and maintain the ovens.[86] "We're not trying to catch up [to other Canadian firms]," said union president Paul Grezel, "but the men are entitled to a living."[87] Just hours after a new contract was signed on 7 May 1982, management notified union officials that the plant would not reopen to capacity and that 1,270 union members would be laid off as of the following Sunday. Management blamed the union, the union believed workers were being punished, and the provincial government placed the blame on "the sick Canadian economy."[88] In the following days, nearly 1,500 steelworkers, office employees, and tradespeople in Sydney applied for unemployment.[89]

With the majority of plant staff on layoff, the city's attention turned to a prospective order from Canada National Railways (CN). The company was expected to announce a major purchase order, which would allow the mill to reopen at capacity. Throughout the late 1970s, Allan J. MacEachen worked closely with management of CN to ensure orders for Sysco rails.[90] The 1982 order was no different; in June, Premier Buchanan confirmed that a substantial rail order had been received.[91] Forty workers were recalled on 2 August. The majority of the 1,500 workers were not recalled until September – after nearly four months on EI. Local 1064 also acquiesced to austerity measures; executive pay was cut, and the workload of the union secretary was reduced to only two days per week.[92]

Precarity increased between 1982 and 1986 as available work was scaled to market demand. In February 1983, another major layoff was narrowly averted when CN renewed their order.[93] This coincided with the plant-wide implementation of a variety of additional cost-saving actions, such as improved man-hour control, restrictions on purchasing supplies, inventory reductions, and energy conservation.[94] Sysco was once again phased down for the summer months and operating at only half-capacity with approximately seven hundred workers on the job.[95] Even after the plant returned to full capacity, management announced that the coke ovens would be temporarily shut down. Sixty-six employees were laid off until coking facilities were reopened in November 1985.[96]

Sysco had now been through two major attempts at modernization. Despite the challenges of this process, some significant changes had taken place by the mid-1980s. One of the blast furnaces was entirely rebuilt in 1984, although its heightened capacity could not be put to use until the open hearths were upgraded.[97] BOF steelmaking had still not been put into practice, and the older open hearth furnaces remained in operation. The product line now consisted of ingots, rolled blooms, cast blooms, slabs, rails, and tie-plate – although rails were now the primary product.[98]

Just three days after Christmas in 1985, Buchanan and federal minister of industrial expansion, Sinclair Stevens, called a press conference in Sydney. "Good news for Sydney," is how they described the terms of a new agreement reached between the federal and provincial governments. Phase II of modernization negotiations were underway, and it was expected that an agreement would include another $150 million commitment to upgrade Sysco facilities.[99] Although one newspaper editorial remarked that the premier was curiously "soft on Sysco workforce size," Local 1064 President John Callaghan "was confident that the widely predicted slashing of the workforce could be avoided with cheaper steel production and the new product lines that will be possible."[100] The plan for BOF production was scrapped for a second time, with the new recommendation being for the installation of an electric arc furnace operation.[101]

Electric arc furnaces use a mix of iron and scrap to produce hot metal. In a fully electric operation, this replaces the need for blast furnaces. Adrian Murphy describes the process:

> They had a 100-ton electric arc furnace; they make the steel in that, bring it up, pour it into this casting moulds, and by the time that heat finished they'd have another one going up. They'd keep it continuous. Of course, that was the name of it, continuous, and if they had have got it working properly, it probably was a good thing. But I mean, it eliminated the blast furnace, it eliminated all the blooming mills, you know? So, it eliminated

all the open hearth from six furnaces to one. So you could imagine the downsizing that was done there.[102]

There were fears that this would eliminate more jobs at the plant, but the province assured the union and the community that the plan was to use both electric arc and blast furnaces to produce hot metal – even though this was not the recommendation that had been offered by the province's steel consultants.[103]

In 1986 and 1987, some provincial politicians began calling for a reassessment of the commitment to Sysco. Although the modernization agreement had been signed, Nova Scotia Finance Minister Greg Kerr spoke to newspapers in October of 1986 and called into question the efficacy of the Sysco deal.[104] The plant's debt was of major concern, and he feared that modernization would not render the mill profitable. In the following months, a public relations battle began to take shape. Members of the provincial business class spoke out against the nationalized mill. Sydney's mayor, Manning MacDonald, was vocal in his support of Sysco and the steelworkers; in 2015, MacDonald recalled that his opposition to planned shutdowns was based upon economic value. If Sysco were to disappear, he believed, the residents of Cape Breton would be left worse off.[105]

Meanwhile, Tippins Incorporated, an American company based in Pittsburgh, was awarded the contract for Phase II. The company would supply expertise in the installation of an electric arc furnace, bloom-casting facility, ladle-refining station, upgraded rolling mill facilities, and a universal mill. The universal mill would broaden the product line of Sysco to include "mine arch bars."[106] According to steel engineers Fumio Tomizawa and Edward C. Howard, electric arc furnace production – the keystone piece of this portion of the Sysco modernization – allows for significant improvements in productivity while "reducing labor cost by use of labor saving equipment."[107] Dravo Automation Services of Pittsburgh were subcontracted to explore the automation of production through specialty computer software, which would allow for greater flexibility among both steelworkers and salaried employees.[108]

In the midst of contract negotiations in February 1988, Local 1064 announced another plant-wide strike. At issue this time were wages, compensation for coke ovens employees, and improved retirement plans for any workers laid off as the result of the modernization process. Callaghan remarked that the steelworkers were not seeking wage parity with other Canadian steel concerns, but that a wage increase of 65¢ per year would prevent Sysco workers from falling even further

4.4 Coke ovens, Sysco, 1987. Photograph by Gerry Langille, Reference 90-255-19687, Beaton Institute, Cape Breton University.

behind.[109] Conflict over wage rates is revealed in the collective agreements; between 1976 and 1984, each contract included the following language: "The Company recognizes the principle of the parity of wages within the Steel Industry and will attempt to achieve this […] The Company intends to embark upon a complete modernization of the whole plant which it is expected will achieve an economic base comparable to competitive companies. When such productivity is achieved, such wage increases can be contemplated."[110] After 1984, Sysco contracts no longer included this language.

Breaking from common practice during other strikes, coke ovens workers walked off the job in 1988 and refused to provide a skeleton crew. Callaghan told the press, "The coke ovens workers feel that they've been led down the garden path. They've told the executive, don't ask us to go in because we're not going."[111] These employees did not only feel alienated from management, but also from Local 1064 – a sentiment that is interrogated further in the next chapter. On

5 February, Sysco management announced that the coke ovens would be closed permanently. More than 120 workers were left unemployed, and although a contract agreement was soon reached, demolition of the coke ovens was scheduled to begin immediately.[112]

Closing the coke ovens was a major indicator that the new mill would not be an integrated plant in any respect. Promises of a dual electric-arc/blast furnace operation would require coking facilities, and many viewed this closure as an early indication of a planned major layoff.[113] It was only one year later that PC cabinet minister Donald Cameron announced that Sydney Steel would not be operating, in any sense, as an integrated plant after the modernization. At the end of the decade, it would operate as a 100 per cent electric arc operation.[114] The blast furnaces and open hearth were immediately scheduled for closure and more than eight hundred employees received layoff notices.[115] This series of upgrades was completed in 1989, and by 1991 there were only approximately seven hundred employees remaining at Sysco.

During the 1970s and 1980s, successive PC and Liberal governments oversaw an uneven modernization campaign that accrued hundreds of millions of dollars in debt with little to show for it. With compound interest, this figure ballooned to $785 million by 1991, and decades of unprofitability had firmly positioned the mill as an "industrial dino-saur" in the minds of many provincial voters – particularly on the mainland. In 1991, ostensibly offering Sysco an opportunity to bounce back after the extensive modernization process, Premier Donald Cam-eron announced that Nova Scotia would forgive the entire Sysco debt. Steelworkers celebrated, as many believed it signalled a fresh start.[116] But the announcement did not symbolize a new commitment to public ownership – indeed, it preceded a plan to privatize the mill, which was revealed by Cameron on 24 January 1992. He described:

> Over the last few years, real progress has been made. Today, in Sydney Steel, Nova Scotians have a world-class mill with the potential to produce a range of speciality products at competitive process. But the Government and Board of Directors of SYSCO are convinced that now is the best time to sell Sydney Steel. We believe that the private sector can manage this facility better than the government can.[117]

When the Liberal Party once again regained control of the Nova Scotia legislature in June 1993, they retained this policy prescription. Between 1993 and 1999, several private firms were courted in the attempt to unload the modernized mill. Manning MacDonald, a Liberal MLA dur-ing the 1990s, describes these years as a sort of *status quo ante bellum.*

The Liberals agreed to support the plant until such time that a private buyer could be found. This state of affairs collapsed in 1999 when the Tories again came into power with a mandate to close the mill if an opportunity to privatize did not immediately present itself.

Epilogue: Post-Fordism at the Electric Arc Mill

Operations at Sysco had changed significantly by 1990. In electric arc production, scrap metal is fed into the furnace and a high-voltage electrical current is applied to melt down the raw material. This creates hot metal that can be reworked to production requirements. Limestone is used in this process and serves a similar purpose as in an integrated mill – to absorb some of the impurities of the melted steel and form a thick slag to be sloughed off during transfer. According to a Sysco skills adjustment study, "There are very few men working on the furnace while the heat is being made [...] The operators of the electric arc furnace sit in a cab or pulpit above the furnace and constantly monitor computer displays. Adjustments, if not automatic, are done through inputs to the computerized controls."[118] The hot metal is fed through the continuous caster to create blooms, before proceeding to the universal mill.

At the universal mill, the steel blooms are rolled into rails. They are reheated using the reheat furnace before being moved through the rolling furnaces. The main process at the universal mill occurs while the rough blooms are transformed into rails; this required two "universal roughing passes," two "edging passes," and one "semi-universal finishing pass." This process shapes the rail to the size and specifications dictated by the production order. Unlike the electric arc furnace employees, workers at the universal mill have jobs that correspond to their former employment in the rolling mills. The skill study notes, "The big transformation of the production work here [...] has been the introduction of computer control [...] if the technology is working according to design, operations are mostly automated."[119] The automation of production, with workers employed largely in a maintenance and organizational role, was central to modernized operations at Sydney Steel.

"It's a new start with a product that will be a lot lower priced. We'll be leaner," promised Sysco President John Strasser in a 1989 interview with *Atlantic Business Magazine*.[120] In the words of one magazine editor, "There's a new attitude that exists [at Sysco], and the new 'buzzword' is *profit!*"[121] Along with a new process of work based upon automation and computerized production, workers at Sydney Steel had to come to terms with an entirely new organizational structure. Full production was forecast at 219,000 tons of steel, with an operational workforce of 709 employees.[122] With these transformations of the labour process came a firming-up of managerial commitment to post-Fordist organizational strategies; Dave Ervin recalls the attempted merger of job classifications after modernization:

> Unfortunately, like I say some of the problem is with the union, but unfortunately some of the jobs on the steel plant ... they're so, bound up in history. Like, okay, if I'm an electrician, I need an electrician helper to help me do a job. No matter how simple the job is. The helper goes with me. Same with the millwrights, same with the plumbers [...] I took a course on this at Dal (Dalhousie University). CLC, Canadian Labour Congress, put on this course, on basically combining jobs. The modern workforce [...] They were just too – caught up in history. And history changes. And a lot of them couldn't realize that. And that's the main reason the plant closed. That last contract they signed could have solved a lot of those problems ... going from 22 pay rates down to about, 5 or 6 ... but a lot of the guys there were against it.[123]

In the new configuration, production could quickly be started or halted to correspond with global steel markets. As with other post-Fordist firms, this would involve employing only a small core of full-time maintenance workers, while a larger number of flexible employees could be hired on or laid off as dictated by demand. While this transition came at a cost of more than eight hundred jobs, the adjustment study notes: "For those who will be continuing to work at the plant, technological changes have mean [sic] that much of the knowledge and skills accumulated over the years will no longer be of direct practical use, and new skills and expertise have had to be acquired by a group of mostly middle-aged workers."[124]

These changes required retraining. Employees had the option of signing up for evening courses, while the company sent another small group to Germany to experience production in an upgraded plant. New automatic systems, computerized controls, and methods of steelmaking created a situation where generations of skill and knowledge were suddenly outdated.[125] While Braverman postulates that Fordism strips workers of both craft skills and workplace control, the development of post-Fordism and flexible or lean production has led to a further rethinking of skill in the modern workplace. This was a new economic world, characterized by contingent employment, stagnant wages, and the ever-present threat of capital flight.[126] Yuko Aoyama and Manuel Castells take a different approach, arguing that the "new economy" reflects an up-skilling of the labour market to correspond with the developments of an information- and knowledge-based economy.[127] Oral history testimony allows us to move beyond this dichotomy to reveal workers' subjective experiences of skill and identity that emerged alongside the changing labour process.

Workers' accounts of Sysco between 1967 and 1989 refer extensively to the active characteristics of work. Workers from the blast furnaces, open hearth, and rolling mills explain production in sense-based and active terms. From freezing on the high cranes to sweating in the open hearth or stick-handling a crane overtop of a crowded shop floor, work was dialectically produced and felt by workers' bodies. On-the-job practice is viewed as essential for the development of the skills and know-how that were required, and workers often questioned the applicability of outside training to the specific work process at the mill. Leslie MacCuish, a Sysco employee who was retrained after the modernization, spoke unfavourably about the transition:

> Us fellows should have been taken when the furnace was being built, the furnace guys go with the furnace guys, and the L.R.F. fellows and caster fellows. We should have been taken and put on them jobs where they were building the furnace. Different parts of the furnace. We'd know where to go if there was trouble. We'd know what to do. We got computers there, sure. Stuff like that. Half of us guys don't know anything about computers.[128]

Others reflected on the new skills required:

> JOHN MURPHY: This new mill is all computerized and where we used to go up with wrenches and bars and hammers and work our butts off to make these tolerances, they just press a button and the computer does it now.[129]
>
> BARRY BROCKLEHURST: It's more efficient, I think and it's good quality steel product. That's about it, I guess [...] You have to watch out, watch the water supply, make sure no alarms come off. You have to make sure you can get them back on right quick, before losing your steel or breakouts or something like that [...] It's every man for himself, now. There is no carrying on or anything like that. Very little of it. Everybody is scared of everybody else, cutting each other's throat.[130]

Labour process theory has traditionally focused on skill and control as reflections of organizational structures; Marxist and neo-Marxist scholarship argues that post-Fordism has masked the continuation of deskilling and increased managerial control endemic within the capitalist mode of production while the liberal position views work in the new economy in terms of flexibility, teamwork, and efficiency. Duncan Gallie charts a middle ground in his study of work in Britain. Defining skill as "the substantive complexity of job tasks in terms of the level, scope and integration of mental, manipulative, and interpersonal tasks," Gallie argues that the British labour market since the 1990s has witnessed a broad trend of "upskilling" along with a corresponding loss of workers' control.[131] If we accept this definition, the same conclusion broadly holds in the analysis of work processes at Sysco through the late twentieth century. Steelworkers were retrained after 1989 to develop skills associated with a technologically advanced modern steel facility. Despite this, the threat of deindustrialization and job losses contributed to a sense of lost control over the process of production.

Oral histories of work at the plant reveal how such a narrow definition of skill and control cannot be fully applied to workers' subjective understandings of the changing work process. Workers' accounts reveal a deeply held belief that the new labour process represented a fundamental break from the skills and sentiments associated with steelmaking at an integrated plant. This does not simply mean the decline of physical labour or bull work, but the perceived end of active participation in production. Although shop-floor employees at Sysco were retrained in work methods that were more appropriate to the so-called flexibility of the new economy, the loss of traditional approaches to work, training, and older forms of camaraderie felt like an immiseration.

We also must remember that, despite the challenges posed by the turn to post-Fordist production, earlier strategies were likewise difficult. Despite their clear and sometimes fond recollection of the work processes, most Sysco employees remembered their jobs as frequently dangerous, sometimes unhealthy, and oftentimes unpleasant. It should also be noted that oral history testimony in this chapter is drawn from interviews conducted in both 1990 and 2014; interviews conducted in 1990 occurred at a moment of profound trauma at Sysco, with the massive shift in work processes having resulted in hundreds of lost jobs. Although many of those who were interviewed in more recent years continued to view the final modernization as a moment of profound disconnection, those who remained employed at the plant after 1989 spoke of steelwork as a shared experience that continued to hold meaning for their occupational identity.[132]

Chapter Five

Labour Environmentalism: Fighting for Compensation at the Sydney Coke Ovens

From the "re-born" environmentally conscious politicians to the tourist dollar oriented civic administrators – to the sterile medical community. To the ivory tower of the academic community and the comfortable pews of the clergy, the men, women and children cry out for justice – Who will answer? Who will answer?

– Don MacPherson, Coke Ovens Workers United for Justice[1]

The plumes of smoke that billowed from the Sysco stacks have been woven into the collective memory of steelmaking in Sydney. Joe Legge, a former coke ovens worker, recalls, "It was part of your everyday living. People that lived in the Pier, depending on which way the wind was blowing didn't hang their wash up on certain days. Because they knew it would either come in red from the blast furnace or black from the coke ovens. And this was a regular thing ... people lived their lives like that."[2] The smell, described as sulphurous – similar to rotten eggs – is another frequent sensory recollection of those who worked at the provincially owned Sydney Steel Corporation. Residents of Ashby and Whitney Pier, the two neighbourhoods immediately adjacent to the plant, frequently describe closing their windows when the wind changed direction; this was to prevent the smoke from leaving ashy deposits on floors and countertops.[3]

The multicoloured smoke is often positioned as a character in its own right in the stories of Sydney residents. It plays many roles; sometimes it is framed as a silent killer, bringing carcinogenic dustfall to an unwitting community, while in others it is a nuisance – something to be put up with for the sake of jobs and the local economy.[4] However the smoke is represented, in each case it arrives in a story to signal a description of the way things used to be; Sydney, in these stories, was a very different place in the years prior to the plant's modernization. Although the

5.1 Pollution from the Sydney steel plant, 1955. Photographer unknown, Reference 97-439-28287, Beaton Institute, Cape Breton University.

dirty air of the steelmaking past is often contrasted with the community green space that now rests on the Sysco site, several interviewees remarked upon the continued relevance of industrial pollutants to life in the city. Sysco's smoke has not soiled residents' laundry for decades, but its material effects continue to loom large over concerns about environmental justice, workers' compensation, and the public health impact of deindustrialization in the city.

As early as the mid-1960s, researchers began examining the effects of industrial dustfall in Sydney. In 1965, a report commissioned by the Department of National Health and Welfare found that air pollution levels in the neighbourhoods surrounding the plant were significantly higher than normal, and that the levels of fine particulate matter could possibly result in respiratory problems for residents.[5] These findings were replicated in the 1970s, when further studies on air pollutants found that the half-mile surrounding the coke ovens tested especially high for dustfall.[6] The Nova Scotia government restricted public access to many of these early reports until the late 1980s, when a group known as the Coke Ovens Workers United for Justice challenged the province, their union, and management on the issue of workers' compensation for occupational illness. Their resistance, and their insistence upon the damaging effects of shop-floor exposure to coke ovens emissions, would result in an overhaul of compensation practices relating to workplace illness in Nova Scotia. So, too, did their efforts inform public attempts to find accountability for the environmental aftermath of deindustrialization.

An Emerging Consensus: Hazardous Working Conditions in North American Coking Facilities

While the early scientific research focused on possible links between respiratory illness and fine particulate matter, others noted heightened rates of certain cancers among coke ovens employees who were exposed to airborne toxins. In 1970, an occupational health study of 58,828 American steelworkers found that coke ovens employees suffered from heightened risk of "malignant neoplasm of the respiratory system" – lung cancer. This was especially pronounced for those workers employed on top of the battery, where exposure to gas and coke fumes was more frequent. Such a finding, the authors conclude, "[is likely] due to factors in the coke plant environment."[7] Studies of this nature were conducted in steel-producing regions of the world throughout the 1970s and 1980s, and each noted the correlation between occupational exposure to coke ovens emissions and bodily illness.[8]

In Ontario, the Injured Workers Movement challenged the provincial government on these issues as early as 1974.[9] The Elliot Lake uranium workers' strike, largely over issues surrounding compensation and occupational disease, prompted the provincial government to appoint a commission to explore the health crisis.[10] The result of these struggles was the 1978 passage of Bill C70: An Act Respecting the Occupational Health and Safety of Ontario Workers. Robert Storey writes, "For the first time, Ontario workers had the statutory right to know about the substances they worked with, could help promote and ensure safe and healthy workplaces through their participation in joint health and safety committees, and had the right to refuse work they believed was unsafe."[11]

Members of the USWA started to recognize occupational illness resulting from coke ovens work in the United States even earlier, by the late 1960s in some cases. Dan Hannan, an employee at the Clairton Works in Pittsburgh, was instrumental in creating this awareness. Coming from a steelworking family, Hannan's older brother was a labour activist who had been involved in the struggle to organize Clairton for the USWA.[12] Hannan was a coke ovens worker and served as president of his union local, and in 1967 U.S. Steel began a series of modernizations to his workplace. Hannan helped to put together a list of colleagues who had become seriously ill or died as the result of issues with lung capacity or cancers, which would later be presented to federal regulatory agencies. Recognizing an apparent connection between employment in the coke ovens and occupational illness, he started lobbying politicians and union leaders for a solution. Following the passage of the US Occupational Health and Safety Act in 1970, he testified before the OSHA (Occupational Safety and Health Administration) Standards Advisory Committee on Coke Ovens Emissions. Hannan's speech is compelling:

> Each name there identifies a man who worked at a hard job, in the heat of the coke ovens, in the valley of the Monongahela River. Their labor made possible the steel we have used as automobiles or refrigerators, or pins and needles, or brides, or nails to hold our houses together. When we bought our cars we thought nothing of paying an extra $10 or $15 to have a cigarette lighter on the dashboard – but we didn't pay the extra one or two dollars per car it would have cost to clean up the coke ovens and save some of these men's lives.
>
> These men are not statistics. They were human beings, like you and me. And as they worked they, too, had their dreams – perhaps of retirement to enjoy the fruits of their labor. They had wives, and families and homes. They had friends to visit with, and children to advise, and grandchildren to spoil – and no doubt they looked forward to devoting their later years to such pleasures.
>
> [Through OSHA] the American people have spoken. We, the people, are no longer willing to be accomplices to industrial murder.[13]

After this testimony, OSHA released an upgraded set of health and safety standards for American coking plants. These included a series of engineering controls on older plants, designed to reduce emissions and create a safer, healthier workplace. Jack Sheehan, a spokesman for the USWA, said that the union was pleased with the result.[14]

The international union was quite willing to share information back and forth with Canadian locals. In 1976, representatives from Local 1005 at the Steel Company of Canada (Stelco) contacted the union international offices for information on American compensation claims for occupational illness among coke ovens workers. The Hamilton union sought compensation for the widow of a coke ovens worker, "L. Skuranec," who passed away from cancers of the rectum, lungs, and bone.[15] Her claim had been denied in Ontario; the provincial Workers' Compensation Board writes that, despite 37 years working on top of the coke ovens batteries, "Mr. Skuranec's death resulted from non-industrial condition and was not related to nor characteristic to the type of work he performed while in the employment of Stelco."[16] The union provided information drawn from the research of William Lloyd – an epidemiologist who worked closely with the union on coke ovens claims – as well as American guidelines for coke ovens compensation, USWA health and safety statistics, and articles detailing the emerging health concerns stateside.[17] Newspapers in Hamilton soon picked up the story, with headlines in the *Spectator* proclaiming, "Killer Coke Ovens" and "Coke Oven Death Alarm Ignored."[18]

These events did not immediately prompt a reaction in Nova Scotia, although a 1976 op-ed piece in the *Cape Breton Post* laments, "sadly ... the information appears to have made no noticeable impact on those who should be concerned about it here: Sysco itself, Local 1064 of the United Steelworkers Union, and the Nova Scotia Workmen's Compensation Board."[19] Concern surrounding occupational and community exposure to steelmaking emissions continued to grow as more local reports were released. In 1977, the *Report of the Sydney Respiratory Health Survey* revealed that coke ovens emissions exceed the "maximum desirable level of ... sulphur dioxide over one hour" by more than 45 per cent, and the maximum level of "suspended particulate matter" by 97 per cent. The authors of this survey concluded that these statistics were likely to "[have] some measurable negative effect on respiratory function for the residents of Whitney Pier and Ashby" – not to mention those employed on top of the coke ovens batteries.[20]

The reluctance among some members of Local 1064 to challenge the province and company on issues of environmental justice was related to the precarious situation at Sysco during the early 1980s. The union had taken some steps to bring issues of health and safety to the attention of management in 1979, when officials presented a document to Sysco asking "that the Coke Ovens Department Management take a closer look at Safety in the Department regarding [...] emissions." The document also describes the heightened rates of cancer found within coke ovens employees, but remarks: "We realize that with a plant as old as ours it is very hard to implement engineering and pollution machinery right away, but we feel there are some areas where improvements can be made immediately."[21] With the importation of new technologies and the industry-wide turn towards lean and flexible production, labour relations were strained even before the wildcats and strikes of the 1980s.

Following the 1982 strike, Local 1064 faced crises on several fronts. Stopping the bleeding of jobs was the first priority; after several strikes that resulted either in stalemate or defeat, they needed to ensure that operations at the plant would continue. Occupational health and safety, which had long been a foundational plank in the union's mandate, was about to reach another flashpoint. As the result of the two-year coke ovens shutdown between 1983 and 1985, many workers in that department began to worry about their future at the plant. While the union continued to address health and safety concerns, some coke ovens workers began to worry that the closure of their department might occur before any agreement on compensation was reached. There were efforts made to bring attention to this situation; Dan Yakimchuk, a former steelworker, describes accessing two restricted provincial studies:

D. YAKIMCHUK: I mean the worst of course was the studies done [in 1973 and 1974] on pollution […] I got a hold of a study that was sent to the union office. It was supposed to be passed around the membership and it was never done. On the effects of pollution, the coke ovens pollution particularly.

M. EARLE: But the union, just to go back to that, the union had this, had got hold of this but they never distributed it to the members.

D. YAKIMCHUK: No. It was in the officers' office. And I got it, I think it was Gramps Kiley [a former union president], when he was in there, he passed it along to me, because him and I were very good friends […] He just passed me a copy, "Don't say where you got it," type of thing. Before that I started wondering why guys were dying, you know … I mean to me it didn't make sense. I mean how come the teachers when they retired didn't die two or three months later? And I seemed to be a voice in the wilderness, because everybody, not everybody, but my members of council, didn't even know what I was talking about […] Because people were really scared of their jobs.[22]

According to Yakimchuk, the ability of Sydney steelworkers to challenge the provincial government on issues of workplace health – specifically on the subject of occupational illness in the coke ovens – was stymied by the constant threat of job loss and unemployment.

Meanwhile, scientific studies were undertaken to ascertain the health impacts of coke ovens emissions on employees and residents of industrial communities. Between 1982 and 1985, three federal research studies examined the public health impact of carcinogenic "polycyclic aromatic hydrocarbons" (PAH) produced during the coking process in Sydney. These reports all made explicit reference to increased levels of

PAH found adjacent to the coke ovens site; Lawrence Hildebrand, writing in 1982, concluded that "the plant does not have environmental controls that meet today's standards."[23] The health impact of these findings were described in 1984, which Atwell et al. confirm:

> Epidemiological findings among coke oven workers [in the United States] show that coke ovens emissions can also lead to the development of non-malignant respiratory disease such as chronic bronchitis and emphysema ... workers exposed to relatively high levels of coke oven emissions develop cancer, especially of the respiratory tract, at rates significantly higher than those reported for other workers.[24]

The most controversial of these three reports was released in August 1985, when J.R. Hickman argued in a federal study that the continued operation of the Sydney coke ovens – barring the implementation of an emission-reduction scheme – would result in heightened levels of cancer among workers and the general public.[25] In addition to this report, Hickman penned a letter to the attorney general of Nova Scotia to illustrate his concerns regarding public and occupational health and the Sydney coke ovens. The attorney general admitted receiving this letter during the discovery portion of an ongoing lawsuit relating to Sysco's environmental impact, but denied that Hickman's findings could be extrapolated to the residents in areas surrounding the plant. "Whether an actual risk exists depends on the degree of exposure," he writes, "Hickman admitted that there were no PAH environmental guidelines at the time. It was not known what exposure levels to PAH's were considered acceptable."[26]

"We'll Go Down Fighting or We'll Win": Sysco Workers Battle for Compensation

Prior to the release of the Hickman report, with the Coke Ovens Department scheduled to reopen in December 1985, the public was also becoming more aware of the environmental and possible public health impacts of continued coke production. In May, provincial epidemiologist Pierre Lavigne attempted to assuage concerns during an interview with the *Cape Breton Post*. He admitted that coke emissions contained heightened levels of PAH, and that the areas surrounding the plant did have much higher rates of lung and stomach cancer; any link between these two facts, he cautioned, was "highly speculative." He also pointed to high rates of smoking among workers in Cape Breton; "the fact that it's an industrial area might not have anything to do [with the cancer rates]," Lavigne argued, though he did recommend the implementation of cautionary emission controls upon the recommissioning of the ovens.[27]

Only a few weeks before the reopening, several articles in the Sydney newspaper began questioning the decision. "Sysco ignoring studies, will reopen coke oven," read the *Post* headline on 4 November; "this ... will expose workers and nearby residents to carcinogenic chemicals at levels which scientists have concluded are dangerous." Company officials refused to comment, aside from reminding the public that the start up "would create about 50 new jobs at the plant itself, as well as badly needed jobs in Cape Breton coal mines."[28] The new president of Local 1064, John Callaghan, and the Liberal leader of the provincial opposition, Vince MacLean, each released statements supporting the company's decision to reopen the ovens. MacLean remarked that the complete closure of the ovens would amount to "putting a gun to the head" of unemployed steelworkers, while Callaghan cryptically mused on a possible "conspiracy by someone to try and stop the second phase of the Sydney Steel modernization."[29]

The plant's existence as a public corporation fed into the notion, expressed by Callaghan, that there were powerful political forces aligned against the plant – both provincially and nationally. This idea remains visible in oral history testimony, and is perhaps not without merit; as career human resources employee Fred James reflects, mainland voters were tired of supporting Sydney Steel debts with their tax dollars.[30] This idea was further cemented in 1999, when John Hamm – a Pictou County MLA – was elected as premier. Several informants recall the 'Sysco postcard' released by the Hamm campaign; this is described as an image of the plant marked "closed," juxtaposed with a series of empty hospital beds marked "open."[31] As a result, this idea is much more firmly asserted in interviews conducted since the closure of the plant; while Callaghan hints at a conspiracy, former employees interviewed in recent years are much more explicit about perceived backroom efforts to close Sysco.

These suspicions, and the tensions they created between workers, their union, the corporation, and the provincial government are also reflected in the testimony related to the release of confidential emissions studies during the 1980s. Yakimchuk describes the clandestine retrieval of documents revealing the extent of pollution at Sysco; according to Yakimchuk, the union was in full knowledge of this material but kept it from the rank and file.[32] Charlie MacDonald, a member of the union executive, argues that the company had access to these scientific reports but kept the information from the union until the end of the decade.[33]

Don MacPherson, an electrician at the plant and later a founding member of the Coke Ovens Workers United For Justice, described being passed the documents from an anonymous source.[34] In each case, the retrieval of these reports is presented as a "eureka moment" when the full extent of coke ovens illness and risk finally became clear. Indeed, Steven High writes that stories of "liberating" documents from recalcitrant corporations can also represent "an act of defiance in the face of [...] erasure."[35]

While the secreting of confidential documents out of the plant under the watchful eyes of security and management presents an interesting narrative structure for the emergence of resistance among the coke ovens workers, it is likely that this resistance sprang from the material processes of industrial decline. As Arthur McIvor argues, worklessness and deindustrialization each have a direct impact on workers' bodily health.[36] In these instances, deindustrialization is a visible agent in the unfolding contradictions of capitalism. Workers' bodies dialectically exist both as active agents within, and bodily receptacles of, productive forces.[37] Industrial capitalism demands healthy bodies for production, but – in another of its contradictions – produces unhealthy bodies. In Sydney, emerging understandings of the physical impacts of industrial pollution combined with local knowledge of the health effects of the shop floor to provoke bottom-up resistance from outside of the traditional institutional structures of the workplace.

These pressures were not new. Trade unions have long agitated for protection in the industrial workplace, and for good reason. More than three hundred men were killed at Sysco during its century of production. Workplace accidents, explosions, mistakes, and unsafe conditions continue to cause injuries and deaths across Canada. These often result in drawn-out applications, rejected claims, and labyrinthian application processes. Robert Storey writes that these workers "have taken on the task of constructing the passageway even as they move through it."[38] In Sydney, many attribute a gas explosion that occurred in the coke ovens on 25 August 1977 as a key event that inspired a renewed focus on health and safety within the department in later years.[39]

This explosion is recalled clearly by Joe Legge. When we met at his home on Rockdale Avenue in Sydney, it was obvious that he had thought extensively about the circumstances surrounding the accident. Tommy McCarron gave me Joe's name; he told me that Joe had been involved in an accident on the Sysco site, and that he had – in the years since – worked extensively with occupational health and safety. I later learned that Joe often speaks to Work Safe Nova Scotia and to patients at the IWK children's burn unit in Halifax about his experience. On 25

5.2 Joe Legge, 2015. Photograph by Steve Wadden (*Forged*).

August 1977, at twenty-nine years of age, Joe was burned on 65 per cent of his body in the Sydney coke ovens. He describes:

> They were changing a valve in the gas main that took the vaporized gas away from the coking process [...] The safety process at the time called for a back pressure of steam six times greater than the flow rate of the gas [...] So they put the steam on, the gas was shut off, and the safety people took their tests – no gas in the area. But the valve that they were replacing was being taken out and cleaned up because tar had gotten into the key-way [...] But what they didn't know was that the shut-off valve that was supposed to be directing the gas the other way had the same problem. [...] So it's August 25th, 80 degrees, you're in a room about the size of this, sweating bullets. Somebody says, "Shut the steam off a little bit" ... Next thing you know, the steam was shut off [...] The maintenance guys take their bolts out, they just opened the top up [...] So it sucks in 80 degree air, hits 2,200 degree gas in the pipe. [claps hands]. Just that quick.
>
> I was standing with one hand on the chain hoist, that was supporting this valve, and there was two mechanics taking the bolts out [...] And I

heard [snaps fingers]. And that was the ignition point within the pipe. Within seconds the flame came up through the top [...] I was standing right above it. It hit me in the chest and tossed me about 15 feet through the air. And the flame went straight up, and hit the roof, and came back down – so the initial concussion – there was 17 people there – the initial concussion knocked everybody down. So when the flame came back down [...] most of them got burnt on the back of their neck, the backs of their arms, the backs of the ears.

With the exception of me. Who got, right in the chest. I got the full blast of it. I landed in the middle of the doorway. So sixteen guys, in panic, ran right over top of me in their efforts to get out. And, uh, I ... managed to get myself out by myself. [...] And Ray Drohan, the electrical foreman at the time, had his car nearby. He had just bought a brand new Buick, with leather upholstery, and he grabbed me by the arm and he said, "Joe, get in the car." And I opened the door and I said, I'm going to ruin all your upholstery!" Because, you know, I had skin all hanging off me everywhere. And he said, "Get the ... in the car!"

I got in the car and he drove me up to the hospital [...] He pulled up to the ambulance entrance, there were two double doors, and I pushed them open. And stepped inside and there was a Doctor and two nurses who were standing there, they had charts in their hands, and when I pushed open the door the three of them looked at me, and made a run for me. And after that I remember waking up two weeks later in the burn unit in Halifax [...] There was eight of us, eight of the seventeen, up to Halifax [...] Wish I could forget [...]

Thirty-seven years ago. I'd like to forget it. Unfortunately, that's never going to happen. The good thing is that I have very few nightmares anymore. For the longest time, I'd wake up two or three o'clock in the morning, going through the whole thing over again. Seeing that ball of fire coming at me. And [pause]. It upsets the whole household. I mean, nobody's going to sleep after that you start screaming. That went on for the longest time. Now, if I'm caught off guard – like I don't watch movies that have explosions or things like that. And sometimes, it's only every now and then you get caught not being aware of something and all of the sudden Bang-o, it's there and you're, "Oh, shit," you know? Your subconscious starts working and the next thing you know, there's a nightmare coming.[40]

Joe went back to work at the plant five years later, and stayed with Sysco until the final closure. Although his case was quickly adjudicated by workers' compensation – as he explains, "there was no way they were going to look at me and say, 'you're faking this'" – legislation at the time covered only physical disabilities that would prevent some-one from working. He received 18 per cent disability. One of the maintenance men injured in the same accident had burns on his arms; he received 35 per cent disability. While Joe's scars are more visible than those of workers suffering from occupational illness, both sets of experiences reveal the shortcomings in the Nova Scotia compensation system during the late 1970s and 1980s.

In December 1985, the Coke Ovens Department reopened after a long closure, but by the end of the month the future of the integrated mill was once more in question. Alongside the announcement of Sysco's Phase II modernization funding, Premier John Buchanan revealed an ambitious plan to clean up and remediate the polluted landscape of the Sydney "Tar Ponds."[41] The full circumstances of these clean-up efforts are discussed in another chapter, but concurrent environmental concerns, coupled with the possibility of an electric arc operation that would negate the need for coking facilities, meant that employees were again plunged into uncertainty.

Workers' fears were soon realized. In August 1986, Buchanan and federal Environment Minister Tom McMillan announced that the coke ovens would be closed down permanently in July 1988. Coking operations were quickly becoming linked, in the minds of the public, with community and environmental pollution. The government promised Local 1064 representatives that nearly 200 jobs would be created to offset the 120 positions lost by this decision, and assured coke plant workers that they would have the right of first refusal.[42] Scepticism reigned; Don MacPherson penned an open letter to Premier Buchanan:

> The general view of most steelworkers is that we are in the final throes of a complete phase-down, if not indeed a phase-out of steel operations at Sysco [...] Now we face, under the pretext of the tar ponds clean up, closure of the Sysco coke ovens [...] Steelworkers would consider continuous iron production without a coking plant laughable, were it not so tragic [...] Mr. Premier, a policy of "keep them in the dark on a diet of horse manure" is fine for growing mushrooms but it does nothing to alleviate the spectre of further mass unemployment at Sydney Steel.[43]

The union acquiesced to the plan with cautious optimism. On 24 July, Buchanan promised Callaghan a feasibility study on the construction of a new coke ovens operation. Such an operation would implement necessary emissions controls and offset concerns over lost jobs.[44] These events ultimately led to the creation of a group called the Coke Ovens

Workers United for Justice – a "vigilante committee" composed of steelworkers Don MacPherson, David MacLeod, John Rocket, and Bernie Sharp, who sought recognition of industrial illness.[45]

There were three concurrent issues that resulted in the formation of this organization. First, many steelworkers did not believe the government's claims that the modernization and tar ponds remediation would create enough quality jobs for former employees. Second, there were a number of issues relating to seniority among coke ovens workers that would have to be resolved for the purposes of workers' pensions.[46] The issue that garnered the majority of the committee's attention, however, was related to workers' compensation for current and former coke ovens employees. The Nova Scotia Workers' Compensation Board (WCB) did not designate the coke ovens as a hazardous workplace despite decades of evidence, and the system for illness compensation was largely dedicated to dealing with pneumoconiosis – black lung – among the island's coal miners.[47]

Deindustrialization provoked a set of circumstances wherein a long-standing "high threshold culture" in the Coke Ovens Department was subverted by bottom-up protest. With similarities to the experiences of workers in other high-risk industries, Sydney's coke ovens workers were habituated to accept a high-risk threshold throughout their working lives – tied, as they were, to innate notions of working-class masculinity.[48] Facing the possible closure of the coke ovens and the spectre of occupational disease, the men in Coke Ovens Workers United for Justice stepped outside these traditional boundaries to action to demand recognition. As an institution, Local 1064, wary of the economic instability wrought by job losses, was slower to act. Some on the executive felt that MacPherson and the others were acting out of turn, and that compensation for the coke ovens workers was simply one of many issues facing the Sydney steelworkers at the same time. Nonetheless, trade unionists did eventually come to challenge the high-risk-threshold culture at the mill. By 1988, Local 1064 had joined forces with the coke ovens activists to challenge the province directly on issues of workplace health and occupational illness.

The Nova Scotia WCB frequently started from "no" in their assessment of coke ovens workers and occupational illness claims. In 1986, a Sysco employee named Joseph Louis Assoun applied to the WCB for industrial bronchitis. In a letter from W.J. Penney of Sysco Personnel Services to the WCB, Assoun's work history is described: fourteen years at the coke screening plant and "around the battery operations," with an additional year labouring in other departments before returning to the coke plant. Nonetheless, Penney writes, "We are not aware of any hazardous environmental exposure Mr. Assoun would have been in contact with."[49] Assoun's claim was denied. "It was felt that his long history of smoking was the main etiological factor," explained R.J. Allen of the WCB, "his industrial exposure did not significantly contribute to his particular medical problem."[50]

Coke Ovens Workers United for Justice organized a concerted letter-writing and media campaign surrounding the compensation issue in 1987. As the result of this pressure, Cape Breton Liberal Member of Parliament Dave Dingwall became involved in the discussion. In a letter to Sysco President Ernie Boutilier, Dingwall cautioned Sysco to act as a good corporate citizen and to behave in the best interests of the community it serves. "Furthermore," he writes, "could you also indicate to me as to why the Sydney Steel Corporation is repudiating statements made by some of the workers who have been affected negatively by the emissions coming from the Coke Ovens?"[51]

Political attention from local MLAs and MPs made both the company and union officials uncomfortable. Boutilier explained that the company was "concerned for the welfare of all ... employees," and that they were exploring assistance options for coke ovens workers. Any changes to the pension structure for former employees were related to negotiations with the steelworkers' union and, according to Boutilier, could not be discussed publicly. He also writes that the WCB's denial of coke ovens workers' compensation claims was the result of "a medical examination, and a review of medical evidence, not on the basis of any statement by the company."[52] Such a claim is at odds with the content of W.J. Penney's 1986 letter to the WCB in the Assoun case. Charlie MacDonald largely supports Boutilier's position on the pension issue; in a 2015 interview, he describes how MacPherson and the Coke Ovens Workers United for Justice were unaware of ongoing negotiations between Local 1064 and Sysco management – many of which dealt explicitly with the questions of coke ovens compensation.[53]

Nonetheless, the existence of an ad hoc, extra-union committee organizing around issues of workers' health and compensation was unusual. Some of the other members of Local 1064 felt, as MacDonald did, that the union was already addressing these grievances through the proper channels and that MacPherson's efforts were simply playing into the hands of those seeking to smear Sysco. Whether or not this was the case is unclear, but the actions of Coke Ovens Workers United for Justice did have some other tangible effects. In April 1988, a letter on behalf of the committee was cited in the Assoun appeal to the WCB. The board found that industrial exposure *did* likely play a role in Assoun's illness, awarding him partial disability payment.[54] By the summer of

1988 MacPherson and MacLeod were asked to join the Compensation, Health and Safety Committee of Local 1064 to add their expertise regarding the coke ovens issue. The men were asked to study employee records held in the steelworkers' hall to find evidence of occupational illness among coke ovens workers.[55] They agreed.

MacPherson and MacLeod began drafting a cursory list of coke ovens workers who had passed away during the previous twenty-five years. With similarities to Hannan's efforts in Pennsylvania years earlier, these did not include employees killed as the result of industrial accidents, automobile deaths, or surgical deaths of a non-occupational nature. Eighty-five names were listed. Of these, forty-eight were marked as having passed away as the result of cancer.[56] With these numbers in hand, MacPherson and the union felt empowered to bring the issue to the attention of the federal government. In a letter dated 3 October 1988, MacPherson wrote to the federal minister of the environment:

> A preliminary survey [...] show[s] a 60% cancer mortality rate, or four times the national average [...] One might ponder the reaction of the New York Times, Washington Post, and World Health Organization when they receive copies of the documentation. The inability of [...] Sysco, the Nova Scotia Department of Labour, the Federal and Provincial Departments of the Environment, to come to grips with this disaster, leave us no choice but to take the issue to a National and International level.[57]

Over the next three months, members of the union sent letters to national and provincial politicians. NDP leaders Ed Broadbent and Alexa McDonough were supportive of the steelworkers' efforts, pledging to broach the issue with the respective ministers, while the federal Minster of Energy, Mines and Resources Jake Epp reminded MacPherson that the issues at hand were provincial responsibilities.[58]

On 15 March 1989, Nova Scotia Minister of Labour Ron Russell announced several possible reforms to the Workers' Compensation Act. These included reformulating the benefit calculation from 75 per cent of gross salary to 90 per cent of net salary, although workers' groups believed that this could result in fewer payments overall. Russell also indicated that the government might make it easier for workers to apply for compensation as the result of lung cancer, but not for other types of occupational illness related to coke ovens employment.[59] MacPherson immediately released a statement decrying the proposed changes as a "lukewarm" effort at drawing attention from the ongoing coke ovens workers' dispute. Local 1064 reiterated their demands publicly:

We're demanding full, comprehensive coverage for all affected coke ovens workers, provisions that would exceed coverage granted to ovens workers in Ontario [...] We don't think that the workers here should have to suffer because of government inaction that borders on criminal negligence.[60]

The proposed changes would do little for those on the union rolls of coke ovens claimants, which by July had reached 32 claims by bereaved family members and 335 claims by living workers.[61] It also appeared that Russell was preparing Sysco workers for disappointment, cautioning petitioning workers, "What's fair to me may not be fair to you. Unfortunately that's the way the world works."[62] Nonetheless, two coke ovens widows – only named in the local newspaper as "the widows of Wilfred Piercy and Joe Magee" – received approval for their compensation claims in November. This decision was hailed as a possible test case for the majority of workers' claims as the women's husbands were not employed on top of the coke battery but in other sections of the coking plant.[63]

A series of small victories followed in early 1990. On 2 January the front page of the Halifax *Chronicle Herald* announced that the WCB had upheld the decision in the Piercy/Magee cases. This decision recognized that all major sections of the coking plant could be considered a "hazardous workplace," not simply the top of the batteries.[64] Although the WCB quickly asserted that these decisions did not set a precedent for the cases still under review, MacPherson was buoyed by the terms of the finding – though he remarked that of the one hundred claims already processed, only twenty-five had received partial disability awards.[65]

It was also in January that MacPherson was contacted by producers of CBC's national television program *The Fifth Estate*. They were interested in producing an episode devoted to the workers' fight for compensation at Sysco. Only a week before the episode went to air, the WCB crafted another press release; the board had been waiting for employment records from Sysco before adjudicating cases, but as of 14 March they decided to move ahead with claims processing.[66] In addition, the labour minister invited those workers who had already been denied – numbering around seventy – to reapply. The WCB would now be applying "the benefit of the doubt," meaning, "if the factors in favour of a worker's claim are just as likely as the factors against, the matter is resolved in the worker's favour. MLA Paul McEwan pointed out that this was nothing to celebrate; the benefit of the doubt was already supposed to have been applied to every application.[67]

By April, the steelworkers' union and former members of the Coke
Ovens Workers United for Justice had obtained a series of important
concessions from the reluctant provincial government. Aside from
announcing the re-examination of formerly denied applications, Russell had also agreed that the WCB would not only be compensating
workers suffering from lung cancer, but also from other diseases associated with coke ovens employment. These included industrial bronchitis, lung collapse, chronic respiratory ailments, and non-cancerous
disease.[68]

Although Local 1064 and Don MacPherson would never achieve their
goal of "full, comprehensive coverage for all affected coke ovens workers," they did make gains on behalf of workers and families suffering
from industrial disease in Sydney. Further, their fight for compensation had a lasting impact within the community; the popularization of
a public discourse surrounding issues of ill health and industrial loss
would result in the emergence of localized protest and collective action
through the next decades. The coke ovens workers' response to deindustrialization provided a platform for resistance that was eventually
adopted by other residents in the city.

Rejecting the "Health or Jobs" Dichotomy

[The coke ovens were] pretty good to me ... I brought up a family there. Bought
a home, bought cars, so I guess I can't complain ... but by the looks it might be
pretty ugly for me, too.

– Joe Keller, Sysco coke ovens worker, 1990[69]

In 1995, amid an ongoing epidemiological study in Sydney, Nancy
Robb published an article on the health impact of the Sysco coke
ovens in the *Canadian Medical Association Journal*. "Were jobs more
important than health in Sydney," was her question; yes, essentially,
was her conclusion.[70] This question, often considered fundamental in
public discourse surrounding deindustrialization and public health,
obscures more than it reveals. As Arthur McIvor has noted elsewhere,
to offer the notion of a binary opposition between "jobs" on the one
hand and "health" on the other presents a false dilemma – it ignores
the power differentials that exist between workers, government, and
corporations.[71]

To present jobs and health in a dichotomous relationship overlooks
the long history of working-class environmentalism that sprouted from
shop-floor experiences since the nineteenth century. Chad Montrie has
effectively dismantled the notion that the environmental movement

only found purchase after the publication of Rachel Carson's *Silent Spring* in 1962; rather, he skillfully traces workers' efforts to challenge environmental degradation from the earliest days of industrialization in the United States.[72] Nonetheless, as Andrew Hurley notes in his study of environmental inequalities in Gary, Indiana, there was also a fundamental shift in the American popular perception of environmentalism dating to the mid-twentieth century. At that point, he argues, three competing strands of environmentalism emerged: middle-class suburban, urban workplace oriented, and urban African American.[73] As a result, industrial workers and middle-class environmentalists are often perceived among the general public as possessing uniquely disparate goals and objectives; such a view is sometimes underscored by workers' attempts to challenge industrial flight and the material dispossession of deindustrialization.

The environmental justice movement, a term coined by Robert Bullard in the early 1990s, began exploring the intersections between environmental degradation and the social conditions experienced by subaltern populations as early as 1982.[74] In the United States, this often meant exploring issues of environmental racism and the marginalization of working-class African American neighbourhoods that were facing issues relating to pollution or environmental decline.[75] Internationally, there has been attention paid to the class dimensions of environmental activism; notably, Joan Martinez-Alier explores grassroots resistance to environmental exploitation in impoverished areas of the global south in her book *The Environmentalism of the Poor*.[76] Rarely do these international studies examine shop-floor environmentalism; more often, they position ecological activism as a community-based social response to the immiseration and exploitation of global capitalism.[77]

Canadian research into environmental justice often focuses on the layers of racial peripheralization that are experienced by Indigenous peoples and First Nations groups as the result of ecological destruction.[78] When environmentalism in industrial communities is explored, shop-floor experiences are often ignored for community-based perspectives. In S. Harris Ali's discussion of political economy and toxic pollution in Sydney, for example, environmental remediation efforts are considered to have begun only in 1991 with the emergence of the provincial corporation The Sydney Tar Ponds Clean-Up Inc.[79] Working-class environmentalism must be incorporated into these studies through an intersectional framework; the efforts of the Coke Ovens Workers United for Justice and Local 1064 were directed explicitly towards resisting both deindustrialization and bodily harm resulting from industrial pollution. Their resistance continued beyond the loss of the workplace to

directly inform an emergent community-based environmental movement in the 1990s, which is the focus of the next chapter. With cases
remaining before the courts, the organization of Sydney's coke ovens
workers against economic erasure and ill health remains an important
part of deindustrialization's "aftermath" in the former steel capital of
Atlantic Canada.

Chapter Six

Bury It, Burn It, Truck It Away: Remediating a Toxic Legacy?

Cancer
Ocean pollution
Killing
Enormously terrible
Outstandingly awful
Vicious
Evil
Nasty

– Protest sign, Sydney, 1999[1]

The smoky air of the integrated mill was only a memory when the city turned its attention to another by-product of its primary industry – this time, emerging from underneath the feet of its residents. In late April 1999, dark orange ooze was found seeping into the basements of homes along Frederick Street in Whitney Pier – just a few hundred yards from the site of the former coke ovens and the Cape Breton Regional Municipality landfill.[2] Two weeks later, after receiving news that the material had tested positive for nearly 50 parts per million (ppm) of arsenic, four families of the seventeen on the street were asked to leave their homes and given the option of staying at the Delta Hotel "until more appropriate accommodations could be arranged."[3] When three more families left the following day, packing what little they could, locals could not help but draw comparisons to the incident at Love Canal, New York, in 1978 when hundreds of families were relocated as the result of toxic pollution.[4]

The Frederick Street relocation – and the eventual demolition of homes – was the culmination of more than a decade of community concern and protest relating to the contamination of Muggah Creek,

6.1 Juanita McKenzie holds a photograph of her home on Frederick Street, 2014. Photograph by Steve Wadden (*Forged*).

known locally as the tar ponds, which flowed alongside the Sysco site into Sydney Harbour. State-funded "remediation" efforts began in the mid-1980s, but the failure of consecutive clean-up plans and a growing literature documenting the health impacts of pollutants found within the site provoked a crisis in the community.

Corresponding with the coke ovens workers' fight for compensation during the late 1980s, public awareness began to build relating to a possible threat – invisible but deadly – emanating from the grounds of the former coking plant and the adjacent tar ponds. As Katrin MacPhee writes of labour environmentalism in Canada, "working class concerns about industrial pollution bled into a wider environmental consciousness outside the bounds of the workplace."[5] Despite the working-class basis for local environmentalism, the notion that the Sydney steel plant could be characterized wholly by its "toxic legacy" also began to gain traction. Elizabeth May and Maude Barlowe give voice to this perception in their book *Frederick Street: Life and Death on Canada's Love Canal.* They write:

For 66 years the plant had polluted the 500 acres it had been given. It had indiscriminately dumped huge amounts of toxic waste on the entire community and any area downwind. Owners and acronyms had come and gone – from DISCO and DOMCO to BESCO and DOSCO [...] but the pollution remained [...] In 1968, the steel plant should have closed. If each worker had received a million dollars in compensation, the cost would have been less than the subsidies poured in to keep the mill afloat. More important, many lives would have been spared. But this was a steel mill that would not die, even if it killed everything around it.[6]

The concept of a toxic legacy remaining long after the direct causes of pollution have disappeared reveals another iteration of the city's identity – one that is correlated with the uncertainties triggered by deindustrialization and economic precarity. By the mid-1990s the illusion of industrial permanency had already been spoiled; instead of "the steel city of Atlantic Canada," Sydney became synonymous with the health and environmental aftermaths of industrial production – home to "the worst toxic waste site in Canada": the Sydney tar ponds.

This shift, and the public health crisis that it invoked, produced an acute sense of fear among residents living alongside the tar ponds and former coke ovens. People began to feel unsafe in their own homes as they became more aware of the possible threat of pollution; the sense that unseen toxins were impacting the bodies of residents and their families preyed upon the mental – as well as the physical – health of community members. One former resident of Frederick Street describes:

> The "Fear" I speak of began in the spring of 1998, as [planned remediation] began on the coke ovens site [...] I remember it being around the first week of April. I woke up not feeling so well [...] I had a severe headache, felt nauseated, and was a little dizzy. Shortly after, my mouth began to feel really dry, my eyes were burning and my whole body was aching. [...] I gathered enough energy to leave my home to run some errands [...] Upon returning home [...] I began feeling all the symptoms again.[7]

After the provincial election in 1999, when the PCs were elected under a promise to close or sell Sydney Steel, many also feared an abdication of governmental responsibility. This reflects a common anxiety within post-industrial communities; when private corporations depart, sometimes being split up and made into subsidiaries of other, larger companies, whose responsibility is the environmental damage that remains?

The relationship between these fears, the deindustrialization of Sydney Steel, and proposed remediation options for areas of the former integrated plant and the tar ponds intersected in the public sphere during these years. One of the first state responses to the question of pollution on-site came with a provincial plan to incinerate tar ponds contaminants between 1986 and 1996. Although many steelworkers were supportive of a clean-up effort, occupational knowledge revealed the likely existence of additional undetected contaminants that would prove a logistical problem. This local knowledge was not taken into consideration, and by 1996 – with the project over time and nearly $15 million over budget – the preliminary incineration plan was abandoned.

When locals rejected another top-down remediation option – encapsulation of the contaminants – the federal and provincial governments mandated a community-based organization to consider options and offer proposals. The disparate interests at play within this organization, the Joint Action Group (JAG), reflect the challenges of maintaining cross-class environmental activism. These lines of division were made more visible by contemporaneous provincial attempts to privatize Sysco.

In addition to this history, the accounts of two women who were relocated from Frederick Street in 1999 provides stark evidence of the continuing costs of industrial production and post-industrial "remediation." Debbie Ouellette and Juanita McKenzie, who had no direct connection to Sysco aside from living next door, continue to suffer the bodily aftermath of these processes nearly twenty years after they left their homes. Their activism reveals the intersections of class and gender that come into relief among grassroots community protest groups. So, too, do their efforts illustrate how the types of knowledge produced by working-class people are called into question by state and institutional actors. That there has been no official recognition of the damage done to these women and other residents is shameful; their experiences reflect the bodily violence done to working-class people during deindustrialization – with mental and physical scars remaining long after industry disappears and brownfield sites are remediated into green fields.

Occupational Knowledge and Incineration, 1986–1996

Scientific reports detailing Sydney's heightened levels of polycyclic aromatic hydrocarbons (PAHs) were used by steelworkers in their fight for compensation; although the state was initially unwilling to deal with their claims, some of these early studies did prompt a response. Testing conducted by the Department of Fisheries and Oceans in 1980–1 concluded that lobsters within the south arm of the Sydney Harbour contained much higher levels of PAHs than did other coastal crustaceans.[8]

This resulted in a moratorium on lobster fishing in the area, and, as J.H. Vandermeulen writes, "subsequent environmental surveys of various potential PAH-sources in the area indicated the Sysco coking facility and nearby 'tar pond' in Muggah Creek as the likely sources of hydrocarbon contamination."[9]

It was clear by the early 1980s that contaminants were negatively impacting the environment around the plant. The Nova Scotia government contracted Acres International to "conduct a drilling program to obtain samples of the contaminated sediments and underlying strata in the Tar Pond" and propose possible solutions.[10] In four phases, Acres assessed the extent of PAH contamination in more than 700,000 tonnes of soil and sediment surrounding the coking plant and organized a series of recommendations designed to stem the flow of pollutants from the tar ponds into the harbour. The company offered three options: in situ encapsulation of contaminants, off-site disposal, or incineration; burning the material, Acres argued, was "by far the most attractive" option.[11]

On the basis of this study, federal and provincial governments proposed a joint clean-up of the tar ponds site in December 1985. The decision was formalized on 7 November 1986, when representatives from each signed a $34 million agreement.[12] Coinciding with Phase II of the Sysco modernization, the clean-up was expected to occur over a ten-year period.[13] Acres was awarded the contract for project management, and they outlined a multifaceted remediation program:

> The dredging will proceed in a step-wise fashion beginning at the south end of the Tar Ponds [...] The dredged material will either be trucked or moved by slurry pipeline to a prepared site on the adjacent Sysco property. The sediment will be de-watered, blended if required and combusted to produce electric power which will be fed into the provincial power grid.[14]

Superburn Systems Ltd of British Columbia was sub-contracted to design and construct the necessary incinerators in 1989. They agreed to construct a "300 T/day revolving fluidized bed incineration plant" at an estimated capital cost of $16.5 million; these incinerators were promised to destroy PAHs "with an efficiency of 99.99 percent."[15]

The problem with this plan, which steelworkers were quick to point out, was that it failed to account for other possible contaminants. A 1984 study by Ocean Chem had found heightened rates of the carcinogenic polychlorinated biphenyls (PCBs) at the mouth of Muggah Creek and in several other areas.[16] These compounds, invented in 1929 to make plastics, pesticides, and hydraulic fluids, were banned in Canada since

1977 – but they had been in regular use within transformers at the steel plant since the 1930s.[17] PCBs required exposure to a much higher temperature than did PAHs to ensure their destruction. In addition, Acres drilled and analysed thirty-two bore holes throughout the tar ponds site in 1987; of these, varying levels of PCB contamination were identified – though they were under the 50 ppm threshold.[18] Don MacPherson, former leader of Coke Ovens Workers United for Justice, argued in 1990:

> They talked about the tar ponds situation, what it contained was PAH material, benzopyrene [...] that sort of thing, sludge. Now, being an electrician on the steel plant for twenty-six years, I knew that PCBs were ... for many years, for generations, [the tar ponds] was the dump site of this transformer coolant when it was being changed [...] If it was 40 or 50 gallons, they used to dump that in the sewer system. And it would end up in the tar pond. If it was 300 or 400 gallons, they used to save that.[19]

Charles MacDonald reflected upon a similar experience:

> CHARLES: We used to go working [...] down on the big transformers three or four days at a time, mucking out the old sediment and stuff.
> MICHAEL: The PCB's?
> CHARLES: Yes, of course, PCB's [...] People used to take it home and rub it on their arthritis[20] [...] We used to take that stuff and just dump it in the sewers after a change. If it was a lot, like if we changed a big transformer [...] they had a little wagon [...] But if you had a small amount, 10 or 20 gallons, you just dumped that down the sewer. That went out in the harbour. They didn't tell anybody anything in that vein.[21]

With these common occupational experiences, it is unsurprising that some steelworkers were sceptical of the incineration plan. In fact, plant welder Leon Colford directly relates the ongoing tar ponds clean-up efforts with the earlier campaign of the coke ovens workers:

> There is a move by the people, and they're going to the city alderman and they're telling them that they are not going to put up with PCBs being burnt in that Superburner. They are not [...] The word is: "What they didn't finish at the coke ovens, they're not going to finish it down in the Pier." They're not going to dump it on us and finish us off [...] They did harm in the coke ovens, they're not going to do it again [...] They're going to their Alderman and the next thing it will be in the news media because we certainly don't want to see PCBs burnt in the Pier area.[22]

These accounts reveal a set of local and global solidarities that influenced how the planned incineration was perceived within the community. Richard Newman, writing of the protest movement at Love Canal, argues that there were two broader trends that influenced working-class activism in that instance: "Americans' rising environmental consciousness and deindustrialization."[23] These trends also influenced the early tar ponds clean-up, but they cannot be divorced from the specific local conditions created by the coke ovens workers' public fight for compensation and an increasing popular awareness of the health impact of the pollutants found within the site. These experiences, combined with an occupational understanding of the types of contaminants involved, allowed for a particular form of cross-class agitation to develop.

Awareness of environmental concerns was strong in Canada by the late 1980s; the Department of the Environment, the Clean Air Act, and the Canada Water Act had been in existence for nearly two decades. International events such as the Bhopal disaster in 1984, Chernobyl in 1986, and the PCB fire in Ville de Sainte-Basile-le-Grand in 1988 had turned the world's attention to the impact of environmental disaster.[24] In Sydney, newspaper coverage of the coke ovens workers' struggle and the circumstances surrounding the final closure of the ovens also prompted an increased public awareness of the site's potentially harmful pollutants. In addition to this, the clean-up was intended to "generate 1,400 direct and in-direct person years of employment in Nova Scotia over the ten-year duration."[25] As a result, Sydney steelworkers were less hostile to clean-up efforts than might otherwise have been the case; this contrasts with the Love Canal case study, where deindustrialization pitted workers directly against middle-class environmentalists.[26]

While removing contaminants was not a controversial proposition, the means by which this would be accomplished continued to elicit strong reactions. The location of the incinerator, near the site of the Sysco blast furnaces, was only a short distance from a Whitney Pier elementary school. This prompted concerns regarding whether the sludge could be safely burnt and gave a sense of urgency to steelworkers' recollections of dumping PCB-laden hydraulic fluids into the sewer system. Others suspected that the proposed methods by which contaminated sludge would be transported to the incinerator would be insufficient. Coke ovens employee Bill Graham remarked:

As a matter of fact I don't think they've even come to a concrete decision as to how to extract the material from the Tar Ponds itself. I hear them discussing dredgeline and trucking, and I've heard them discussing a pipeline and pumping. I don't think that after this two years of study,

6.2 Sydney Tar Ponds Clean-Up public information display centre, 1988.
Photograph by Raytel Photography, Reference 88-594-18104, Beaton Institute,
Cape Breton University.

and the facility actually being in the construction stage, that they've even
made a decision on that, which I find very surprising.[27]

Graham's remarks are prescient, but steelworkers' occupational knowledge was not taken seriously; the incineration plan was plagued with
cost overruns and missed deadlines. By the mid-1990s, problems
relating to both the incineration and transportation of the sludge had
manifested. These would call the viability of the entire operation into
question.

Part of the problem was that there were no formal mechanisms by
which local knowledge, occupational or otherwise, could be effectively
communicated to project organizers. Although some steelworkers had
reservations, as did other community-based environmentalists, the
only means of communication available were letters to the editor of
the *Post*, private correspondence with project organizers, or discussions
with local politicians. While some took this route, as Colford describes,

others outlined their concerns informally – in the interviews catalogued with the Beaton Institute "Steel Project," for instance. Recognition of these shortcomings would, in the second iteration of the clean-up, result in the creation of the community-based Joint Action Group in 1996.

On 26 March 1991, the government of Nova Scotia established Sydney Tar Ponds Clean-Up Inc. to oversee the processes of remediation. Its board of directors included John Strasser, president of Sysco, and Ray Martheleur, a steelworker and photographer with decades of experience at the mill.[28] Just six months after the organization issued its first annual report, Acres revealed that PCB tests found several "hot spots" throughout the tar ponds; these had not been visible throughout the earlier randomized testing.[29] According to the report, a 1.2 hectare area of the south pond contained more than 50 ppm of PCB material– qualifying as a hazardous waste. One of the boreholes, located outside a Sysco sewer pipe on Ferry Street, revealed a staggering measurement of 2,066 ppm of PCB within the soil – more than forty times higher than the limit. As a result, this material could not be incinerated.[30]

Meanwhile, residents and steelworkers alike pressed for information on heightened rates of cancers and other illnesses throughout Ashby and Whitney Pier. Dave Ervin, a former president of Local 1064, recalls working to promote "Act! For a Healthy Sydney" as early as 1991, as well as the Atlantic Coastal Action Program after its formation in 1992. Act! was a community-based project, initially proposed by Dalhousie University epidemiologist Judith Guernsey, that sought to promote healthy lifestyles in Cape Breton and examine possible environmental determinants of ill health.[31] The province funded this project after 1993, when another steelworker – Don Deleskie – went on a public hunger strike demanding an epidemiological study of residents.[32] ACT! was officially launched in 1994 as a "health-protection, health-promotion community intervention trial," and its data provided a basis for further studies by Guernsey and other public health specialists.[33]

Another major problem soon presented itself. In 1994, R.V. Anderson Ltd was contracted by the province to explore the delivery system by which the sludge was to be transported to the incinerators. The seemingly contradictory conclusions reveal:

> The equipment and unit processes installed are considered to be appropriate for the intended functions [...] There is, however, some concern that the installed dredging and pumping system is not capable of delivering the contaminated sediment to the fuel cells in the required quantities.[34]

This admission, coming nearly ten years after the clean-up was initially announced, prompted outrage within the community. That $55 million had been spent with nothing to show for it did not go unnoticed; after defeating Donald Cameron and the Tories in the 1993 provincial election, the new Liberal government under John Savage sought an inexpensive path forward for the remediation process. These efforts led them to propose another solution for the tar ponds problem, which was announced to residents in Sydney on 15 January 1996: encapsulation.

"If we don't watch out, we'll be studied to death": Environmental Activism and Public Health in "Canada's Love Canal," 1996–1998

Steelworkers and community members grew increasingly frustrated through 1995 as the clean-up remained stalled.[35] Compounding this was the apparent levity with which some provincial Liberals treated the tar ponds issue. The following exchange occurred on 10 January 1996 in the Nova Scotia legislature between George O'Malley, the minister of supply and services, and Alfie MacLeod, a PC MLA from Cape Breton:

> MacLeod: On December 14, 1995, in this House I asked the status of the plan regarding the clean up of the Sydney tar ponds. The minister responded, "It is in the very near future. In the very near future" that the government would be announcing its plan. Well, it is almost a month later and I was wondering if the minister is any closer to the future now than he was then?
>
> O'Malley: Mr. Speaker, that is a very philosophical question, whether I am any closer to the future now than I was then. I would presume I am just about as close to the future as I was then [...] In serious answer [...] it is my hope that this time next week we will have gone to Cape Breton and made the appropriate statements.[36]

Despite his mirth, O'Malley faced a raucous crowd of angry community members when he arrived in Sydney on the morning of 15 January.

Arriving at 500 George Street in downtown Sydney for a 10:30 a.m. press conference, O'Malley announced a new $20 million commitment to the remediation effort. The incineration plan was to be entirely abandoned. Rather, the tar ponds were to be encapsulated using leftover slag from Sysco steelmaking operations, while the sludge containing the highest levels of PCB was to be transported out of province. "We're going from a clean up to a cover up," shouted Bruno Marcocchio, a local environmentalist.[37] Victor Tomiczek, a member of the Canadian

6.3 Tar Ponds, Sydney, c. early 1990s. Reference 97-521-28369, Beaton Institute, Cape Breton University.

Auto Workers, interrupted O'Malley, "Because it's in Cape Breton, you don't care about our jobs, you don't care about our health, you don't care about our future. You're just going to cover it up. Well it's not going to go away, and we're not going to allow you to do it."[38] According to Sydney mayor John Coady, O'Malley had told him "it was this or nothing" just prior to the announcement.[39]

The next afternoon, the province backed off from that position. Instead, provincial Environment Minister Wayne Adams announced that he would send the plan to an environmental assessment board where the public would have an opportunity to offer input. Marcocchio, who lost his wife and fellow activist Roberta Bruce to cancer in 1992, welcomed the news but demanded a full federal investigation.[40] Adding their voices to those of unionists and local activists were the youth members of the Sydney 4-H club, who organized a letter-writing campaign seeking support for alternative options to encapsulation. In response to one of these letters, Elizabeth May pledged the support of the Sierra Club of Canada; May's involvement helped to place the Sydney tar ponds in the national spotlight and her account of these events form the basis of her book *Frederick Street*.[41]

The proposed burning of toxins in deindustrializing locales is another thread that connects Sydney to other similar areas throughout the continent. So prevalent was the practice that Andrew Hurley has dubbed the period between 1985 and 1994 as the incinerator interregnum, wherein the zealous "appeal of [incineration as a waste-disposal method] coincided with [...] technological advancements facilitating the conversion of heat into steam and electricity, thereby restoring profitability to the method."[42] While the popularity of this method of disposal declined as the result of public opposition and legal constraints, its failure in Sydney was also related to the local landscape and types of pollutants that were involved. After a decade of inaction, followed by the failure of incineration, residents feared that burying the waste would simply be leaving the problem for their grandchildren to deal with.

The emergence of a concerted community-based effort to influence the tar ponds clean-up is also related to changes in how the Canadian state dealt with social movements. Catherine Corrigal-Brown and Mabel Ho argue that the governance style of Prime Minister Jean Chrétien (1993–2003) prompted the federal state to work more closely with community groups as part of an appeal to "ordinary citizens" instead of "interest groups." This was in contrast to these same relationships under former prime minister Brian Mulroney (1984–1993), when the legitimacy of social movements was sometimes openly attacked.[43] The federal position on the Sydney tar ponds reflects this change; although the feds had been in the city to sign the 1986 agreement, clean-up operations had been entirely under the purview of the provincial government throughout the early 1990s. By the summer of 1996, the federal Liberals became considerably more involved in the clean-up process.

When Environment Minister Sergio Marchi travelled to Sydney in August 1996 to tour the tar ponds, he met with representatives from several community groups. Charles MacDonald, the president of Local 1064, was present, as were several former steelworkers, Elizabeth May on behalf of the Sierra Club, Shirley Christmas of the nearby Mi'kmaq community of Membertou, a number of economic development personnel, and Ron Deleskie of a local citizens liaison group.[44] Greg MacLeod of the Tompkins Institute at the University College of Cape Breton (UCCB), who was also present at the meeting, expertly connected the ongoing environmental problems with deindustrialization:

The old [company] from England took out the coal, making profits for investment in England and New York. It left us with environmental problems. It kept the profits and made no investment in Cape Breton.

Again, we have outside companies that want to solve the environmental problems, and make profits, but they will not reinvest in Cape Breton.[45]

The community message was loud and clear, Marchi told the *Chronicle Herald*; on the basis of the minister's urging and the community protest, the province announced that it would not be moving ahead with the encapsulation. Rather, he reported, "We'll have a joint action committee" to recommend solutions.[46]

Marchi's announcement was the first step towards the Joint Action Group – a government-funded community organization with a mandate to examine and influence the tar ponds clean-up efforts. JAG, billed as "one of the first times that citizens are being given a lead role in an environmental cleanup," consisted of a main roundtable of fifty-five members and several smaller working groups such as: governance, site security, environmental data gathering, health studies, and public education and participation. The organization was initially funded by a $300,000 grant, which drew upon municipal, provincial, and federal resources.[47] JAG consisted of representatives from the steelworkers, concerned residents, local politicians, and economic development staff.

Cracks soon began to show. Although initially intended as a space for each of the groups to have their voices heard, sometimes members' positions were at odds with one another.[48] The first meeting of the steering committee devolved into a shouting match, when Marcocchio – the vice-chair of the committee – confronted representatives from JWEL-IT – the company that had initially proposed encapsulation as a solution. According to the *Cape Breton Post*, "Marcocchio approached the two JWEL-IT representatives [...] and after referring to them using a slang word for prostitute, ripped the [paper] handout in half."[49] Despite these growing pains, representatives from the federal, provincial, and municipal governments gathered in Sydney at the end of January 1997 to announce $1.67 million in funding for the JAG program. This included funding for a secretariat, a review of all previous health studies, and environmental monitoring.[50]

Circumstances at Sysco also made it difficult for labour environmentalists to remain united with other partners in the clean-up process. In 1993, the China Minmetals Corporation arranged a deal with the Nova Scotia government wherein they would co-manage the plant for three years; this arrangement was organized with the intention that Minmetals would purchase the plant at the end of this period. Manning MacDonald, who took over the Sysco file in 1996, recalls:

I found out that – when dealing with Minmetals – I wasn't dealing with Minmetals in China, because when they came on board with Sydney Steel they formed a company called 'Min-Canada.' There was an office in Toronto. […] And so Minmetals China, the corporate giant, wasn't really responsible. It was this 'Min-Canada.' And they had no assets. So I soon realized that we were taking all the risk, and [they] weren't putting anything up.[51]

Minmetals announced in 1996 that they were no longer interested in pursuing a purchase agreement and the province began exploring other options for privatization.

Even though the Sydney steelworkers had been at the forefront of combating the environmental impact of industry for years, some felt that they were increasingly perceived as outsiders within these discussions. The uncertainty surrounding Sysco combined with an increasingly popular narrative that consigned industrial work wholly to the "dirty" past meant that some within Local 1064 grew wary of the JAG process altogether.

This narrative consisted of two primary motifs: economic and environmental. Economically, Cape Breton's industries were positioned as perennial losers within the language of an emergent neoliberalism. Political discussions surrounding regional economic development began to focus on the promise of tech-incubators, entrepreneurialism, and fiscal austerity; coal and steel were passé. Steelworkers grew wary of environmental narratives that viewed the operation of the mill as an ongoing problem, one that could be solved only by immediate closure. Pollution had decreased dramatically since the closure of the integrated mill, and some resented the notion that they clung to their jobs to the detriment of their community. Dave Ervin reflects:

I don't have any use for the "rabid environmentalists." You know? "There's only one answer," and it's their answer. There's lots of answers to every problem […] By the [mid-1990s], nobody on the steelworkers' executive wanted to be involved with them. Well, I said, the place is going to get cleaned up one way or another. It's best we be on the inside, you know, tempering what they're doing.[52]

Others felt that "outsiders" were using the tar ponds to advance their own careers and would not pay any more attention to Sydney or its residents once the issue left the national spotlight. Several respondents, speaking anonymously, held this view of *Frederick Street*. As one reflected, "It was great when the Sierra Club first got involved […] they brought media attention that would get things moving […] but Elizabeth May hasn't been back to Sydney in awhile."

This is why the impact of labour environmentalism must be taken into account within popular treatments of environmental and community activism; not only is it disingenuous to ignore workers' contributions, but the imposition of a wholly exclusionary "toxic legacy" narrative of industrial history actively disincentivizes industrial workers from further participation in community-based environmental activism.[53] This should not be read as a claim that the bodily and environmental impact of industry is overstated, but as a reminder that workers, too, bear these scars alongside those wrought by the economic displacement and marginalization of industrial capitalism.

While Local 1064 participated in JAG and other discussions surrounding the clean-up, particularly as these related to possible on-site jobs for laid-off steelworkers, by the end of the 1990s the employees at Sydney Steel were also facing economic threats. Disagreeing with the tactics of other local environmentalists, described by one former steelworker as "marching into an office and screaming for the head of the person in charge," some stepped back from the process. Others, such as Eric Brophy, Don and Ron Deleskie, and Dan Yakimchuk remained staunch in their working-class environmentalism; these steelworkers would not only fight for environmental justice on the shop floor and within the union, they would become vocal supporters of the Frederick Street residents as the extent of pollution within the community became clear.[54]

Despite the cross-currents emerging within JAG, Sysco, and Local 1064 remained invested in the clean-up. In July 1998, JAG officially signed a memorandum of understanding with municipal, provincial, and federal governments. This formally outlined a mission statement: "To educate, involve, and empower the *community*, through partnerships, to determine, and implement acceptable solutions for Canada's worst hazardous waste site and to assess and address the impact on *human health*."[55] The mandate included a Study and Assessment Phase, wherein health and environmental studies would be conducted on-site, and a Recommendation phase, in which JAG would present official recommendations of remediation options to government stakeholders.[56] Even prior to the signing of the MOU, work had begun on the assessment phase – provoking an immediate crisis for the working-class residents of Whitney Pier who lived closest to the former coke ovens site.[57] In two accounts of these events, the continuing spectre of deindustrial remediation becomes terribly visible.

"I live with it every day: It's not something that goes away": Debbie Ouellette, Juanita McKenzie, and the Aftermath of Remediation

Although the homes on Frederick Street have been demolished and the landscape of the former coke ovens has since been transformed into a

6.4 Debbie Ouellette, 2005. Photograph by Steve Wadden (*Forged*).

community green space, the memory of spring 1998 remains rooted in place for former residents. It was at this moment when Debbie Ouellette's "Fear," and nearly two decades of personal and legal struggles, began. Steven High writes, "Oral history provides us with an invaluable opportunity to see ruination from the point of view of those most directly affected."[58] In the case of two former Frederick Street residents – Debbie Ouellette and Juanita McKenzie – the ruin wrought by decades of industrial production, the fraught political processes coinciding with deindustrialization, and the contentious community-based efforts to solve the tar ponds problem remain as relevant in 2016 as they were in 1998.[59] For these two women – neither of whom have a familial or occupational connection to Sysco – the psychological scars of 'remediation' will never disappear.

Debbie Ouellette

In June 2016, I met Debbie outside of what was once her home on Frederick Street. Over the next hour, we talked about her experience as we drove to a number of locations: nearby streams, the now-empty spaces that used to be filled with the homes of her friends and neighbours, and – finally – the site of the former coke ovens. It was Debbie who proposed conducting the interview in this manner; most of the interviews for this project took place across tables in the kitchens and living rooms of participants. As recent literature on "new mobile methodologies" describes, the mobile interview can offer special insight into the connections between place, space, time, and memory.[60] Although the distance between sites precluded us from walking, Debbie's control over the location of the interview at different points of her story offered a deep "atmosphere of place." Her spoken memories of life on Frederick Street were contrasted with the now-empty landscapes before us.[61]

"These are new trees. These are all new trees that were planted. This is a new brook. When we were here, nothing looked like that," she says, gesturing to the altered landscape that was once her front yard. Looking across the grassy expanse towards where the Sysco coke ovens once belched their smoke, she describes the symptoms that began to plague the street's residents as the earth was disturbed during the assessment process: "severe headaches, nausea, sore throats, burning eyes ... The headaches were so bad, I thought I had a brain tumour [...] So that's when we decided to get together as a group."[62] Debbie and I drove away from Frederick Street, towards an exposed bit of water trickling through the newly constructed ditchwork. Here, we got out of the car and the conversation turned to her changing perceptions of the environment:

> [After we started getting sick], I looked up here and started seeing this yellow, this yellow goo coming over the embankment. And I said, "Oh my God, what's that – where's it coming from?" And I said, this brook this year ... Everything was different. The colour was different. Everything. The trees were turning orange. Everything looked different to me that year [...] My concern at that time was getting my kids out of there safely. I didn't care about money. I just wanted them out of there.[63]

After residents brought their concerns to the media, politicians, and JAG in 1998, the provincial government contracted CANTOX Environmental Inc. to "conduct an independent human health risk assessment of the Frederick Street area."[64] On 12 August 1998, this report was released to residents; although tests identified "elevated concentrations of several heavy metals (lead, copper, molybdenum) and some PAH (including naphthalene)," the authors concluded, "No measureable adverse health effects in local residents are predicted to result from

6.5 Human health hazard sign, 2014. Photograph by Steve Wadden (*Forged*).

long-term exposure to chemicals in the Frederick Street neighbourhood."[65] As an "additional issue," the report notes, "the signs posted
on the coke ovens perimeter fence [erected in 1997, reading Human
Health Hazard] are a considerable source of anxiety," as is the fact that
"when environmental work is conducted on the coke ovens site, the
individuals wear protective gear (ranging from a dust mask to a full
protective suit)."[66]

Chain-link fences marked "human health hazard," located just yards
away from residents' front doors, and nearby workers in "moon suits"
have indeed become part of the collective memory of Frederick Street
and the remediation process. As Debbie recalls:

> I lived on Frederick Street for thirteen years and there was never a fence
> around the coke ovens site [until 1997]. People used that site as a short cut.
> The kids played over where. And when the fences did go up, signs were
> posted with these words that said HUMAN HEALTH HAZARD.
>
> ...
>
> I remember driving on the overpass and noticed a man cutting the grass
> on the Coke Ovens site covered from head to toe in a white-suit. Why were
> we treated differently than the guys in white suits? [67]

These occurrences contributed to a sentiment expressed succinctly by another former resident: "somebody knew something we didn't."

Evidence continued to build; Frederick Street residents experienced a variety of symptoms through the fall of 1998. Judith Guernsey, who had initially been involved with Act! in the early 1990s, published some of her epidemiological findings: men and women in Sydney suffered far higher rates of various cancers than did their counterparts in mainland Nova Scotia.[68] By January, the International Institute of Concern for Public Health released a study challenging the conclusions of the CANTOX study; the Sierra Club of Canada commissioned this report, which identified several significant methodological limitations of the earlier study. Through all of this, Juanita, Debbie, and other Frederick Street residents continued to attend JAG meetings and lobby government officials for a solution.[69]

Debbie recalls what happened next "as though it was yesterday." She related the story to me as we stood next to a watery ditch, alongside what is now Spar Road – a section of highway running along the former Sysco site, watching a piece of machinery clear left-over slag away from the nearby railway tracks:

> We had another heavy rain [...] And our son Steven happened to go down the basement. And the orange stuff seeped up through one of the pipes on the floor [...] We had never seen that before. And I figure now that the coke ovens were the source [...] Of course, I wasn't home when [Environment Canada] came, it was pouring down rain. And they knocked at the door and my husband let them in. And he didn't know anything about this [chuckles] it was me that was doing the talking [...] They took samples [and the next week] They said, "Yes, arsenic was found in your basement" [...] I got off the phone, and I headed out to Juanita's [...] and she said "What's wrong?" [...] I said I just got the arsenic results back from my basement and they're really high. She said, "do you want to go to a JAG meeting?" I said sure [...] And before I walked out [of the JAG meeting] I said ...

At this point in the interview, seventeen years after the events described, Debbie began to cry.

> If my kids get arsenic poisoning ... From living in their own home. There will be hell to pay. And I walked out ... Emotionally and physically, I was totally exhausted [...] I didn't know what was going to happen next [...] I came back home [one afternoon] and I walked in the house, no word of lie, and I still don't remember who passed me the phone. And I said "Who is it?" And it was [MLA] Michel Samson. And he said, "Debbie, we have

a room at the hotel for you and your family to move into." And I said to
Michel [...] "Thank you very much, but I will never be coming back to
Frederick Street."[70]

As we returned to the car and began to drive back towards the area of
Frederick Street, Debbie told me about the aftermath of the relocation.
They had stayed in the Delta Hotel until after the provincial government announced a purchase offer to residents living alongside Frederick Street and the nearby Curry's Lane.[71] According to the provincial
government, "Offers for homes [were] based on the value of a similar
home away from the Coke Ovens site [...] [This offer] is voluntary and
is not being made because of a health risk. Residents may remain in
their homes if they wish."[72] The refusal to admit any fault, offer any
compensation, or provide alternative homes for Frederick Street residents has continued; former residents have continued to make sacrifices.[73] In Debbie's case, this meant moving to a small home next door
to a brothel in Glace Bay. Although she has since moved again, Debbie
has continued her fight to force the province to recognize that the toxins found around the Frederick Street area and in the basement of her
former home were the direct result of the historical operations of the
Sydney Works. In 2018, Debbie reached a confidential settlement of her
lawsuit against the federal and provincial governments.

Juanita McKenzie

Juanita was also among the original six Frederick Street residents who
began agitating for information and action on environmental issues. In
addition to Juanita and Debbie, there was Louise Deveaux, Ronnie and
Debbie MacDonald, and Rick McKenzie. I met Juanita in her apartment
in Ashby for our interview. She was born in Newfoundland, although
she grew up in North Sydney until the age of sixteen. The ever-present
smoke of Sysco surfaces early in our discussion; "I always remember
seeing the plume of orange smoke. And Sydney, to me, back then, was
a dirty place. I didn't know [the city]. I just knew that orange smoke."
She eventually moved to Sydney and in 1984 her family purchased a
home on Frederick Street.

Her memories of the events leading up to the Frederick Street relocation are nearly identical to those described by Debbie. Along with
Debbie and four other residents, Juanita helped to lead the fight against
toxic pollution in her neighbourhood. Juanita's entry into environmental activism occurred when the fencing and "human health hazard"
signs were being erected around the coke ovens site:

I came home that day [...] and they were putting a fence up. And there was this guy there in the white [Haz-mat] suit, and anyone that knows me knows I always have my camera with me [...] And I took out my camera and I took a picture of this guy [...] And I went over to him and there was a sign. It said, "Human Health Hazard," and I said, "What's going on?" He said, "Well, you can't come over here." And I said to myself, If he's dressed like that, and I'm dressed like this ... If something's toxic, how can it just stop at the fence? So I went to a meeting they were having for JAG and the mayor, that night. And I was really upset [...] So I went up to the mayor, and I was getting nowhere with him, he was kind of brushing me off. And I just stuck out my hand, for him to shake my hand, and I said "My name is Juanita McKenzie and you're going to be hearing a lot from me." And I turned around and walked out. And my husband wanted to kill me [chuckles].[74]

As in the case of Lois Gibbs at Love Canal, Debbie and Juanita became leading voices among their neighbours in challenging popular conceptions of the tar ponds issue.[75] This is not radically distinct from other cases throughout Canada and the United States, where working-class women have turned to environmental activism to challenge threats to their health and the health of their families. As Phil Brown and Faith Ferguson write, "In their efforts to understand the hazards and to draw attention to the consequences of toxic exposure, these women activists come up against power and authority in scientific, corporate, and governmental unwillingness to consider their claims or address their concerns."[76] In accounts of their early activism, both Juanita and Debbie speak of challenging authority at JAG meetings – in Juanita's account, this meant responding directly to the mayor's perceived indifference.

As we have seen in the response to Black Friday, Sysco's male steelworkers often marshalled popular conceptions of traditional masculinity in their resistance to deindustrialization. This is not uncommon; as Ronnie Johnston and Arthur McIvor describe, workers in the UK have also challenged deindustrialization in terms of the corrosion of traditional masculinity.[77] In similar ways, female toxic waste activists have sometimes centred their resistance upon a perceived threat to traditional femininity – based within the home, the family, and the body. Standpoint feminist analysis may also be applied to Juanita's and Debbie's undertaking of leadership roles in their fight for the residents of Frederick Street. The ways in which these women have constructed epidemiological and environmental knowledge from their own experiences of class and gender – and how this knowledge was expressed to neighbours, family members, and authorities – reveals a particular form of "front porch politics" that emerged in response to the refusal of the state to take citizens' health concerns seriously.[78]

Both women discussed the role of popular epidemiology in oral interviews about their activism; Juanita describes purchasing the first computer on the street for the purposes of studying the health impacts of PAHs, PCBs, and arsenic. Debbie was kind enough to forward me dozens of documents related to the tar ponds, coke ovens site, Frederick Street, and public health in Sydney. These included all of the state-funded environmental reports dating back to the 1970s, as well as newspaper articles, her written recollections, and photographs of the coke ovens and tar ponds sites. In studying the problem in this way, both women felt more authoritative in their efforts to challenge the recalcitrance of the state, offer unique and informed insight at JAG meetings, and argue their position against efforts to discredit their experiences.[79]

Motherhood played an important role as a mediating identity throughout this process. Debbie and Juanita's stories are centred upon their children; in Debbie's account, it is when her children are first mentioned that she becomes visibly emotional. The notion that her children would be directly harmed by exposure to toxic material, and that nobody in power seemed particularly interested in immediately resolving the problem, is described as a flashpoint for her activism. Juanita identifies a tension between the perceived safety of the home for her children and their friends and her own growing awareness of the dangers posed by the soil beneath their feet. This is fairly commonplace in narratives of white, female, working-class toxic-waste activists. As Celine Krauss describes:

> The traditional role of mother, or protector of the family and community, served to empower these activists [...] from the beginning, their view of this role provided the motivation for women to take risks in defense of their families and overcome their fears of participating in the public sphere.[80]

Through this rearticulation of power relationships, drawing upon power in the private sphere to inform resistance in the public sphere, these women began reaching out to form activist relationships with other groups in the community.

Juanita reflected upon receiving both support and condemnation when they took their concerns public; some residents in Whitney Pier believed that she was harming property values and that her health issues were overstated. Critiques were often gendered in nature. She recalls, in the early days of Frederick Street activism, being told that the group was "making a mountain out of a molehill," or that they were unnecessarily emotional. Throughout, state and environmental officials had their accounts positioned as "objective" and "factual," while the Frederick Street women were constantly questioned about their recollections and symptoms. Others in the city offered solidarity. In a story reminiscent of the coke ovens workers' earlier accounts, Juanita remembers:

> I woke up one morning and there were papers on my step, and I have no idea to this day where they came from. And it was all these ... had been some kind of, something that had been done back in the 60s, I believe, they had done a study on all of the poisons and toxins on the Sydney steel plant. And they hid it. But this person had this and gave it to me. And, like I said, I don't know where it came from.[81]

As with Dan Yakimchuk's earlier description of receiving the secret documents – air-quality studies from the 1970s – there is an indication that somebody was attempting to keep secret the full scale of toxicity, environmental degradation, and ill health. In expressing her experience in this same way, Juanita reveals a sense of solidarity with Sysco workers – particularly those suffering illness or disease resulting from exposure to on-site toxins. Later in our interview, this comparison is explicitly stated.

The majority of steelworkers, Juanita explains, were supportive of the Frederick Street protesters. She believes that this was the result of their own struggles with occupational illness and disease – though she understood that they were unable to explicitly join the protest movement over fears relating to deindustrialization. She notes that many steelworkers were also residents of the Pier:

> The majority of them knew the truth. And they were on the plus side of things. They knew that they were – they were sick. A lot of them were sick, too. [...] They were just another statistic and they knew they were going to be gone. They [knew they] had to work and they had to shut their mouths, that's just my opinion on it anyway [...] But you know what? The local people in the Pier who worked on the coke ovens, worked on the steel plant, are some of the finest people in the world. And, and they were taken as much advantage of as ... as the rest of us. [...] They knew it.[82]

Juanita, like many others within the community, recognizes a particular form of working-class solidarity that existed between Sysco employees and those who lived in the neighbourhoods around the plant. This was not simply the result of coinciding economic interests, as the steelworkers' efforts to maintain production at the plant were sometimes unappreciated by other local environmentalists, but they emerged from a shared sense of having been victimized by an extractive industry that relied on local labour and resources for decades before leaving residents and workers to deal with an environmental and health disaster. The fear expressed by Harry Waisglass and Andrew Hogan to the Atlantic Development Board in 1966 proved prescient more than thirty years later; Cape Bretoners – steelworkers and Sydney residents alike – were left "with nothing but ashes in their mouths and carbon dioxide in their lungs."[83]

A Double-Sided Coin

Just as deindustrialization is a constituent part of unfolding global capitalism, so are its aftermaths continually experienced by the affected in the years and decades after closure. The proposed remediation of the tar ponds and coke ovens sites during the final fourteen years of production at Sysco reveals several concurrent lessons that relate to local and global experiences of deindustrialization.

First, occupational knowledge should not be discarded in favour of scientific proposals for remediation; although steelworkers had asserted for years that PCB-containing materials had been disposed on the site and that the methods proposed for transferring the sludge to the incinerator were likely insufficient, it was not until more than $55 million had been spent that the state officially recognized these realities. Not only were workers in the midst of being decentred from their economic (and physical) place within the city, but the dismissal of their voices during the early phases of the remediation process also reflects a deep institutional antipathy to working-class ways of knowing and proposed solutions. This antipathy was in further evidence during O'Malley's contentious press conference, when incineration was rejected and encapsulation was presented as a fait accompli.

While the JAG process reveals the growth of a community-focused effort in the remediation process, prompted in part by the Chrétien administration's comparatively accommodating attitude towards social movements, the seemingly endless political discussions, conflicts between interested parties, and bureaucratic wrangling contributed to a popular association of industry and its aftermath with wastefulness and incompetency. The notion that environmental remediation contracts were being offered to off-island companies for work that continually ran over time and over cost caused some to speculate that the period was simply another stage in the region's exploitation by "come from away" capital. The simultaneous collapse of the Minmetals purchase agreement and the emergence of a toxic legacy narrative that sometimes obscured the contributions of steelworkers and their families also meant that some became reticent to maintain cross-community solidarities. Each of these factors would become fertile ground for politicization, and by July 1999 the question of Sysco's future featured promptly in the ongoing provincial election.

Finally, the processes of deindustrial remediation holds a profound and terrible impact for residents. Debbie's and Juanita's accounts reveal the connections that remain between place, memory, and deindustrialization within the framework of the environmental remediation process. They describe a transformation from complacency to toxic waste activism, prompted in part by the official rejection of their accounts, their perception of bodily health, and their lay understanding of the connections between their symptoms and the disturbance of the tar ponds and coke ovens sites. In their stories, the processes of deindustrialization represent economic violence – but its violence is also markedly physical. This reality remains certain and inescapable, and it will continue throughout the lives of former residents. The violence, and the reprehensible, plausible deniability maintained by the province in relation to the site's toxins and health effects, is powerfully expressed in the following exchange between Juanita McKenzie and myself in 2016:

LACHLAN: So were you glad to have gotten out of there? When you did?
JUANITA: ... [audible sigh] ... That question kills me ... I lost my
    daughter ... seven years ago. She died of colorectal cancer ...
LACHLAN: I'm sorry.
JUANITA: She was thirty-three years old. And the day before she died,
    she said to me. She said, "Mom, did Frederick Street do this to me?"
    And I said I don't know. And I *don't* know. I can't say for 100 percent
    certainty [...] Frederick Street is like a double-sided coin for me. I have
    a lot of good memories of Frederick Street. Frederick Street will always
    be my home. That was my home. My ... my children grew up there. My
    grandchildren. I have all my memories of my daughter that passed ... are
    there. And ... how? How does a thirty-three-year-old die from colorectal
    cancer? You know? I lost my kidney. A couple of years after we moved
    from there I had kidney cancer. I have problems now, with other things
    [...] My husband had a heart attack. [...] Frederick Street has a lot of
    good and bad memories for me. We had a beautiful home there. We had
    a pool in the backyard. The water might have been bad, but I mean,

6.6 Juanita McKenzie and daughter, Michelle McGuigan, with photo
of Juanita's late daughter, Tonya Kelley-Lepe, 2014. Photograph
by Steve Wadden (*Forged*).

my … my house was where the kids came […] And I have a lot of good
memories of Frederick Street. Yet Frederick Street, you know, turned out
to … to be a bad thing for me too. I think it took a lot from me. It took a
lot mentally from me. It took a lot physically from me. And it took my
daughter too, I think. […] I live with it every day, it's not something that
goes away …

LACHLAN: So what do you think now when you, you know, look at
  everything that's been done there and …

JUANITA: I go down there a lot. I find peace down there, actually. I find
  my … I find my daughter there, which is strange enough … I drive by
  it a lot and I think of Ronnie and I think of Louise and I think of my
  daughter. I think of what we gave up … to save other people, as far as
  I'm concerned. […] We fought for what we thought was right and, you
  know, our names might not be over there on the steel plant but by Jesus
  we deserve it […] We were the most unassuming people you'd want to
  meet in the world. But you know, we fought for what we believed in […]

I think back on Frederick Street and I think back lovingly on it … because we've just moved around ever since. And I've never really been content since […] Like I said, I drive down there every now and again […] And it's just sad. When I look at it it's a sad street to me […] I drive by there and I see Ronnie leaning on his fence, having a beer, Friday night […] what a man. I see Laurie, our next-door neighbour, sitting on her step. I see the kids at the pool. […] I see Debbie's kids, out playing […] I see, I see things as they progressed until we were taken away from there. And Debbie, God love her, she's fighting […] But I lost it. I don't like fighting for it any more. Because it took everything from me. And people don't realize that. I might have started the fight, but I lost the fight – even if in some ways we might have won. So that's about it.[84]

On 12 May 2004, nearly four years after the final rail was rolled at Sydney Steel, the federal and provincial governments announced a $400 million renewed clean-up plan. This was to be accomplished through the removal and destruction of PCBs from the tar ponds, the in-place treatment of the remaining contaminated material using biore-mediation or solidification, engineered containment, and "site restora-tion" for future use.[85] This plan would ultimately destroy and solidify the remaining toxic material, before the design and construction of a community park – now named "Open Hearth Park" – on the site of the former steel plant. Today, after thirty years of remediation propos-als, the site exists as a green space. But for former steelworkers and residents such as Debbie Ouellette and Juanita McKenzie, the bodily and environmental impact of deindustrialization and the remediation process will never fade away.

Chapter Seven

From Dependence to Enterprise: Economic Restructuring at the End of the Steel City

We do not want to work on remediation. We want to make steel.
    – Murdoch McRae, 1064 recording secretary, 6 April 1999[1]

I had made a very firm commitment that the budget we introduced in the spring of 2002 would be balanced. [...] In my mind, I had decided that [Sydney Steel] was never, ever going to be not subsidized. I could see no way forward that it would not be subsidized. And I said, "Shouldn't we be putting our money in something else? That has a possibility of return?"
    – John Hamm, 29 July 2015[2]

On the morning of 28 July 1999, employees of Sysco awoke to the news that the province's Progressive Conservatives (PC) had won a majority government with twenty-nine seats in the legislature. Liberal and New Democratic Party (NDP) contingents had only mustered a combined twenty-three seats throughout the province.[3] The Tories did not fare as well in Cape Breton, with only two PC members elected out of the island's eleven seats.[4] In these two districts, Inverness and Guysborough-Port Hawksbury, the PC and Liberal races were extremely close – only separated by 327 and 134 votes respectively. The NDP also picked up a significant number of votes throughout Cape Breton. With their electoral victory, the new government under Premier-Elect John Hamm was well positioned to implement its campaign promise to privatize or close Sydney Steel.

The Tory position on Sysco evolved from an announcement made earlier in the year by John Hamm. A Liberal minority government, elected in 1998, had announced a $44 million line of credit for the mill. While the Liberals had committed to selling the plant since taking power in 1993, several purchase agreements had fallen through

during the decade. Unwilling to close the plant, Sydney Steel continued operating indefinitely. On 23 March 1999, Hamm revealed that he
had examined the newly tabled Sysco business plan and found it to
be seriously lacking. "Now is not the time to be sinking millions more
into capital expenditures. Now is the time to close the book on Sysco ...
and to open a new book – one which promises a real future for Cape
Breton."[5] This marked the first time since nationalization that the leader
of a major party in Nova Scotia officially called for the closure of the
Sydney steel plant.[6]

Political commenters framed the decision as a political gambit. The
mill had not achieved profitability after the electric arc installation.
That reality, coupled with the long history of failed modernizations,
subsidies, and losses had soured voters in mainland Nova Scotia on the
notion that the mill could one day be profitable. Parker Donham writes:

> Conventional wisdom holds, incorrectly, opposing Sysco would carry
> an onerous price [...] Even if you assume all parts of Cape Breton love
> Sysco equally, the mainland, where Sysco is despised, still has four times
> as many seats [...] In any case, Hamm's Conservatives placed last in all
> but one of Cape Breton's ridings last year and they aren't expected to be
> a factor here next time. So there is little downside in Hamm's adopting a
> policy position most mainlanders regard as blindingly obvious common
> sense.[7]

Hamm's announcement was also perceived as a sign that the Tories
would either withdraw their support from the Liberal minority or Premier Russell MacLellan would call a snap election sometime in the
spring or early summer.[8]

In May, Manning MacDonald – now in charge of the Sysco file under
the Liberals – revealed the government's plans for the mill. Defending
continued operations while privatization was explored, he writes:

> Sysco has nothing to hide. Sysco wants to show its wares. Sysco and its
> workers want to show off what it is. Not what people think it is. Let's,
> once and for all, bury the folklore that paints Sysco as a belching dinosaur.
> Let's see it for what it is – an opportunity for Nova Scotia to make jobs,
> not make-work; an opportunity to replicate at Sysco the successes of the
> Halifax Shipyards and Trenton Car Works. Sysco is a modern facility – an
> asset to be exploited, not closed.[9]

The Liberals were defeated on 18 June after the PCs refused to support
a budget that included nearly $600 million in health-care spending.

Fiscal responsibility from health care to Sysco was the primary electoral campaign issue – and Hamm had established himself as the sole
candidate willing to close the mill.

Although the Tory victory concerned union members and others in
the community, there was not the same sense of looming civic devasta-
tion and shock that characterized Black Friday more than thirty years
earlier. Nowhere in the days following the election were the concerted
calls for community resistance that emerged in 1967. While one letter to the *Post* laments the "bleak" future for Sydney Steel, the author
expresses larger concerns over the high cost of university education
and the partisan nature of provincial politics. In this letter, the fate of
Sysco is simply one among many issues facing Cape Breton and Nova
Scotia.[10] According to Fred James, the community response was quite
distinct:

> LACHLAN: When you were talking about Black Friday, you said you
>   remember exactly where you were [...] Do you remember where you
>   were when John Hamm was elected, on the promise to close the steel
>   plant?
> FRED: Well it's not really the same kind of thing, because we saw that
>   coming – you know? [...] It didn't surprise me. You've been living with
>   the axe over your head for all those years, so you kind of prepared for
>   anything. Although it's always a jolt when it comes. But still, you hang
>   on to the hope that it will be ... Because so many steelworkers had that
>   doom and gloom prophesizing for their whole life. You can't put your
>   life on hold because the plant's going to – you think the plant might
>   close. You have to just live your life, and do the best you can. And so I
>   think that was the general feeling with most of the people. [...] You hear
>   what's going on, and you just continue on and you hope for the best.
>   And deal with whatever comes out of it and do what needs to be done
>   when the time comes.[11]

Manning MacDonald highlights the sense of resignation that had settled into the community by 2000:

> LACHLAN: When that election happened, and they said they were going to
>   close Sydney Steel, was that similar to, like, in '67 when they said they
>   were going to close it, or?
> MANNING: No, no. Quite the opposite. People were resigned to the fact. The
>   only people that cared about it after all the machinations about losing
>   money and everything were the steelworkers themselves and people
>   like me who put a lot into it, and our government did, to try and keep

it open. The general public here were conditioned to the fact that it was going to close under a new government. They knew it was coming. And the workforce was down to 800 at that time.

LACHLAN: So, less of an impact?

MANNING: Yeah, well it was 4,000 when '67 was there. Or probably a little bit more than that [...] And the guys running for office said, you know, we're going to shift direction down here. We're going to create all kinds of other economic activity to take the place of Sydney Steel. Well, Sydney Steel's gone and the government, to my knowledge didn't create a thing. But they got rid of the plant.[12]

The long, slow decline in employment at the Sydney Works reflects a reality first articulated by Daniel Bell in his 1973 *The Coming of Post-Industrial Society*. Bell describes how the industrial era would follow the same broad contours first charted by pre-industrial societies. Advances in technology allowed humans to supersede their reliance on labour-intensive agriculture, which prompted fewer workers and higher rates of production. With technological advances in modern industry, workers would similarly vacate positions within the factory – leaving production unaffected – for jobs within the "post-industrial" service and knowledge sectors.[13] While the first point is reflected through the restructuring and modernizations at Sysco, the second has not come to pass. Frank Webster, expanding upon Bell's vision of post-industrialism, writes:

As productivity soars, surpluses are produced from the factories that enable expenditures to be made on things once unthinkable luxuries: for example, teachers, hospitals, entertainment, even holidays. In turn, these expenditures of industrial earned wealth create employment opportunities in services, occupations aimed at satisfying new needs that have emerged, and become affordable, courtesy of industrial society's bounty.[14]

Instead, a set of economic, and ideological axioms – broadly termed neoliberalism infected our political discourse with the fantasy of market objectivity.[15] As industrial employment declines, workers are asked to do more with less; under neoliberalism, the state, its functionaries, and the wider public are expected to do less with less.

The economic character of this myth is based upon the tenets of financial and industrial deregulation, the privatization of state-held industries, and the withdrawal of the state from traditional areas of social responsibility.[16] But neoliberalism is more complicated than simply the direct implementation of a political and economic plan of governance.

Rather, it must be understood "not as a fait accompli, but rather as an ongoing process of struggle and compromise through which the meaning of neoliberalism is both re-examined and reaffirmed."[17] In this sense, neoliberalism – like deindustrialization – must be considered as a *process* and not as a bounded practice or set of clear policy prescriptions. It was from this shifting intellectual and political landscape of the new millennium that the will to close Sydney Steel was finally able to bear fruit.

"Devco University" and Neoliberal Development, 1984–1999

The growth of the public sector in the postwar period is inseparable from twentieth-century political economy. Public institutions provide a critical backdrop to the deindustrialization process, and they have sometimes been referred to as "safety valves" for cities suffering from high unemployment, high poverty rates, and low tax bases. Public sector employers provide both short- and long-term employment and can help to facilitate the turn towards alternative economic drivers.[18] In 2007, for example, American hospitals were the top employer in five of the top ten cities with the highest rates of poverty. In Philadelphia, education and health services together accounted for a full 26 per cent of the city's total employment in 2002.[19]

Universities act as gateways to local and regional labour markets, and in working-class cities they are sometimes viewed as a means of escape from the factory, mill, or mine; this point is reflected in Christine Walley's *Exit Zero*, where she reflects personally upon the transitions in identity undergone by a working-class university student.[20] In Cape Breton, the island's university has been a major part of its economic fabric since its earliest iterations. Its contributions can be divided into two periods, each reflecting a particular set of institutional and political pressures. In the first, encompassing the years between 1952 and 1984, the institution existed as a complement to the "free industrial society" envisioned by its founders. After 1984, corresponding with a national turn towards neoliberalism and the designs of various federal and provincial agencies involved in Cape Breton, it became a local instrument in the rhetorical shift towards entrepreneurialism, self-reliance, and the promises of the new economy. This is broadly in keeping with trends established at other Canadian institutions, which Fuyuki Kurasaw argues were positioned as "a major platform for the generation of territorial wealth and corporate profitability [...] simultaneously cast in the role of innovation incubator, engine of economic growth, and source of corporate profit."[21]

Higher education in Sydney was closely tied to the fortunes of heavy industry since Xavier Junior College held its grand opening in January 1952. Students came from Sydney and the surrounding mining communities; education, for these men and women, represented an opportunity not afforded by the coal mines or steel plant.[22] Moses Coady, a Roman Catholic clergyman and notable cooperativist, described the importance of educational institutions for industrial communities:

> [The founding] proves that there is still very alive in our people the possibility of progress within the democratic framework of society and, what is more important, the conviction that [Cape Bretoners] must have adequate instruments for the achievement of their full destiny. The past history of Cape Breton is proof that people of many races and cultures can come together for the development of a free industrial society.[23]

The notion that a local educational institution could provide the bedrock for economic diversity and the establishment of a "free industrial society" remained visible into the 1960s. In 1961, religious leaders wrote an open letter to Prime Minister John Diefenbaker and Nova Scotia Premier Robert Stanfield on the subject of the ongoing coal crisis. They argued for the establishment of a modern progressive trade school and demanded that "the Department of Education put on a compulsory course on the Maritime Economy in Grades 11 and 12 as an experiment for the next ten years."[24] The college's promoters believed that the history of industrial Cape Breton, its relation to capitalist production, and its place within the Canadian national economy were necessary to understand in light of the contemporary problems facing the island's residents. One course offered in 1965 devoted an entire semester to the historical analysis of capitalism – including "the theory of competition as opposed to its apparent reality."[25]

On 1 July 1974, Xavier Junior College merged with the Nova Scotia Eastern Institute of Technology to create a new institution: the College of Cape Breton (CCB). The number of students taking credit courses in Sydney numbered 1,068. With long-term growth predicted, the suitability of the small downtown campus came into question.[26] Early plans to purchase more property downtown from the Department of Defence fell through, and the institution instead bought a large plot of land approximately 10 kilometres away from the city centre – between Sydney and Glace Bay. Residents would come to view this decision as a mistake; the city's downtown core and the surrounding neighbourhoods would never experience the economic benefits that are associated with spatial proximity to a university or comparable institution.

The federal government, through its role in the Cape Breton Development Corporation, was directly implicated in these events. In 1971, Tom
Kent – then president of Devco – announced a $500,000 loan to comple-
ment a pre-existing $500,000 grant to support the initiative. Robert Morgan
writes, "DEVCO realized [early on] that the higher education of the local
population was an essential component of any economic expansion."[27]

Some mainlanders reacted negatively to perceived federal favourit-
ism towards industrial Cape Breton. Irene Henry, a town councillor
in Antigonish, derided CCB as "Devco University" in a 25 May 1974
interview:

> [Antigonish is] on our own. We're outside of DREE, we haven't factories
> so we have always had to struggle to exist and we are not going to quit. St.
> F.X. is our big employer. We have to pay for everything we have.[28]

Another concerned citizen, Peggy MacDonald, penned an editorial
drawing attention to the ongoing state intervention:

> CJCB [radio host] Earl Smith came on strong to piously chastise Antigonish
> for its "vested interest" opposition [to the planned campus expansion in
> Sydney]. Somehow, it was quite respectable for Sydney to fight for its
> "vested interest" in the steel plant. [29]

Despite the opposition, CCB was granted the ability to offer BA degrees
in 1982. In recognition of this change, the institution added "university"
to its title, officially becoming the University College of Cape Breton
(UCCB). Soon, the scope of federal involvement in UCCB would expand
dramatically; by the end of the 1980s, the institution was poised as a
major actor in a renewed development strategy for "post-industrial"
Cape Breton.

Hopes for the island's coal industry were temporarily bouyed by
the second global oil shock in 1979–80, but Sysco continued to bleed
jobs. It was also at this time that federal involvement in industrial Cape
Breton began to shift away from the Keynesian strategies employed in
the postwar period.[30] During the lead-up to the 1984 federal election,
Progressive Conservative (PC) candidate Brian Mulroney promised
a reconsideration of regional economic development methods. Business interests had expressed concerns that the Department of Regional
Industrial Expansion was too centralized and focused too extensively
on sectoral growth.[31] Mulroney and the Tories were voted into office on
4 September 1984; with this, Canada joined in the neoliberal revolution
underway in both the US and the UK.

The language found within the Tories' economic planning documents reveals the contours of this transition. Michael Wilson, the new minister of finance, described the renewed interest of the government in establishing bottom-up aid for small business and entrepreneurship.[32] In Canada, this would take the form of tax cuts designed to facilitate the reallocation of resources to the most productive ends possible.[33] In Cape Breton, it meant the withdrawal of federal support from two heavy-water plants, which employed approximately seven hundred workers.[34] The impact of this decision, James Bickerton argues, "could not have come at a worse time: 700 jobs would be lost when the Island was suffering a 25% unemployment rate."[35] The federal cabinet was also almost immediately looking towards the possible privatization of Sysco, although this was an unofficial position.[36] As a planning document reveals:

> The Cabinet Decision required that the provision of federal funding be subject to the Province of Nova Scotia agreeing to seek a private sector investor for SYSCO and that the steel making technology employed be such as to attract a private sector partner.[37]

The Mulroney administration soon moved to decentralize regional development. Sinclair Stevens, the newly appointed minister for regional economic development, announced a plan to relieve some of these economic pressures that had been pushing Cape Breton towards crisis. Enterprise Cape Breton was created to administer and oversee a tax credit to promote the growth and expansion of local businesses. Governor General Jeanne Sauvé also announced during the 1986 speech from the throne:

> An Atlantic Canada Opportunities Agency (ACOA) will be constituted to facilitate and coordinate all federal development initiatives in the area. This agency will make fuller use of the expertise available in the Atlantic region and invite the maximum participation of other governments and organizations in the area.[38]

Enterprise Cape Breton merged with ACOA in 1987, although the following year the industrial development wing of Devco was turned into another crown corporation – Enterprise Cape Breton Corporation (ECBC).[39] UCCB was soon embedded within these processes as a local partner; in 1990, the institution received $200,000 in ECBC funding for the creation of a laboratory devoted to the ongoing tar ponds remediation efforts. This was the beginning of an extensive relationship between the university and the federal "alphabet soup" development agencies.[40]

An official memorandum of understanding (MOU) was signed between UCCB and ECBC in 1991. The purpose of this agreement was to seek the beginning of a new era in Cape Breton – "the first steps toward creation of a technological and entrepreneurial culture on the island and to rebuild a devastated economy."[41] This new cultural mindscape, intended to supersede the old industrial ortgeist, would be built upon the basis of university partnerships with private firms.[42] With this, the university took on a new role within the deindustrializing city; rather than the "free industrial society" that Moses Coady envisioned during the institution's earliest years, the university would now serve as an instrument for moving beyond the trappings of industrial society altogether.

Very quickly, the language used to facilitate these changes identified the working-class cultures and practices on the island as a problem. One ECBC planning document describes Cape Breton as a region where "public demonstrations [are seen] as an acceptable response to change"; where an "assumption exists that outsiders will solve the island's problems"; and that "lacks an entrepreneurial culture."[43] Such ideas continue to be widely expressed, and they draw upon deeply rooted stereotypes about Cape Bretoners. The Cape Breton "folk" in these readings, are simply not suited to the globalized, entrepreneurial economy – but they must be disciplined into accepting its new realities.

There stereotypes are not new; as Ernie Forbes describes, they have been marshalled as explanatory apparatuses for circumstances as disparate as regional support for prohibition, the apparent conservatism of Maritimes suffragettes, and the purported tardiness of the region in developing social welfare programs. In castigating these explanations as unsatisfactory, Forbes writes:

> One should be under no illusion that myths disappear simply because their basic inaccuracies are exposed by a scholar. Myths become popular when they serve the purposes of those transmitting and/or receiving them. They will tend to endure as long as they are useful.[44]

And endure, they have. Development groups within Nova Scotia also adopted the language and ideals of neoliberal restructuring, an impulse that remains visible today. As recently as 2014, the Ivany Report warned:

> This lack of solidarity as a province undermines constructive dialogue about our future and makes us a more difficult and risk-averse place to

do business and built communities. It seems apparent that if Nova Scotia is to find ways to meet its current challenges, there will need to be change on the cultural level as much as in economic structures and government policies and programs.[45]

The bold strategy identified in the Ivany Report does not differ in intent from those employed twenty-five years ago by Voluntary Planning – another provincial advisory group consisting of regional business people, labour organizers, and community activists. This document identifies seven core values and articulates an overall goal designed to guide Nova Scotia's economic strategy. The "core values" of this system are: private sector–driven, outward looking, value added, technologically advanced, performance oriented, environmentally sustainable, and regionally sensitive. The stated goal is "to build an economy that is based on *competitive success* so we will be able to sell more goods and services in the global marketplace." The authors remark:

> We must develop in Nova Scotia a competitive culture, a shared sense that we are all competing with each other and with those in other parts of the world to be the best at whatever we do.[46]

The Voluntary Planning document recommends that the province refocus its attention on the promising future of high-tech enterprise.[47] UCCB, with its combination of academic and trades education, was positioned advantageously in light of these proposals. The agreement with ECBC allowed the university to cooperate with federal agencies in charting a new way forward not only for industrial Cape Breton, but also for the Maritime Provinces.[48]

Federal and provincial strategies began to hinge upon the language and intent of an ascendant neoliberalism by the 1980s. Cape Breton, a region already suffering from the dual shocks of deindustrialization in steel and coal, seemed ready-made as a case study for the implementation of these strategies. Interestingly, and counter to neoliberal orthodoxy, the state played a significant role in the proposed transition. Development agencies in cooperation with the university directed funding towards chosen private sector actors in the new economy. This was intended to foster a transition away from reliance upon state-owned industrial firms, such as Devco and Sysco, which would ultimately allow for their disintegration. While ACOA remains in place, Devco, Sysco, and ECBC have since closed – and the promised post-industrial miracle has not emerged to take their place.

By May of 1992, the MOU had already resulted in nearly $700,000 of additional federal funding allocated to UCCB. This included $500,000 dedicated to the creation of a Chair in the Management of Technological Change, and an additional $182,000 towards further research in the technology sector. The university worked closely with ECBC to encourage the establishment of high-tech companies in Cape Breton and a Technology Advisory Group was created to help members of the community and other entrepreneurs with the planning and execution of tech start-ups. As Patterson and Biagi write, "in creating TAG, one of ECBC's original goals was to encourage partnerships between the University College and the private sector."[49] The development of closer relationships between universities and private firms was also fundamental to the spread of market ideology. That these ideas would take root in the modern university is not surprising – "Business schools at prestigious universities like Stanford and Harvard, generously funded by corporations and foundations, became centres of neoliberal orthodoxy from the very moment they opened."[50] What distinguishes the Cape Breton experience, again, is the extent to which the state was involved in such affairs.

Jacqueline Scott, appointed as president of UCCB in January 1993, sought to expand upon this strategic impulse. Scott was a staunch supporter of neoliberal restructuring in the Cape Breton economy and within the university. Between 1996 and 2009, she sat on the board of directors for the Atlantic Institute for Market Studies – a quasi-right-libertarian think tank that favoured pro-market reforms.[51] Brian Lee Crowley, the institute's founder, has written extensively on the works of Friedrich Hayek, the "morality" of the market, and the importance of market-based solutions for the problems facing the region; the think tank was designed to bring these ideas to bear on Atlantic Canada.[52] Deeply rooted cultural and attitudinal handicaps, Scott would later write, were primary factors in preventing the Island's industrial communities – and, indeed, its First Nations residents – from achieving prosperity. She writes:

> [Some First Nations leaders] believe that "the government victimized us and, under the treaties, it owes us a living" or that government should provide jobs through grants and subsidies to enterprises – a sentiment that is, indeed, shared by many non-aboriginals in Cape Breton's industrial communities.[53]

Throughout the decade, the university expanded its focus and partnered with more than one hundred local tech projects. It also reshaped its internal structure; on-campus programs now included the Bachelor of Technology in Environmental Health, Nautical and Chemical Sciences, and Petroleum Studies. A program in Community Economic Development was unveiled in 1998. By this point, the university was much more than simply a go-between for federal development agencies and local business – it was positioned as a research and development incubator. In 1999, the University College established its Department of Economic and Technological Innovation to "facilitate the transfer of research and development to the private sector, for commercialization, and to promote economic diversification.[54] Research clusters included centres for computer-assisted design, GIS/GPS research, IT, petroleum development, and technology and enterprise. Although research in many of these areas has continued, the centres they supported are no longer active at the institution.

Trying to Light a Candle with a Wet Piece of Paper: The Death of Sysco, 1999–2001

In the fall of 1999, with UCCB ostensibly positioned as the agent of change that would help to guide Cape Breton into the post-industrial future, all that remained was for citizens to accept this change with open arms. This would necessitate the closure of the two firms that had, by this point, become associated in popular imagination – on the mainland and among chattering politicos on CBC's *Talkback* radio program, at least – with the failure of industrial interventionism.

John Hamm, on the other hand, strongly rejects the idea that the decision to close Sydney Steel was based on any intended implementation of an ideological system. Rather, he believed that the subsidization of Sysco simply did not fit within a program of targeted economic development. In fact, the former premier spoke highly of Stanfieldian interventionism – but only if it is geared towards the proper economic drivers:

> I am a believer in business incentives, but only the ones that work. And some of them worked very well, I mean, the best [historical] example we have in our province is Michelin. Michelin came [to Nova Scotia] with business incentives. They didn't come here out of the goodness of their hearts.[55]

Rather than continuing to support the steelworks in Sydney, increasingly seen as a drain on provincial coffers and portrayed as an industrial dinosaur in development literature, the PCs focused their plan on the much-touted "new" economies of the twenty-first century.

NovaKnowledge, an association of knowledge economy groups supported by provincial and federal grants, produced a report in 1999 in which they lauded the decline of federal and provincial spending in Nova Scotia. This decline, including the closure of Sysco and Devco, would apparently provide opportunities for the private sector to create sustained, job-creating economic growth. Traditional government spending, on the other hand, would "retard the development of the competitive, business-oriented mindset."[56] Instead, subsidy dollars could be redirected to other sectors; in October of 1999, for example, the province provided $3 million to Scotiabank Atlantic for the training of nearly three hundred employees for positions at the company's Halifax call centre.[57]

The provincial government was not set on closure; indeed, they continued searching for prospective buyers for the mill. Hoogovens Technical Services Technological & Operational Assistance Inc. had been commissioned by the Liberals in 1998 to bring the plant to a level of operation that would appeal to global steel firms, and they continued the search under the Tories.[58] Some workers were sceptical of the company's intentions, particularly surrounding the $700,000 per month fee paid by the province for their services. The following exchange occurred in a group interview with former steelworkers in August 2015:

> GERRY McCARRON: They brought Hoogovens in before ... when we were trying to sell it [...] brought a group of about thirty of them in. And each guy went into different departments and [...] they're going to correct our problems [...] We lost more money under these guys then we did with our own guys running it [...] They paid these guys ...
> SHELDON ANDREWS: Top dollar
> GERRY: Top dollar. To come in and try to run things.[59]

Concerns over the remuneration of outside management firms reflect the worry that international firms were simply interested in Sysco as a means to profit from closure and liquidation. Even when a possible sale appeared on the horizon, employees wondered if a private owner would simply shutter the plant and sell off equipment after gaining control. Manning MacDonald recalls these fears: "It's the same old story. If something is vulnerable, there's always somebody willing to come in the door and make you an offer you can't refuse."[60]

Sysco employees knew that they were vulnerable. Several significant factors, which have been examined throughout this book, meant that their labour was no longer considered indispensable within their community; nor could they count on the sustained public support that had emerged during previous shutdown attempts. As a result, Local 1064 soon had to engage in "effects bargaining." To ensure that members would receive appropriate remuneration should closure occur, members began pressuring the provincial government on the issue of workers' pensions.[61]

They were right to be concerned. A number of firms expressed interest in purchasing Sydney Steel during the final months of 1999, but none moved beyond the initial bidding stage. Bill McNeil, the president of Local 1064, met with members of WCI Steel, a subsidiary of New York–based Renco Steel Holdings Inc. The steel executives indicated that they would be interested in Sysco only if higher production rates could be attained and lower man-hours negotiated; this would require significant layoffs.[62] Although this sale did not move beyond preliminary interest, WCI Steel declared bankruptcy just three years later and absconded with a $117 million shortfall in the pensions of its American employees. Had this company decided to take on the Sysco operations, a similar fate could easily have befallen Sydney steelworkers.

On 31 December, Hamm arrived in Nova Scotia with good news. The plant was to be sold to a consortium of companies under the Ohio-based "Research Group." The workforce would be reduced through attrition, but the firm hoped to employ approximately 150 steelworkers. Following this press conference, steelworkers in the audience remained subdued. The collapse of the Minmetals sale in the 1990s had made steelworkers wary of pinning their hopes on any "fly-by-night" operation. After all, the agreement specified an 15 April closing date – it was not yet a done deal. Local 1064 now turned their attention towards bargaining for a government commitment to their pensions. As one worker remarked following the announcement, "where will the older workers be left if in three years or so the privatized steel company fails and the government declares itself free of obligation to them?"[63]

By mid-January 2000, this deal collapsed and liquidators from Ernst & Young began to prepare for the demolition of the plant.[64] Roger Faulkner, a representative from the national chapter of the USWA, visited Sydney and revealed that the union had separately contracted out an American company, Locker Associates, to try and find other possible buyers for the plant.[65] With no serious offers on the table, Sysco workers began to take more direct action in search of a solution to the ongoing pension issue. In the chill of late February, more than five hundred steelworkers and their families crowded the doorway at the Provincial Building in Sydney. One expressed his thoughts in an open letter to the premier:

> I was hired at Sysco on March 12, 1979, and I've worked sporadically ever since. I am 47, with 21 years seniority and only 5 years of actual work time and credited pension service. While on layoff I began my own small business in Ingonish. I received a registered letter to return to work at Sysco in 1991 so I decided to do that, giving up on my business project. I worked eight weeks and was laid off again. And that's the story of my life. I am living between welfare and Employment Insurance. [...] At this point in my life I cannot leave the area to look for work. Who would spend the time and money to train me at my age? [...] Now it's time for [the premier] to protect me and my family.[66]

The provincial government set up a bidding process for potential buyers and began negotiating with the union regarding pensions. The union was wary of these assurances; Hamm, the executive believed, was stalling for time and making empty promises. The union revealed:

> The executive met and decided to [begin protesting] John Hamm [...] as the province is causing untold stress to steelworkers and their families. We agreed [...] to send a bus to opening of Legislature On Mar. 28 [...] Also planning a trip to Hamm's office in Pictou with support from Trenton Local 1231.[67]

The response reveals the precariousness of the situation faced by Local 1064. Any misstep could risk collapsing a possible purchase agreement, which removed most of the traditional mechanisms of workers' ability to shape policy through strike or protest. One member spoke out about the abnormality of the situation; in usual contract negotiations, trade unionists would have the ability to withdraw their services. This tactic would be useless as a protest mechanism against either the proposed closure of the plant or as part of pension negotiations. The member argued, "We cannot and must not do this, as it would look like we closed the plant. The government is looking for any excuse."[68] Nonetheless, Hamm remembers that the steelworkers' protest in Pictou did have an impact:

> And to be perfectly honest, despite the fact that it was a very, very emotional issue. They did not treat me badly. I remember one time [...] my MLA office was downtown, New Glasgow. Bus loads of them came to New Glasgow to protest outside my office [...] But government played a

role in [Sysco], so government can't just suddenly say, "We don't have a responsibility." [...] I said to them on the picket line, I said "We will treat you fairly." Now, they might have had a different idea of what fairly ... But what I meant was, you know, first of all the pension fund was in terrible shape; number two the benefits weren't really adequate, and I didn't think they were [...] And number three, if we could arrange it, employment with a new employer.[69]

Negotiations surrounding the Sysco pensions continued into May. The union sought clarification on a number of issues; notably, they pressed for an early retirement incentive package after twenty-five years of service, a drug plan for retirees, and $2,200 per month. The government, on the other hand, pushed for $1,500 per month for all employees with thirty years of service in the event of a closure, a retirement window for those with twenty-seven to twenty-nine years, and severance packages for those with fewer than twenty-seven years' service.[70] John Kingston, the Atlantic Provinces representative for the USWA, explained the union's position:

> Without fear of contradiction, the Steelworkers in Sydney were closer to and competitive with wages and benefits paid by the Industry prior to the Province assuming ownership in 1967. Thirty-three years later we are on an average $5.00–$6.00 below that mark in wages; pensions are $10.00–$20.00 per month times years of service behind the industry.[71]

At the same time, two other companies expressed interest in organizing a purchase arrangement. North American Metals (NAM), a subsidiary that had been involved in the failed Research Group deal, and the Swiss-based Duferco both put forward operational proposals. Local 1064 favoured the NAM proposal, which included the maintenance of five hundred positions, while Duferco sought a "leaner" operation of only two hundred employees.[72]

In the midst of these discussions, the final rail was rolled at Sysco on 22 May 2000. This brought a century of steelmaking to an end, and occurred without much fanfare.[73] While the final order was completed, steelworkers and management continued to entertain the possibility of a private sale. Workers in other occupations and areas of the country frequently recall with great clarity the final shift, but this was not the case in Sydney. The overbearing possibility of a private sale not only robbed steelworkers of the ability to actively resist closure through striking or walkouts, but also ensured uncertainty surrounding whether or not there would be further work at the plant. Gerry McCarron and Dave Nalepa recalled:

DAVE NALEPA: Well, we knew when the last rail was rolled because I
remember that night, it was the four to twelve shift, and as soon as the
thing – they started working on dismantling right after that.
GERRY: Well, we knew it was the last rail rolled – but there was always still
that glimmer of hope that before they started pulling everything apart
that maybe a sale could happen – but something would have had to
fallen out of the sky.[74]

Nearly 250 workers were laid off the next day. Executives from Local
1064 continued to believe that a deal would be reached. Duferco and
the NAM proposals were under consideration and members of the
union executive met with Teresa MacNeil – chair of the Sysco board –
to discuss the possibility of new rail orders. NAM planned to maintain
operations at the rail mill, while the Duferco proposal was based solely
on the production of slabs.[75] Meanwhile, the scheduled protest in New
Glasgow went ahead.

Approximately 130 steelworkers picketed Hamm's office, although
attendees would later regret that there had not been more participation. Roddie Livingston, speaking at a 1064 membership meeting, said
"people are not interested in taking part in rallies, this must change."
Others echoed these sentiments, with some remarking that pressuring
the government would lead to a better pension agreement and continued interest in procuring a sale.[76]

On Wednesday, 22 June, Ernst & Young officially recommended that
the province accept the Duferco offer. Matt Harris, speaking on behalf
of the liquidators, argued that this purchase agreement was the only
possible option; the sale would see the buyer pay $7 million upfront
and an additional $15 million in bonds.[77] Before this could be finalized,
however, the company demanded that a pension agreement be negotiated with the provincial government and that a contract be agreed
upon with the plant's unions.[78]

Pension negotiations began immediately. In the first week of
August, some steelworkers took matters into their own hands; a group
of about one hundred younger workers blocked the gates at Sysco
for the first time since the provincial election. As steel production
had already ceased, this only impacted a few remaining employees
in management positions and scheduled deliveries of scrap metal –
though it also delayed the shipment of the final rail order. These workers felt that they were being left out of the deal, and they demanded
that the province drop the eligibility requirement from twenty-seven
to twenty-five years of service.[79] Steelworkers held another protest on

11 September, this time disrupting a garden party held for Nova Scotia Lieutenant Governor Myra Freeman at UCCB.[80] Bill McNeil reflects on the eventual agreement:

> So, that's the way it worked out ... The guys with thirty years of service got the total, the full pension. And the guys with thirty years of service down to twenty-five were prorated. And the guys after that got severance packages ... And the union agreed that these younger guys would get the work at Duferco.[81]

With the pension issue settled, Duferco began serious negotiations with employees from CUPE, the USWA locals, and salaried staff. This bargaining did not take long; by Halloween, CUPE workers, salaried employees, and the steelworkers had agreed to the terms of a five-year Duferco contract. Under this contract, nearly two hundred former Sysco workers would have continuous employment; the union agreed that those men who were ineligible for pensions would receive the first opportunity for work. These jobs were categorized into five base wage groups, ranging from $15.50 per hour to $17.22 per hour.[82] This offer, for many former employees, appeared to be a done deal; according to Gerry and Dave:

> GERRY: We all got together, the management, and we actually picked the workforce – we had it all lined up for when –
> DAVE: Yeah. I had the HR side of it done. We probably had – 90 per cent of the employees picked and a lot of people had signed up, and all the salaried people had all signed up, with letters and contracts.
> GERRY: Jackets ordered. Jackets with Duferco-Sydney.[83]

But this deal, like so many before, would not come to pass. The final stage in the sale process required a contract between Duferco and Nova Scotia Power – a former provincial crown corporation that had been privatized in 1992. The inability of the two companies to reach an agreement on power rates caused the entire deal to collapse on 18 January 2001. John Hamm reflects:

> They came that close to buying it. And it was only afterwards that I found out why the deal fell through. And it wasn't really their fault. They, in their business plan, had to negotiate the electricity rate with Nova Scotia Power. And they came within half a cent of bridging the gap. But they couldn't bridge the gap. And that gave them the out.[84]

Table 7.1 Monthly Crude Steel Production in Canada, 2000 (thousand tonnes)

Jan	Feb	Mar	Apr	May	Jun	Jul	Aug	Sep	Oct	Nov	Dec
1,460	1,401	1,534	1,339	1,443	1,428	1,420	1,397	1,335	1,408	1,315	1,114

Source: International Iron and Steel Institute, *Steel Statistical Yearbook*, 2001 (Brussels: Committee on Economic Studies, 2001), 48.

"Steel Era Ends," read the *Post* headline the next morning; "Sydney's designation as a steel town ended Thursday."[85] It was this event, the collapse of the Duferco deal, which most respondents view as the final end of Sydney Steel; in 2015, very few interviewees expressed the belief that another serious buyer could have been found in time to maintain production at the plant.

A global downturn in the steel market was forecast at the end of 2000. Market uncertainly likely also played a role in the decision by Duferco to halt the Sysco sale agreement. In Canada, crude steel production had already slowed by the end of the year, and a predicted slowdown in the automotive sector indicated that prices would remain low. An inventory glut had depressed the market and forecasts for 2001 continued to predict a nearly 7 per cent fall in demand. According to the OECD report on steel markets, "Canadian producers will be facing a difficult situation that was not seen since the early 1990s and that is expected to result in layoffs."[86] It was a bad time for any company to consider purchasing a steel mill. Matt Harris announced, "There is no remaining credible option out there to operate Sysco."[87] As of 1 June 2001, all remaining employees of Sydney Steel were officially off the company's books; the steel industry in Sydney had come to an end.

Eulogy

Ten years after the collapse of communism, the world had moved on. American capitalism reasserted its primacy in all fields. Europe moved towards the US model following the apparent discrediting of Marxism, and Asia – including the Indian subcontinent – had broadly adopted the prescriptions of the World Trade Organization. The dominant intellectualism was that of practical resignation; capitalism had won – or at least scored a major victory – and the left would have to contend with that hard reality.[88] It was into this international environment that the "discourse" of neoliberalism became predominant; Pierre Bourdieu writes:

It is so strong and so hard to combat only because it has on its side all of the forces of a world of relations of forces, a world that it contributes to making what it is. It does this most notably by orienting the economic choices of those who dominate economic relationships. It thus adds its own symbolic force to these relations of forces. In the name of this scientific programme, converted into a plan of political action, an immense political project is underway.[89]

The ideological contours of this project are particularly relevant to the circumstances surrounding both the final closure of Sydney Steel and the evolution of UCCB in the rapidly deindustrializing city. Both institutions represented poles of the changing landscape; Sysco is framed, within this discourse, as a symbol of the old economy – and old working-class ways of thinking that, like the landscape itself, must be "remediated." As Jackie Clarke argues, "while this language of class death registers a process of social and economic restructuring that is real, it does little to get to grips with the fact that the people who populated the old industrial order still exist."[90] In contrast, UCCB was institutionally positioned to soothe the transition from a city dependent upon state employment towards a private sector economy.

Sysco employees keenly felt their displacement; "trying to light a candle with a wet piece of paper" is how Charles MacDonald describes attempts to get the community involved in trying to keep the plant open.[91] When asked why a sense of resignation permeated the plant's final months, employees offered several answers. Fred James reveals:

I think there were a number of factors [...] Probably the biggest single factor was the fact that the number of employees had been reduced so much, I mean we were down under eight hundred people at that point in time [...] So it didn't have the economic impact [...] The other thing, I think, is that people were in a position that they had come to terms with it. That it was inevitable. They had, for '67, well – thirty-some years – thirty-three years, I guess – watched millions and millions of dollars pumped into the steel plant, and still didn't turn it around. I know you could write books and volumes on why, and what have you, but that's the bottom line right there. After all those millions of dollars pumped into it, it was still losing money. And they couldn't say that was going to stop. So I think the people were much more willing to accept ... the demise of the steel plant in 2000 [...] And [sighs] ... I never experienced it myself, I mean face to face, but I was hearing that there were a lot of business people, even in Sydney ... that were saying, you know, alright, enough's enough.[92]

Bill McNeil agrees with many of these points:

> I was talking to Premier John Hamm [...] and he told me right out, he said, "Look, Bill," he said, "there's organizations within the City of Sydney that want to see it closed." He said, "It's not only Halifax that wants the plant closed [...] Now he told me that himself. In the good times, there were five thousand men working on the plant. That went down to three thousand in the 1970s, then to 1,200 workers in the 1980s. There was a strike in 1988 and the steelworkers did receive a great deal of community support at that time. Then, after 1988, it was down to just eight hundred. And the Duferco deal was only likely to have around three hundred employees. But after awhile as the workforce dwindled down we just didn't have the support. We tried, of course, it's just ... it wasn't going to happen. But anyway, the feeling was "get a pension [...] if somebody wants to work with Duferco, let them run it."[93]

A number of themes remain common to discussions of final closure at Sydney Steel. That Sysco suffered a "death by a thousand cuts" through frequent layoffs and the long-term failure to diversify and achieve profitability is frequently articulated. The age of the workforce is another; the majority of workers qualified under the pension arrangement and those who did not were generally in their mid- to late forties. Dave Nalepa explains: "[In 1967] you had young guys and old guys at the plant. You had the whole slew. When we closed, you just had old guys. There were no young guys. There was no, you know, the son of so-and-so, is twenty-two, is working in the melt shop." This lack of younger workers, who would perhaps have been more invested in the continued operation of the plant, is another reason frequently given to explain the inability to organize effectively against closure.

In these answers, the absence of resistance is contingent upon the decline in employment at Sysco and the displacement of the plant from the economic and cultural centre of the community. Workers were fearful of acting as barriers to the market; they believed that traditional forms of resistance would scare off potential buyers. These attitudes did not simply spring from the period between 1999 and 2001, but developed alongside the global dismantling of the Keynesian welfare state and the ideological turn towards "flexibility" and "lean production" in North America and Europe.

Marx wrote, "Men make their own history, but they do not make it just as they please [...] but under circumstances directly encountered, given, and transmitted from the past."[94] As Sydney steelworkers responded to these global forces, the decision to close the plant was similarly circumscribed. That is not to say that such a decision was inevitable, but rather that the closure of Sysco had become a hugely appealing political option in a marketplace of ideas dominated by the voices of an ascendant neoliberalism.[95] While John Hamm does not personally view the closure through the lens of neoliberal ideology, his decisions – like all things – were shaped by prevailing notions about political economy, government intervention, and the shape of the future. Other sectors, such as technology, appeared to be more promising and a better investment for taxpayer dollars.[96]

If we consider G.I. Smith's decision to nationalize the Sydney steel plant in 1967 as the natural culmination of a regionalist/interventionist development ideology, Hamm's resolution to close the plant in 1999 was framed within a set of popular ideological axioms about the market, production, and society that were nearly the polar opposite of those that surrounded the issue on Black Friday. Neoliberalism must be understood as a set of epistemic commitments that hold as a primary ambition the redefinition of the form and function of the state – not its destruction.[97] The closure decision was more than simply an impartial analysis of where public dollars would be better spent. It was developed as the result of a decades-long ideological construction whereby the employees of Sysco, the residents of industrial Cape Breton, and the citizens of deindustrializing regions throughout the world were popularly castigated as symbols of a bygone era.

Noam Chomsky describes policy prescriptions under modern capitalism as being chosen from within a particular spectrum of "acceptable opinions."[98] In Nova Scotia, alternative solutions to the problems of deindustrialization were either ignored or pre-emptively dismissed as backwards-looking by a canon of development literature that presented the issue as a dichotomy. Cape Breton, in these narratives, *must* transition wholesale from dependence to entrepreneurship – nothing else would be acceptable. This is why the language of the neoliberal project is so odious. It affirms Social Darwinist assumptions while lobbying for specific political/economic solutions.[99] If the transition from coal and steel to the restructured capitalism of entrepreneurship, knowledge, and innovation were to fail, this could simply be blamed on the inability of the population to move beyond their industrial mindscape; the project itself could – and did – continue without question.

The importance of UCCB to this process cannot be overstated. The institution, following Mulroney's re-envisioning of regional development during the mid-1980s, provided an in-community link between research dollars and the nascent private tech industry. A primary goal of these activities was to shrink Cape Breton's reliance on federal and provincial expenditure, which would be accomplished not only with the establishment of private–public partnerships at the institution but also through inculcating a more entrepreneurial and business-friendly cultural orientation. There were also efforts to attempt these cultural revisions through the public school system on the Island. As one Cape Breton County Economic Development report from 1994 recommends, "UCCB [in conjunction with local schools] should develop a series of teacher/administrator in-services, teacher retraining programs, and information services for students based upon the new economy of Cape Breton."[100]

This lengthy process, culminating with the final closure of Sysco and the ascendency of UCCB as a prime mover within the island's much-lauded new knowledge economy, must be considered in terms of both top-down ideational constructions and bottom-up responses to the material circumstances of capitalist reproduction. Hans-Jürgen Bieling argues, "It seems very alluring to adopt a view that emphasizes the prominent role of intellectual leadership in social and political strug-gles [...] [However], the ideas and perceptions – the content of common sense – which emerge from the 'bottom up' in these processes [are by no means simply secondary]."[101] Restructuring in two institutional "poles" of the community – the steel plant and the university – reveal how com-munity members' responses to the material economistic changes of late twentieth-century Canadian capitalism can differ drastically depend-ing upon their position within popularly constructed discourse.

If the goal of neoliberal restructuring in industrial Cape Breton was to produce significant private sector employment, it was an abject fail-ure. In 2015, the island's unemployment rate remained between 15 and 20 per cent – far higher than anywhere else in the province. If, on the other hand, the goal was to implement an ideological project of mar-ket restructuring then it has been an unmitigated success. Federal and provincial governments have since abdicated responsibility for Devco and Sysco, ECBC was closed by the federal government in 2014, and the provincial Liberal government of Stephen MacNeil has recently enacted further austerity measures – including an attempted wage freeze imposed on 75,000 of the province's public sector workers.[102]

Perhaps, as a result, it should be no surprise that the language of economic development from the early 1990s remains so remark-ably consistent today. The solutions proposed twenty-five years ago to the problems of regional deindustrialization are still described as bold and fresh ideas. Strategists bemoan the lack of an entrepreneur-ial spirit among Cape Bretoners and other residents of the Maritimes more generally, while pushing for Nova Scotians "to endure major sacrifices – such as cuts to rural services, so that money can be invested elsewhere."[103] As University of Prince Edward Island political scientist Peter McKenna told John Ibbitson of the *Globe and Mail* in March 2015, "our region lacks the energy, entrepreneurial spirit, and the desire for a fresh start."[104] The reasons for this are clear; Forbes's words still ring true: myths will endure as long as they are useful.

Chapter Eight

Making History from Sydney Steel, 2012–2016

I had to go to the steel company site and look up these old personnel records. I went on the steel plant for the first time since retiring. I got in that main gate and I turned right and the tracks weren't ploughed – the railway tracks when you come in. From 1965 to that point I had never ever seen that. In my life. And I filled up. It just … it sounds like such a stupid little thing … it just struck me, all that history, all the families that fed their children and maybe put their kids through university and all the rest of it for almost one hundred years. And it's gone. Gone. Even today sometimes … a memory will be sparked and, and, I'll feel the sadness.[1]

– Fred James, 2013

Demolition of the plant began almost immediately. By the end of July 2001, work crews staffed with former steelworkers began dismantling what remained of the Sydney Works. Reusable assets were organized for auction and the province sought private buyers to begin recouping some of the funds that had been spent on the Sydney Steel Corporation over the years.[2] In 2003, Zoom Developers of India purchased several large pieces of equipment from the Sysco site; the company hired teams of former workers to dismantle and organize the universal mill to be shipped. During this process, the last fatality on the Sydney Steel site occurred. On 23 September 2004, Roy Marchand – a former steelworker – was killed when a falling steel beam struck him in the head.[3]

Community divisions remained. Questions over the environmental and health impacts of the site again erupted as work was carried out. Throughout the early 2000s, local environmentalists and members from the Sierra Club continued pressuring government to resolve the issue. Some of these divisions were visible on 30 August 2001, when a crowd gathered outside the plant to watch the destruction of the smokestacks

8.1 Steel cutters, 2005. Photograph by Steve Wadden (*Forged*).

at the Open Hearth Department. After several quick explosions, three of the stacks had fallen – but two remained standing. Charles MacDonald reflected, "They just don't want to lay down and die, it seems [...] The worst part is that this shouldn't have happened. The fact that Cape Bretoners let this happen is sickening."[4]

On 12 May 2004, government representatives announced yet another renewed commitment to the clean-up of the Sydney tar ponds and the remediation of the area surrounding the former steel plant. Adrienne Clarkson, in the 2004 speech from the throne, revealed that the Canadian government would provide approximately $280 million to aid in these efforts. The Hamm administration agreed to fund the remaining $120 million. Stephen Owen, the minister for public works and government services of Canada, told gathered reporters that the project would include a combination of high-temperature incineration and on-site encapsulation.[5] The demolition of Sydney Steel structures concluded in 2007, and by the end of the decade the remediation phase of the tar ponds and coke ovens sites was also drawing to a close.

The Sydney Tar Ponds Agency, a federal crown corporation created to oversee the clean-up, stated in 2011 that the planned end use of the site was to take the form of a community green space. Envisioned as a "central park" for Sydney, the design would include trails, bike paths, and public art, and would act as a connection between Ashby, Whitney Pier, and downtown Sydney. Today, this green space bears the name "Open Hearth Park."[6] Open Hearth Park and a corresponding historical film about the Sydney steel plant, titled *Heart of Steel* (2012), continue to exist as public history representations of the deindustrialization process more than ten years after final closure.[7] Such cultural forms are ripe for analysis in the aftermath of deindustrialization. Popular culture is widely understood as a semiotic site where ownership over the legacy of the industrial past is contested and where place-identities are shaped.[8] As soon became clear in Sydney, the process of naming the park and representing its past would prove controversial as it ignited tensions between labour history, public history, and environmental history on the site of the former mill.

What's in a Name?

On Labour Day weekend at the end of August in 2013, hundreds of Sydney residents gathered at the Sydney Steel site to hear a variety of local musicians, purchase food from a gourmet street fair, and participate in multicultural events organized by members of the Mi'kmaq, Acadian, eastern European, and black communities of Cape Breton.

The capstone event of the weekend took place at dusk on Saturday evening, when a procession of former steelworkers –some dressed in their Sysco work clothes – walked through the park under a banner bearing the event's name, "Stronger Than Steel." This title was meant to represent survival; the reclaimed land has come to signify reuse, remediation, and adaptation.

The purpose of the Stronger Than Steel event was twofold; it was a celebration of the conclusion of the $400 million tar ponds and coke ovens remediation project that had been announced in 2004 and it served as the official opening of Open Hearth Park. Government representatives were on hand for the festivities. Diane Finley, the Canadian minister of public works and government services, offered credit to her own government for its hand in the process. "Thanks to the leadership of the Harper Government," she began, "this has been the most successful contaminated site remediation project in Canada's history and we're proud that it was completed on time and on budget."[9] Provincial NDP minister Maurice Smith spoke of remembering the industrial history of steel and coal on the island and honouring those who took part, but also of looking ahead "to a brighter future." This is perhaps easier said than done.

Before the park opened, the first commemorative efforts had already taken shape. In March 2013, a competition was announced for students from local elementary, junior high, and high schools. Students were invited to submit proposed names for the park, along with an attached essay, story, video, photograph, or song that explains their reasoning for their choice. Frank Corbett, deputy premier of Nova Scotia, explained, "Providing students with the opportunity to name the new park gave them a meaningful role and voice in helping to shape the community's future."[10] The Sydney Tar Ponds Agency described the criteria of the "Sydney Park Project" naming competition: "We're looking for upbeat and original name submissions that show pride in Cape Breton's history and hope for the future. Names from all local cultures are welcome, but we won't be considering people's names for the overall park site." The organizers preferred that the park have some form of collective significance beyond memorializing a single person.

In public history, the act of naming is political. Meanings are contested, memorializations can include or exclude particular groups, and place-identities shift in response to present conditions.[11] Of course, no place remains static through time. Locations and demographics are constantly shifting; but the stories, commemorations, and heritage that remain can give an impression of great stability.[12]

8.2 Football practice at Open Hearth Park, 2014. Photograph
by Steve Wadden (*Forged*).

Steelworkers' perceptions of the park reflect such a transition in
place-identity, and these processes are often uncomfortable. While
almost everybody interviewed for this project expressed a positive attitude towards the park, this was often qualified through a discussion of
mitigating factors. Some expressed the opinion that a steel plant should
still be operating on the site, while others expressly took issue with the
process by which the name was chosen. Fabian Smith describes:

> Well, they gave [the responsibility of naming the park] to the children. And
> that's fine. But to me, with all the money they spent … they were taking away
> a steel plant. Dozens of guys got killed there … Why would you put Open
> Hearth Park? It's only one of the dirtiest departments on the plant. Why is it
> not named Steelworkers' Memorial Park? To me, that says it all. As I told you,
> I worked with this guy, one day, and twenty-two hours later he was dead. I
> mean to me, that's still … things like that take a lot out of you, that's something
> you never forget. It should be people like him that the park is named after.
> Steelworkers' Memorial, you know? But anyway, it's too late now.[13]

Naming controversies periodically emerge in response to the creation of public sites or commemorations. Although it was children who ultimately named the park in Sydney, some respondents felt that the site held such significant meaning that the decision should have been undertaken with more care. This is revealed through the frequency in which our conversations soon turned to the numbers of men who were killed at the plant, close calls on the job, or direct experiences of workplace injury.

Perhaps more stinging is the realization that the input of steelworkers, their families, or their union held no more weight in the decision than did the general public. Submissions were posted to a website for the Sydney Park Project, and the top five were selected by a committee of project and community representatives. These included members from the municipal council, provincial and federal representatives, a representative from the African Nova Scotian community, a member from the First Nations community, and members of the tar ponds clean-up committee. A shortlist was created, and online voting began in May 2013.

Demographically, former steelworkers were unlikely to participate in this type of online selection. The democratization of commemorative sites represents another step in the displacement wrought by deindustrialization. Workers are displaced economically, first through decline, then by closure. As employment at the Sydney Works continued to decrease, so too its workers found themselves pushed further to the margins of the city's social and cultural landscape. This process is visible both in the "toxic legacy" and the perceived place of Sysco workers within that narrative, and in the language of neoliberal economic development popularized during the 1980s and 1990s. Open Hearth Park, though named after one of the central departments in the steelmaking process, does not necessarily communicate the sense of collective experience that many former workers seem to prefer.

Students throughout Cape Breton submitted more than two hundred proposals. These included options such as Heartfield Park, Sydney Pleasant Park, We Rise Again Park, and more. The social media campaign that corresponded with the contest offered an opportunity for broader participation. Here, some contemporary concerns relating to memory and commemoration came to light. On 12 April 2013, James Duane Marchand – whose father Roy was the man killed during the demolition in 2004 – had the following online exchange with the Sydney Park Project social media coordinator:

JAMES MARCHAND: My Dad was the last man to fall on the job there. [I] think this [park] should be named after the men who gave their lives to feed their families. Keep in mind that we lost fathers, sons, brothers, friends – for this place to make steel.

SYDNEY PARK PROJECT: Thanks, James many of the proposed ideas coming in absolutely commemorate the contributions, efforts, and incredible accomplishments of the men and women who worked in the Steel industry in Sydney [...] Making steel was often a dangerous job and impacted the lives of many Cape Bretoners and their families over the years.[14]

Michelle Gardiner, whose husband Kevin was employed at the plant, added:

Remember, too, many of us are still young. My husband worked for 13 years in the "plant." I had a family member working in the steel plant from the day it opened [...] Do us all proud by giving it a name that reflects respect for those who lost their lives and the heart of steel that beat in everyone who lived through the good times and bad to keep the hot steel flowing for 100 years. Believe me it wasn't easy those last ten years when she was on the auction block and you didn't know your future from 1 day to the next.[15]

From the beginning of the competition, it is clear that those who were connected to the operations of Sydney Steel hoped that the memory of work at the plant would be prominent in whichever name was chosen.

Others used the campaign to publicly express concerns over the tar ponds remediation. Shane Paul, commenting on a *Cape Breton Post* article about the naming competition, offers, "The 'Just Cover It Up Park' made possible by the federal government!" Anonymous posters offered sarcastic suggestions: "Tarpark," "Carcinogen Creek," or "Mutation Legacy Park."[16] These refer to the fears that the 2004 encapsulation and incineration plan has simply "covered up" the toxic site. Such fears have also been expressed in a number of oral history interviews; Debbie Ouellette, for example, mentions that she will not attend any community events held in the park.[17] The toxic legacy is visible in these proposals; the site, for some, remains more firmly associated with the environmental and health costs than with the history of steelmaking.

In early May, five finalists were revealed: Rob Sinclair's Grade 6 classroom at MacDonald Elementary School in Dominion proposed Open Hearth Park; Piley Poqtamkiaq Park (trans. New Beginning Park) was submitted by Lori Anne Leroy's Grade 9 class at We'koma'q Mi'kmaq

School in Whycocmagh; S.P.A.R.C.K. Park was recommended by the Grade Primary class at Harbourview Montessori School in Westmount; and Phoenix Park was proposed by Katelyn McPherson, a Grade 10 student at Riverview High School in Coxheath. Few of these include descriptions of direct connections to the steel plant; indeed, the winning entry – Open Hearth Park – was submitted by students from a nearby former coal town.

The conceptual renewal of the site was obviously an appealing notion for the selection committee. Three of the finalists explore themes related to rebirth and remediation. Katelyn McPherson, in her description of "Phoenix Park," explains the site as characterized by a Phoenix rising from the ashes. She writes, "A land that was devastated from a century of steel industry is given a new life and rises out of the ashes of the former – a beautiful new park is born."[18] Similarly, the students who proposed Piley Poqtamkiaq Park describe their submission: "We picked this name because the tar pond project has given the Sydney/Pier area a new beginning and start to heal mother earth."[19] S.P.A.R.C.K. Park stands for "Steel Park Renewal for the Community and Kids. In their video submission, these children included a musical motto for the new site:

> Our new park will be a sign
> That the past is the past
> And the future is mine
> It's a place for recreation
> A symbol of hope for our generation[20]

Two other finalists explore some connections between past and present with explicit reference to the site's industrial history. History Heroes Park proposal commemorates coal miners and steelworkers, "whose labour is at the centre of Island history," but also remediation workers, the animals that live in the park, and the Mi'kmaq "who hunted and fished there long ago."[21] "Open Hearth Park," which won the competition with more than twice as many votes as the second-place finisher, refers most explicitly to the experiences of former steelworkers. But this choice, too, was lauded for its broader themes. An editorial in the *Post* describes, "From a contemporary 'branding' perspective, it is hard to find two more welcoming words than 'open' and 'hearth.'"[22]

Each of the final selections reflects the tensions that continue to exist between public history and labour history. Based upon state efforts at remediation through the Sydney Tar Ponds Agency, the desire to commemorate working-class history on the site is combined with efforts

to celebrate the present and future of a community green space. Lucy
Taksa has been critical in her assessment of Australian industrial heritage sites, writing, "public history, at least in the context of redeveloped
industrial heritage, reflects an urge to create a collective memory that
mythologizes the past and construes it as a foreign country in which
workers' collective struggles are concealed beneath the large machines
that once enslaved them."[23] Open Hearth Park does not contain the
same sort of exclusionary focus on industrial machinery that Taksa
describes, but the selection of possible names does reflect a sense of
disruption between the industrial past and the current challenges facing post-industrial Sydney.

This disruption is visible in the sensory recollections offered by several former employees as they describe visiting Open Hearth Park. Fred
James, in the quote that begins this chapter, explains his perception
that something was very wrong upon his first seeing the unploughed
Sysco railway tracks. Adrian Murphy discusses visiting the park and
attempting to reorient himself based upon buildings, departments, and
gates that no longer exist:

> ADRIAN: I was there a couple of times with my brother who worked there
> for thirty-plus years, too. And trying to visualize. And the only thing we
> can base our point of origin is the tunnel going through five-gate. There's
> a tunnel that was directly across between the Open Hearth and the
> Blooming Mill, and I just stop right there and to the left I'd see, well the
> little furnace was right there, then you'd have the Old Mill, then you' d
> have the Open Hearth, and drive down a little place and this was where
> the Blast Furnace and ... Yeah, it's unbelievable. Unbelievable.

These accounts expose a deep sense of place attachment, but an attachment that is rooted within a set of social and productive relations that
have no referent in the present. This is why Adrian, and several other
former Sysco workers who relayed similar stories, try to rearticulate
themselves within the disappeared landscape of the plant. In the existing scenery, replete with green grass, walking tracks, and children's
play equipment, former workers confront the recognition that place
and identity are constantly being radically unsettled, that the very
notion of a static place to call one's own has always been a fiction, and
that memory can promote the acceptance of new place-identities rather
than congealing into nostalgia.[24]

The former worksite is now organized around a series of walking
paths. In addition to a playground and two sporting fields, there are
several historical panels, a memorial site, and pieces of public art that

refer to the site's industrial history. The Coke Ovens Sculpture, a conceptual art installation that stands nearly 30 feet tall, was installed in Open Hearth Park just three days before the Stronger Than Steel celebrations. Designed and constructed by Gordon Kennedy, a Cape Breton artist who spent the first years of his career in British Columbia, the sculpture consists of four central figures, each facing the cardinal compass points. This represents the distinct nationalities that made up the workforce in the Coke Ovens Department.[25] A smaller memorial site, officially named Steelworkers' Memorial Park, exists within Open Hearth Park. Here, a monument bearing the names of 308 steelworkers who were killed on the site rests alongside several benches.[26]

When historical material is present, as it is in the panels that crop up alongside the paved trails of the park, the site's identity is positioned as part of a continuum. This history does not begin with the founding of the mill in the late 1800s; rather, the first panel describes the contours of the land as it existed under the proprietorship of the Mi'kmaq before their purposeful displacement from the site in the early twentieth century. The sparse text perhaps leaves room for further context, but the foundational notion – that the site existed prior to its industrial life – also gestures towards a multiplicity of identities that could come to characterize the location in the future. Other panels describe the former mills and departments, while some explain the steelmaking process, but the overall sentiment of transition is one that works.

The site brings to mind a term coined by Sherry Lee Linkon, "the half-life of deindustrialization."[27] Linkon describes how the influence of industrial production remains within the culture and landscape of communities long after the industry has itself vacated. My own research, in many ways, is based upon my experiences growing up not in the shadow of the mill, but in the shadow cast by its absence. For the children who now play on the equipment at Open Hearth Park, even that linkage between the plant and Sydney's present will seem tenuous. Rather, their perceptions will be informed by the longer view visible within the public history of Open Hearth Park. While the political circumstances surrounding industrial absence are perhaps not examined within the landscape, for its purposes the site does a good job of connecting its past, the experiences of steelworkers who laboured there for a century, and its present iteration as a community green space.

Deindustrialization on Film: *Heart of Steel*, 2012

Another representation of the site's industrial history, a 42-minute film that was released to correspond with Stronger Than Steel, does not reflect these interconnections. *Heart of Steel* was funded through the Sydney Tar Ponds Agency as part of the remediation project. Its opening shots are an exercise in juxtaposition; immediately following scenes depicting the integrated mill in full operation, the viewer is treated to the plush greenery and coiffed fields of the present-day. "Birds flock here now," proclaims the narrator. "When the government funded clean up project finishes, the former Sydney Steel site will be a placid refuge."[28] Randy Vallis, the federal director for the remediation project, told the *Chronicle Herald* in 2012 that the film sought to "capture the story of steelmaking" because "the last vestiges of steelmaking are about to disappear."[29] In the film, the problems associated with the end of the steel industry are nowhere to be found; they, similar to the landscape, have been remediated. The men and women who once worked at the plant are represented as vestiges of an industrial past. "Ghosts linger," reads a voice-over, as Gerry and several other former steelworkers are shown walking onto the site. "Once, on these vacant lands, the epic saga of the Sydney steel industry unfolded.[30]

The film does incorporate significant testimony from workers at the plant, but when this begins to discuss present concerns the narrative quickly moves ahead. In the first five minutes of the film, several steelworkers are seen walking around the former plant site and brief excerpts describe women's experience at the coke ovens during the Second World War. Ray Martheleur gestures towards some discomfort with how the mill came to an end. "I would definitely like to see the plant in operation now," he says. This statement is not followed up on; instead, the film transitions to a discussion of the plant's earliest years.

Issues of ethnic conflict, racial prejudice, or discriminatory hiring strategies are also glazed over. Although, as Ron Crawley writes, "antagonism between the long-established residents of the Sydney area and the incoming 'foreigners' was evident from the beginning," the film deftly sidesteps these stories.[31] The closest it comes to identifying these divisions is when former steelworker Sid Slaven remarks upon the tradition of "Catholic" and "protestant" sections of the plant in its early years – although the reasons for this are not discussed. John Murphy, who was also interviewed for the film, reflects that "everybody got along," and "there was none of this racism or ... you're this and you're that, everybody was equal." Garfield Moe, an African Canadian steelworker, explains: "we had a United Nations long before it was ever thought of being."[32]

This representation of ethnicity and religion on the plant is particularly puzzling because it directly conflicts with workers' oral testimony collected during the Steel Project in the 1990s. In a 10 January 1990 interview, for example, Murphy discusses the pattern of employment in the different departments of the plant: "It was called the patronage system," he says. "Nepotism."[33] Similarly, Dan Yakimchuk describes discriminatory hiring practices occurring at the plant in the 1950s: "I worked for about three years or so in the general yard because that is where you had to start, especially if you weren't in the right either political or religious denomination [...] In the mechanical, as an ethnic person or a black person you never got the opportunity."[34] These attitudes, writes Elizabeth Beaton, existed to some extent at the steel plant as late as the 1970s.[35]

Deindustrialization, too, prompted the structural continuation of discriminatory hiring long after such practices were made illegal. The seniority system in a deindustrializing mill plays a role in this process. As workers are laid off, those who maintain seniority are the first to be hired back should the opportunity arise. In the case of Sysco, with some workers maintaining seniority from periods when women, blacks, or Indigenous peoples would not have been considered for work in particular positions, the mill's decline prompted an effective continuation of these practices. With the workforce having dropped from several thousand in the 1960s to less than one thousand by the 1990s, there were always enough people looking for work from the seniority lists that new hires were sparse.

There were instances where this process was overcome. Alana Mac-Neil was one of the few women to work in steel production at the Sydney Works in the decades after the Second World War. Although other women were employed in the general office and in administrative or managerial roles, it was rare that they would find work in steel production or quality control. Alana describes having come to Sysco as a clerical worker, organized under the USWA clerical union Local 6537. In 1995, her union merged with Local 6516, the metallurgical lab union. As a result, she was able to keep her seniority and became available for work within the mill. She soon moved into the lab, where she worked inspecting the Sysco rails on the line.

> ALANA: I was working shift work, but it was good work. I'll tell you, it was a learning curve. It took while. I was the first female that came in, Denise [another woman in a similar circumstance] came after me, I was the very first one that went down there. And I was working and I could feel ... not daggers, but you feel eyes on you there were people ... There was people that wouldn't trust me. I think some of the men, from old ways, thought that I was down there to spy and make sure everyone was working, not taking an extra break or ... I really think they were. It took a few months

before they got to know me, you know, I'm here working for a pay cheque, too. I'm just "one of the guys." And once that turned around it was a whole different – I got respect, I was, you know … No harm ever came to me, don't get me wrong, but at first it was just to break that barrier. You know, all of the sudden there was this female, you know?[36]

In *Heart of Steel*, all issues relating to ethnicity, religion, or gender are wholly explained as concerns of the distant past, while more recent issues are downplayed. The film engages in "smokestack nostalgia" – it presents a depoliticized view of life in and around the mill that contains few direct connections to present conditions in the post-industrial city.[37] As these conversations unfold, the viewer is left with the distinct sense that the industrial past and the post-industrial present have been entirely divorced from each other.

Resistance and political agitation are visible in the film's treatment of the Parade of Concern. The community's participation in the event – "right from the old retirees right down to babes in arms," in the words of former steelworker Syd Slaven – is discussed, as are the potential devastating economic consequences for the city's residents.[38] This does not extend to the continuing effects of the mill's final closure. The parade is framed as a successful, albeit temporary, moment of resistance. "Mistakes were made about modernizing the plant, strikes hurt productivity," asserts the narrator. "Even the millions of government dollars spent modernizing the plant couldn't make it profitable in the face of cutthroat international competition."[39] Decline, in this view, was inevitable; international competition was too powerful for Sydney Steel to overcome – even under the control of the provincial state. The uncomplicated presentation of the mill's eventual closure allows for further distancing from the present. Any suggestion that Sydney should have remained a steel city is rejected as a position at odds with the realities of the globalized twenty-first-century market.

Workers' accounts of the final closure are the strongest portion of the film. Garfield Moe describes his feelings in 2000:

Yeah. I made a living out of it. My father before me made a living out of it, and I think it should be there for the other guy to make a living […] To drive over the overpass now and see no fire, no smoke coming out of the stacks … it'll make you wonder.[40]

In Moe's account, there is both a sadness surrounding the loss of the mill and a question regarding the necessity of its erasure. Steven High identified similar sentiments in his study of Sturgeon Falls. He writes,

"If place attachment is a symbolic bond between people and place, this bond is often severed in time of sudden social or economic crisis such as a mill closing. People then attempt to re-create these attachments by remembering and talking about these places."[41] Again, the film fails to connect these sentiments to the present. Instead, they are positioned as the final remnants of a distant past – one that holds no relevancy for the dire economic situation existing in Cape Breton today.[42]

The final section of *Heart of Steel* examines the environmental legacy of industrial pollution and the tar ponds. The extensive pollution that characterized the site during the 1990s is briefly described, but this is relayed only as a set-up for the complete success of the remediation and solidification efforts. The contentious politics of the clean-up, the remaining health effects that plague those who lived and worked around the site, and its unforgettable impacts – such as those that remain with Juanita McKenzie and Debbie Ouellette – are ignored.[43] Contrarily, the entire clean-up process is positioned as an unmitigated success; the ability of citizens and their government to work hand in hand to overcome the toxic legacy is entirely restorative.

This intense focus on environmental and geographical remediation is not uncommon in state-driven representations of former industrial sites. Linkon describes this approach as a "variation on smokestack nostalgia, one in which images of deindustrialization serve not only as representations of the past but also as a resource for imagining the future."[44] This brings to mind the case of Anaconda, Montana, where remediation projects of "turning brown into green" have been criticized for papering over legitimate social and political concerns in the aftermath of deindustrialization. In Anaconda, much of the image making has been what Kent Curtis describes as "an elaborate show of smoke and mirrors.[45] In these representations, "post-industrial" describes not the absence of industry, but an opposition to it altogether. Residual aspects of industrial life are ignored, and in some instances are presented simply as backwards-looking reflections of practices, people, and events that are best left behind.

In the final moments of *Heart of Steel*, John Murphy treats the viewer to an insightful commentary on the history of work, and the working-class identities that emerged from experiences at the plant. These will continue in Sydney, he believes, though they may exist in a changed form. "It's history," he says, "It's all in a book. It's on a DVD, somewhere. It's in a song. The older people, generation, they remember. My daughter's 17 years old and she knows nothing of the steel plant. She knows I was a former steelworker. She knows her grandfather, both grandfathers, were former steelworkers. And that's it."[46] Murphy's daughter, along with an entire generation of Cape Bretoners, occupy a middle space in the deindustrialization process. This generation does not have the occupational experiences of industrial work, but they directly experienced the "displacement and disorientation of deindustrialization" first-hand.[47]

This has certainly been my experience, and this book can be read as an attempt at understanding the aftermaths of deindustrialization that remained starkly visible throughout my own childhood. Its impacts can still be felt today. Out-migration continues unabated among islanders of my generation. In 2012, almost 20 per cent of Cape Breton's population was more than sixty-five years of age. Underemployment, contingent work, and unemployment are significant factors in driving our youth away.[48] The recent downturn in the Alberta oilfield has caused many to return home, though federal crisis allowances for EI claims have not been extended to Cape Breton. Our crisis, apparently, has already been normalized.[49] Further attention to the creative output of this generation offers an opportunity for future research. Linkon's recent work reflects this type of approach; she concludes that "those who have inherited the economic struggles and blighted landscapes of deindustrialization have the opportunity to use the complicated past [as] a problematic resource that both shapes and highlights the contradictions of the present and future."[50]

Cultural representations of industry remain an important source for the historical examination of deindustrialization. In the introduction to a recent special issue of *International Labor and Working-Class History*, Tim Strangleman, James Rhodes, and Sherry Linkon describe how film, photography, or landscapes can reflect and influence forms of memory and perspective. Through these media, they write, "we can gain insight into the continuing struggle over the meaning of industrial work and its loss, for displaced workers, their families and communities, and outsiders."[51]

Open Hearth Park and *Heart of Steel* each reflect a particular view of deindustrialization. The park presents the industrial past as but one iteration of the site's changing identity. While the plant no longer exists, in this narrative, its impact cannot be separated from the site – or the city – in the present. *Heart of Steel*, by contrast, positions the industrial past as a foil for the post-industrial present; this perspective is rooted in Whig conceptions of history, where the site's progression from industrial to post-industrial was as inevitable as it was apolitical. Any continuing concerns over how the decline of Sysco was handled or how its closure is directly related to the political and economic problems on the island today are themselves castigated as relics of the past. They, like the workers shown in the film, are "ghosts" of a bygone era.

8.3 Truck mirror silhouette, Whitney Pier, 2014. Photograph
by Steve Wadden (*Forged*).

Each of these, when read as cultural products, reflects the limitations
and continuities of working-class memory and industrial structures of
feeling. According to John Kirk, Sylvie Contrepois, and Steve Jeffreys,
"heritage practice in former industrial areas offers 'versions of the past'
that imply new identities in contexts often marked by the 'old' [...]
The past is constituted for the purposes, primarily, of the present."[52] In
Sydney, these issues have by no means been decided. These memories
remain contested. Another group of citizens – consisting largely of former steelworkers – has recently attempted to garner support for a brick-
and-mortar Sydney Steel Museum at the Open Hearth Park. This group
initially emerged immediately after the plant closure, and – although
they were unable to muster enough support for the museum – their
efforts resulted in a "Sydney Steel Museum Website," which includes
a series of photographs of the plant and demolition, prose by former
employees of Sysco, and other information related to the mill's history.[53]
In their efforts, and in existing representations of the city's history of
steelmaking, we see how "post-industrial Sydney" retains some aspects
of an industrial structure of feeling, now residual, that ebbed and flowed
throughout the twentieth-century history of industrial Cape Breton.

Girl with toy dog, Sydney, 2005. Photograph by Steve Wadden (*Forged*).

Conclusion

The seeds of this project sprouted from the anger I felt towards what I perceived as an injustice committed against residents in my hometown. The plant did not just close; it had *been* closed – by the province, by John Hamm, by Halifax. I remember watching the Sysco demolition as it progressed day by day from my seat on the school bus into Whitney Pier. I remember, later, hearing the names of young people – my peers – from Sydney and the other towns in industrial Cape Breton who lost their lives to drug abuse, suicide, or violence. I remember my friends leaving to begin their lives elsewhere and seeing the prime minister wag his finger at those of us who stayed.

If my anger has not dissipated, it has become more narrowly focused. Rather than assign blame, this book has transformed into what I hope has been a far more nuanced assessment of working-class experience than was initially envisioned. My informants played an undeniable role in this shift. While the Sydney Works is a central character in my work, life continues for those who have been directly affected by both its operation and its closure. The loss of the plant has been a loss for the city and its residents, but so, too, has a century of steelmaking taken its toll. One needs only to look at the hundreds of names on the Sydney Steelworkers' Memorial Monument or listen to the accounts of Joe Legge, Debbie Ouellette, and Juanita McKenzie to recognize the full cost of industrial production. But the lives of those who remain are not fodder for anthropomorphic ruin gazing. Their present concerns, struggles, hopes, and fears are related to life in a post-industrial city, but they are no longer rooted in Sydney Steel.

Gerry McCarron's work history reveals this continuum of industrial and post-industrial life. Today, working for the provincial crown corporation Nova Scotia Lands, he oversees the Harbourside Commercial Park on the site of the former plant. In a December 2015 interview, another former employee joked that Gerry was the "last man standing" from Sysco. There is truth to this. After beginning at Sydney Steel in 1978 in the blast furnace department, Gerry moved to the metallurgical lab in 1982. In 1993, he went on salary in production planning, where he remained until the liquidation began in 2001. While some steelworkers began working on the demolition process under Zoom Developers, Gerry and four other employees were transferred to Ernst and Young – the company that had been hired by the province to oversee the receivership of Sysco. After six years, they began working for Nova Scotia Lands out of an office that used to be part of Sydney Steel. Gerry remains the only Sysco worker to have been continuously employed on the site of the mill to this day.[1]

Although Gerry remains on site, the terms of his current position could not be more different from those during his time as a steelworker. In overseeing Harbourside Commercial Park, he is involved with planning and organizing events on the remediated site and dealing with public and private inquiries. His experience reveals how the issues and concerns of industrial work end up giving way to an entirely different set of post-industrial experiences. In this sense, industrialism is not all encompassing; Gerry is more than a "former steelworker," just as all of the people involved in this project cannot be defined solely by their position vis-à-vis the steel plant.

The larger focus of this book has been to expose the ways in which deindustrialization in Sydney has resulted from the particularities of Canadian capitalism, how this process has been influenced from the bottom up through worker and community-based action, and how its impacts continue to echo in the present. The challenge today is to recognize the significant difficulties that continue to face residents in these communities and begin to move towards possible solutions. In assessing this need, Cathy Stanton problematizes the very notion of the "post-industrial." She argues that in accepting a narrative trajectory – industrial/deindustrializing/post-industrial – we risk masking "the continued elaboration of industrial capitalism in ways that may actually make it more difficult to understand its ongoing trajectories and to resist its most insidious and divisive effects."[2] Using the "post-industrial" experience of Boston, which saw a return to prosperity driven largely by the knowledge sector after industrial exodus, Stanton outlines how the relationships engendered within this "new" economy are actually quite industrial in character.[3]

Stanton's critique of the post-industrial applies directly to cities and geographies that Andrew Hurley refers to as "Info-boom catch basins." In deindustrialized cities that were geographically positioned to take advantage of the nascent tech, financial, and knowledge economies, we have seen the emergence of high-end suburban development, the condo-ization of formerly working-class neighbourhoods, and green-field office construction.[4] This transformation has already found purchase within popular culture; British punk poet John Cooper Clarke writes of the shift from the dusty tenements and working-class pubs of 1980s Salford to the "noodle bars and poodle parlours" of the 2000s in his comparative poems "Beasley Street" and "Beasley Boulevard."[5] Rather than view this transformation as a dichotomy, Stanton asks that scholars become more holistic in our analysis and begin to assess the ways in which "industrial" principles of economy and governance have actually continued to exist long after the shuttering of blue-collar basic manufacturing.[6] Based as it is upon a case study of Boston, Stanton's call for a vigorous re-analysis of our own terms of reference imagines a popular conception of the "end" of deindustrialization's impact that perhaps does not exist within many single-industry rural resource economies where revitalization has been conspicuously absent.

This does not mean that we cannot reassess these terms; like the processes of capital mobility and industrial closure, they must be geographically situated and contextualized. In contrast with "Info-boom catch basins," Hurley describes the conditions in what he terms "plunder zones" – cities where today, more than twenty years after collapse in some cases, there is little sign of economic recovery, poverty rates remain astronomical, and out-migration threatens their very existence.[7] In Sydney, which corresponds more closely with this latter category, "post-industrial" can perhaps be considered as a placeholder. It describes an absence, not only in economic terms, but also of an entire way of life, personal and place-identities, and a working-class culture fixed in the particularities of the shop floor. The industrial structure of feeling that is described in chapter 2 has come irrevocably unspooled. Though it remains in residual forms, its decomposition can be usefully understood in "industrial" and "post-industrial" terms. Though it casts a long shadow, the industrial character of twentieth-century Cape Breton cannot truly be reconstituted. That is not to say that industrial work cannot occur, nor that new forms of class identities and cultures cannot take shape based upon other forms of production; however, the historical forms evidenced throughout this book are unlikely to re-emerge.

Nor would such a direct reconstitution be desirable. Efforts at "reindustrialization" often go hand in hand with anti-union and anti-regulatory practices. I am reminded of a recent flight back to Sydney, where I met a man affiliated with ongoing efforts to reopen the

Donkin Mine between Glace Bay and Port Morien. In 2014, Kameron
Collieries – a subsidiary of the American company The Cline Group –
purchased the flooded mine and announced their intention to restart
production.[8] My aisle mate told me that Cline was flying him back
and forth between Cape Breton and his home in the American Mid-
west to work on the reconstitution of the mine. Apparently unaware
of the island's history, he mentioned that it was nice to work in an area
without the headache of unions or Obama's job-killing environmental regulations. With the Donkin mine current reopened in a province
where the memory of Westray remains a dark cloud, the non-union jobs
it provides will be a paltry salve for the problems facing the Island's
residents.

Despite the stories and memories that are at the heart of this work,
not much of it is visible to those who visit Cape Breton in search
of the tourist experience. Historian Ian McKay has articulated the
anti-modernism endemic to tourist-driven representations of Nova Scotia and Cape Breton.[9] Efforts at reindustrialization exist as backwards-
looking attempts to deny the gains – constrained as they were – of labour
in the twentieth century. In June 2016, I had the pleasure of hearing Bobby
Burchell – the Canadian representative for the UMWA and a New Waterford local – speak to a gathered crowd at the Davis Day ceremony in
Glace Bay. He described how, in recent decades, mining companies in
Cape Breton would traditionally donate wreaths for the ceremony. With
their purchase of the Donkin mine, the Cline Group became the first in
decades neither to send a representative to the Davis Day gathering nor
to donate a wreath.[10] For the Cline Group, presumably, the ceremony represents a locally based working-class practice that does not fit with their
desire for non-union operations and a contingent workforce; in this sense,
Stanton's critique rings true. There will always be new forms of resistance
that respond to material conditions. While these may assume the shape
of past struggles, the political, economic, and ideational circumstances of
the present mean that they will unfold in a markedly different way.

The state also suffers from this anti-modernist view of reindustrialization. Recent attempts to develop the Port of Sydney, driven largely
by the municipal government and Mayor Cecil Clarke, envision the city
as a significant North American seaport. As a recent planning document describes, "The Port of Sydney is located on the east coast of
Canada. The Port's channel and sheltered inner harbour can handle the
world's largest vessels and the Port is positioned on direct shipping
routes to Europe, the U.S., South America and Asia."[11] In a promotional
video created by a consulting firm hired to assess the project, "West
Coast labour disputes" are described as one major reason why such

development is necessary – apparently the Sydney port will be free of such disruptions.[12] In this view, it is not only basic industry that belongs to the past, but the labour movement, class struggle, and workers' agitation for better wages and conditions tout court.

The mayor's assuredness about the Sydney port development would not have been out of place in 1899, when an article in the *Daily Post* reported, "By and by, when Pittsburgh is a village and New York has got to be whistled for to stop a steamboat, Sydney will be the grand seaport of a continent."[13] In this rhetorical turning back of the clock, the potential for reindustrialization is framed as existing outside of and beyond the struggles of the twentieth century. In his recent book, *The Great Exception*, Jefferson Cowie argues, "The political era between the 1930s and the 1970s marks what might be called a "great exception" – a sustained deviation, an extended detour – from some of the main contours of American political practice, economic structure, and cultural out-look."[14] Much of the language surrounding economic development in Atlantic Canada has, in recent years, been informed by the neoliberal notion that working-class cultures developed during this interregnum have resulted in anti-business attitudes that must be overcome. Sydney Steel, with its history of unionism and state ownership, is apparently representative of these attitudes. As one history-themed kiosk on the Sydney waterfront asserts, "100 years of steelmaking. Good-bye to all of that!"

Deindustrialization represents a series of changes and conflicts that occur across time and space and have the ability to provoke both resistance and resignation. Rooted in the material relationships of capitalist production, its impacts are fragmented – with each fragment revealing an aspect of its totality. At the individual level, the scars of industrial work, environmental degradation, and deindustrial remediation efforts continue to plague the bodies and minds of those who have been affected. Working-class cultures and voices are decentred from their communities during these processes; the decline and closure of Sydney Steel reveals a slow unwinding of an industrial structure of feeling that emerged during the struggles of the early twentieth century. State action also constrains and shapes how deindustrialization unfolds. The provincial response to Black Friday resulted in thirty-three years of further production at Sydney Steel and prevented some of the drastic effects of immediate closure that have occurred in many Rust Belt cities in the US. So, too, did federal policies relating to regional economic development promote an economic and philosophical turn towards a promised post-industrial knowledge economy that has failed to emerge in the aftermath of industry.

Looking forward, we must also examine our own historical position. We are now able to "consider a range of social, cultural, and political factors and determine how they continue to shape and structure the lives of individuals, families, communities, and places long after the immediate event of shutdown and closure."[15] While this book takes a step in this direction, there is much room for further research. If the industrial structure of feeling is now "residual" in post-industrial areas, what productive and cultural forms are emergent? Such attention could take the shape of environmental histories that position the human experience of industry and deindustrialization within the broader context of climate and ecological change. Scholarship on the history of capitalism is also worth engaging; as Julia Ott writes, this field remains "deeply concerned with performativity, with the ways economic theories operate as ideology and shape the reality they purport to describe in a neutral fashion."[16] With such a renewed focus, we will be better able to ensure that our scholarship responds to the present needs of our subjects and provides a link between twentieth-century experiences of deindustrialization and twenty-first-century politics of resistance.

Notes

Introduction

1 "One Third of Cape Breton Children Living in Poverty: Report," *Cape Breton Post*, 24 November 2014.
2 David Frank, "The Cape Breton Coal Industry and the Rise and Fall of the British Empire Steel Corporation," *Acadiensis* 7, 1 (Autumn 1977): 3–34.
3 "Tour Bus Makes Stop at Tar Ponds," *Cape Breton Post*, 5 July 2007.
4 The concept of *ruination* has been effectively examined in Alice Mah, *Industrial Ruination, Community, and Place: Landscapes and Legacies of Urban Decline*
5 *Cottonland*, directed by Nancy Ackerman (National Film Board of Canada, 2006), DVD.
6 "Heart-Wrenching Battle against Addiction," *Chronicle Herald*, 6 April 2014.
7 Steve Earle, "OxyContin Blues," Washington Square Serenade, New West Records, 2007.
8 David Wray and Carole Stephenson, "Standing the Gaff': Immiseration and Its Consequences in the De-industrialised Mining Communities of Cape Breton Island," *Capitals & Class* 36, 2 (2012): 323–38.
9 Sherry Lee Linkon, *The Half Life of Deindustrialization: Working-Class Writing about Economic Restructuring* (Ann Arbor: University of Michigan Press, 2018).
10 Barry Bluestone and Bennett Harrison, *The Deindustrialization of America: Plant Closings, Community Abandonment, and the Dismantling of Basic Industry* (New York: Basic Books, 1982); Christopher Johnson, *The Life and Death of Industrial Languedoc, 1700–1920: The Politics of Deindustrialization* (Oxford: Oxford University Press, 1995); Jefferson Cowie, *Capital Moves: RCA's Seventy-Year Quest for Cheap Labour* (Ithaca, NY: Cornell University Press, 1999).

11 In this context, the "third way" refers to the abandonment of social democracy and working-class politics of solidarity that infected many parties of the left during the 1990s. See Denis Pilon, "Review Essay: The Long Lingering Death of Social Democracy," *Labour/Le Travail* 70 (Fall 2012): 253.

12 Craig Heron, *Lunch Bucket Lives: Remaking the Workers' City* (Toronto: Between the Lines, 2015), 555.

13 Pierre Bourdieu, *The Logic of Practice*, trans. Richard Nice (Palo Alto: Stanford University Press, 1992), 54.

14 Simon Charlesworth, *A Phenomenology of Working Class Experience* (Cambridge: Cambridge University Press, 2000), 108.

15 Raymond Williams, *Marxism and Literature* (Oxford: Oxford University Press, 1977), 129; See also Jefferson Cowie and Joseph Heathcott, "Introduction: The Meanings of Deindustrialization," in *Beyond the Ruins: The Meanings of Deindustrialization*, ed. Jefferson Cowie and Joseph Heathcott (Ithaca, NY: Cornell University Press, 2003), 5–7, and Sherry Lee Linkon and John Russo, *Steeltown U.S.A.: Work and Memory in Youngstown* (Lawrence: University Press of Kansas, 2003).

16 John Kirk and Christine Wall, *Work and Identity: Historical and Cultural Contexts.*

17 Glenn Graham, "Regionalism on the Celtic Fringe: How a Peripheral Community Resists, Negotiates, and Accommodates Political and Economic Integration," PhD dissertation (Halifax: Dalhousie University, 2016), 296.

18 Steven High, "Deindustrialization on the Industrial Frontier": The Rise and Fall of Mill Colonialism in Northern Ontario," in Steven High, Lachlan MacKinnon, and Andrew Perchard, eds, *The Deindustrialized World: Confronting Ruination in Post-Industrial Places* (Vancouver: University of British Columbia Press, 2017), 260.

19 Craig Heron, *Working in Steel: The Early Years in Canada, 1883–1935* (Toronto: McClelland and Stewart, 1988), 16–23.

20 Donald MacGillivray, "Henry Melville Whitney Comes to Cape Breton: The Saga of a Gilded Age Entrepreneur," *Acadiensis* 9, 1 (Autumn 1979): 44–70; In addition, Scotia maintained a steel mill in the Cape Breton town of Sydney Mines. This mill would remain in use until the early 1920s. For further information, see James M. Cameron, *Industrial History of the New Glasgow District* (New Glasgow, NS: Hector Publishing, 1960), and Craig Heron, "The Great War and Nova Scotia Steelworkers," *Acadiensis* 16, 2 (Spring 1987): 3–34.

21 Stephen J. Hornsby, *Nineteenth Century Cape Breton: A Historical Geography* (Montreal and Kingston: McGill-Queen's University Press, 1992), 25.

22 E. Roy Harvey, *Sydney, Nova Scotia: An Urban Study* (Toronto: Clarke, Irwin, 1971), 17.

23 Ron Crawley, "Class Conflict and the Establishment of the Sydney Steel Industry, 1899–1904," in *The Island: New Perspectives on Cape Breton History, 1713–1990*, ed. Kenneth Donovan (Fredericton and Sydney: Acadiensis and UCCB Press, 1990), 145–64.

24 John Huk, *Strangers in the Land: The Ukrainian Presence in Cape Breton* (Sydney: City Printers, 1986), 10–11.

25 Sam Migliore and A. Evo DiPierro, *Italian Lives, Cape Breton Memories* (Sydney: UCCB Press, 1999).

26 Robert Morgan, *Rise Again! The Story of Cape Breton Island from 1900 to Today* (Sydney: Breton Books, 2009), 20.

27 Ibid., 19.

28 David Farber, *Everybody Ought to Be Rich: The Life and Times of John J. Raskob, Capitalist* (Oxford: Oxford University Press, 2013), 30–1.

29 "The Steel Boom Comes to Sydney," *Cape Breton's Magazine* 39 (1985): 47.

30 Moira Ross, "Dr. Arthur Samuel Kendall, His Life and Times as a Medical Doctor, Politician and Citizen of Cape Breton Island, 1861–1944" (Master's thesis, St Mary's University, 1998), 5.

31 See David Alexander, "Economic Growth in the Atlantic Region, 1880–1940," *Acadiensis* 8, 1 (Autumn 1978): 47–76; James D. Frost, "The 'Nationalization' of the Bank of Nova Scotia, 1880–1910," *Acadiensis* 12, 1 (Autumn 1982): 3–38; E.R. Forbes, *The Maritime Rights Movement, 1919– 1927: A Study in Canadian Regionalism* (Montreal and Kingston: McGill-Queen's University Press, 1979); Don Nerbas, "Adapting to Decline: The Changing Business World of the Bourgeoisie in Saint John, NB, in the 1920s," *Canadian Historical Review* 89, 2 (2008): 151–87.

32 Frank, "The Cape Breton Coal Industry and the Rise and Fall of British Empire Steel Corporation," 14; See also: L. Anders Sandberg, "Dependent Development, Labour and the Trenton Steel Works, Nova Scotia, c. 1900–1943," *Labour/Le Travail* 27 (Spring 1991): 127–62; Kris E. Inwood, "Local Control, Resources and the Nova Scotia Steel and Coal Company," *Historical Papers* 21, 1 (1986): 254–82.

33 Craig Heron and Robert Storey, "Work and Struggle in the Canadian Steel Industry, 1900–1950," in *On the Job: Confronting the Labour Process in Canada*, ed. Craig Heron and Robert Storey (Montreal and Kingston: McGill-Queen's University Press, 1986), 211–12.

34 Frank, "The Cape Breton Coal Industry and the Rise and Fall of British Empire Steel Corporation," 22. Several smaller producers did remain, although the market was dominated by Besco and, later, Dosco.

35 Gregory S. Kealey, "1919: The Canadian Labour Revolt," *Labour/Le Travail* 13 (Spring 1984): 11–44; Craig Heron, *The Canadian Labour Movement* (Toronto: James Lorimer, 1989).

36 Frank, "The Cape Breton Coal Industry and the Rise and Fall of British Empire Steel Corporation," 33.

37 Gary Burril, *Away: Maritimers in Massachusetts, Ontario, and Alberta: An Oral History of Leaving Home* (Montreal and Kingston: McGill-Queen's University Press), 5.

38 Patricia A. Thornton, "The Problem of Out-Migration from Atlantic Canada, 1871–1921: A New Look," *Acadiensis* 15, 1 (Autumn, 1985): 27–8.

39 Heron, *Working in Steel*, 174.

40 Christine Walley, *Exit Zero: Family and Class in Postindustrial Chicago* (Chicago: University of Chicago Press, 2013), 5.

41 Elizabeth Beaton, "The Beaton Institute's Steel Project," *Archivaria* 27 (Winter 1988–9): 194.

42 Daniel James, *Doña Maria's Story: Life History, Memory, and Political Identity* (Durham, NC: Duke University Press, 2000), 124.

43 Paul Thompson, *The Voice of the Past: Oral History*, 3rd ed. (London: Oxford University Press, 2000): 71–2.

44 Alistair Thomson, "Four Paradigm Transformations in Oral History," *Oral History Review* 34, 1 (2006): 51; Steven High, "Sharing Authority in the Writing of Canadian History: The Case of Oral History," in *Contesting Clio's Craft: New Directions and Debates in Canadian History*, ed. Christopher Dummitt and Michael Dawson (London: University of London, 2008), 20–46; Steven High, Stacey Zembrzycki, and Jessica Mills, "Telling Our Stories / Animating Our Past: A Status Report on Oral History and New Media," *Canadian Journal of Communications* 37, 3 (2012): 1–22.

45 Alessandro Portelli, "What Makes Oral History Different?" in *The Oral History Reader*, ed. Robert Perks and Alistair Thomson (London: Routledge, 1998), 63–74.

46 See also Steven High and David Sworn, "After the Interview: The Interpretive Challenges of Oral History Video Indexing," *Digital Studies/Le champ numérique* 1, 2 (2009), http://www.digitalstudies.org/ojs/index.php/digital_studies/article/view/173/215; Michael Frisch, "Three Dimensions and More: Oral History beyond the Paradoxes of Method," in *Handbook of Emergent Methods*, ed. Sharlene Nagy Hesse-Biber and Patricia Leavy (New York: Guildford Press, 2008), 222.

47 Michael Frisch, *A Shared Authority: Essays on the Craft and Meaning of Oral and Public History* (Albany, NY: SUNY Press, 1990).

48 Linda Shopes, "Commentary: Sharing Authority," *Oral History Review* 30, 1 (Winter-Spring 2003): 103–10.

49 Gerry and Tommy McCarron, interview with author, 7 August 2013; Gerry McCarron, Sheldon Andrews, and George MacNeil, interview with author, 5 August 2015; Gerry McCarron and Dave Nalepa, interview with author, 8 December 2015; Gerry McCarron and Joel MacLean, interview with author, 29 April 2016; Gerry McCarron, Alana MacNeil, and George MacNeil, interview with author, 29 April 2016.

1. Diversify or Die

1 F.L. Estep, report to the Minister of Industry, Halifax, Nova Scotia, regarding operations of Dominion Steel and Coal Corporation [8 April 1944], Nova Scotia Steel and Coal, Trenton Works, Hawker Siddeley Collection, MS-4-106, A-127, Dalhousie University Archives, Halifax, NS.

2 "Carrier Plans to Lay Off 1,400 Indy Workers in Mexico Move," *Indianapolis Business Journal*, 10 February 2016; "Carrier Air Conditioner (part of United Technologies) Moving 1,400 Jobs to Mexico," YouTube Video, 3:31, posted by Joe Brunner, 11 February 2016, https://www.youtube.com/watch?v=Y3ttxGMQOrY.

3 Melanie Bencosme, Jake Heller, and Corky Siemaszko, "Carrier Plant Layoffs: Worker Thought Trump Would Save Her Job. She Was Wrong," *NBC News*, 12 January 2018. https://www.nbcnews.com/news/us-news/carrier-plant-layoffs-worker-thought-trump-would-save-her-job-n836261.

4 Joseph Schumpeter, *Capitalism, Socialism, and Democracy*, rev. ed. (1942; repr. London: Routledge, 2003), 82–3.

5 Eddie Parris, interview by Diane Chisholm, 5 October 1990, Steel Project, MG 14, 206, Box 7, File 62, transcript, Beaton Institute Archives (BI), Sydney, NS; Romeo Sylvester, interview by Diane Chisholm, 12 March 1990, Steel Project, Box 5, File 80, transcript, BI; Adrian Murphy and Mickey Campbell, interview with author, 1 September 2014.

6 Mel Watkins, "Staples Redux," *Studies in Political Economy* 79 (Spring 2007): 213–26; Mel Watkins, "The Staple Theory Revisited," *Journal of Canadian Studies* 12 (1977): 83–95.

7 Roger Hayter and Trevor Barnes, "Innis' Staple Theory, Exports, and Recession: British Columbia, 1981–1986," *Economic Geography* 66, 2 (April 1990): 158.

8 Paul Kellogg, *Escape from the Staples Trap: Canadian Political Economy after Left Nationalism* (Toronto: University of Toronto Press, 2015), 10.

9 Ibid.

10 Kenneth G. Pryke, "Cape Breton: Identity and Nostalgia," *Acadiensis* 22, 1 (Autumn 1992), 169–84; Adrian Ivakhiv, "Colouring Cape Breton 'Celtic': Topographies of Culture and Identity in Cape Breton Island," *Ethnologies* 27, 2 (2005), 107–36; Andrew Parnaby, "Life among the Ruins: Deindustrialization in Historiographical Perspective," *Labour/Le Travail* 72 (2013): 279–93.

11 *Report of the Royal Commission on Coal, 1946* [Carroll Commission] (Ottawa: King's Printer, 1947).

12 Ibid., 13.

13 David Frank, "In Search of C.B. Wade, Research Director and Labour Historian, 1944–1950," *Labour/Le Travail* 79 (Spring 2017): 32.

14 Gail Weir, "The Wabana Ore Miners of Bell Island, Conception Bay,
    Newfoundland: Their Occupational Folklife and Oral Folk History"
    (Master's thesis, Memorial University of Newfoundland, 1986), 30.
15 F. Shea and D.A. Murray, "Limestones and Dolomites of Nova Scotia
    – Cape Breton Island, Part 1," *Bulletin, Nova Scotia Department of Mines*
    (Halifax: Department of Mines, 1969): 1.
16 E.R. Forbes, "Consolidating Disparity: The Maritimes and the
    Industrialization of Canada during the Second World War," in *Challenging
    the Regional Stereotype: Essays on the 20th Century Maritimes*, ed. E.R. Forbes
    (Fredericton, NB: Acadiensis Press, 1989), 174.
17 Clem Anson, "Memo," 21 September 1940, F1157, File 6, Angus L.
    Macdonald Fonds, MG 2, Nova Scotia Archives and Records Management
    (NSARM), Halifax, NS.
18 "Let's All Know More about Sydney Steel," *Sydney Post Record*, 24 July
    1946.
19 Arthur G. McKee & Company, *Report on Steel Industry, Royal Commission
    on Provincial Development and Rehabilitation* (Halifax: King's Printer, 1944),
    31–2.
20 "Sydney Harbour in World War Two," *Cape Breton's Magazine* 13 (1976):
    28–9, and Marc Koechl, "Sailor's Ashore: A Comparative Analysis of
    Wartime Recreation and Leisure in Halifax and Saint John's" (Master's
    thesis, Memorial University of Newfoundland, 2003), 120; Arthur McKee
    & Company, *Report on Steel*, 64–8.
21 "C.M. Anson and Steel," *Cape Breton's Magazine* 28 (1981): 48–9.
22 John Campbell, interview with author, 6 September 2014.
23 Memorandum, "Sydney Steel," 1946, Sydney Local 1064 Correspondence
    and Reports, C-13112, United Steelworkers of America (USWA) Fonds, MG
    28 i268, LAC.
24 There is some evidence that this was part of a broader regional strategy
    that took shape as early as the 1930s, following the company's acquisition
    of Scotia's steel holdings at Trenton. See L. Anders Sandberg, "Dependent
    Development, Labour, and the Trenton Steel Works, Nova Scotia, c. 1900–
    1943," *Labour/Le Travail* 27 (Spring 1991): 162.
25 MG 19, 6. B Beaton Institute
26 McDowell, *Steel at the Sault*, 200.
27 O.J Firestone, *Encouragement to Industrial Expansion in Canada: Operation of
    Special Depreciation Provisions, 10 April 1944–31 March 1949* (Ottawa: King's
    Printer, 1948); Richard Goode, "Accelerated Depreciation Allowances as a
    Stimulus to Investment," *Quarterly Journal of Economics* 69, 2 (May 1955): 191–2.
28 Matthew Tonts, Kirsten Martinus, and Paul Plummer, "Regional
    Development, Redistribution and the Extraction of Mineral Resources: The
    Western Australian Goldfields as a Resource Bank," *Applied Geography* 45
    (2013): 367.

29 Corey Slumkoski, *Inventing Atlantic Canada: Regionalism and the Maritime Reaction to Newfoundland's Entry into Canadian Confederation* (Toronto: University of Toronto Press, 2011), 45–8.

30 Jonathan Aylen, "Plant Size and Efficiency in the Steel Industry: An International Comparison," *National Institute Economic Review* 100, 1 (May 1982): 68–9.

31 This included Belgium, France, Italy, Luxembourg, the Netherlands, and West Germany.

32 Stephen G. Bunker and Paul Ciccantell, *East Asia and the Global Economy: Japan's Ascent, with Implications for China's Future* (Baltimore: Johns Hopkins University Press, 2007), 62.

33 Elver, *Economic Character and Change in the Canadian Steel Industry since 1945*, 8.

34 Bruce Muirhead, "Perception and Reality: The GATT's Contribution to the Development of a Bilateral North American Relationship, 1947–1951," *American Review of Canadian Studies* 20, 3 (1990): 281.

35 L.I. Morgan, *The Canadian Primary Iron and Steel Industry* (Ottawa: Queen's Printer, 1956), 83.

36 Peter Warrian, *The Importance of Steel Manufacturing to Canada: A Research Study* (Toronto: Munk School of Global Affairs, 2010), 34.

37 University of British Columbia Sauder School of Business Pacific Exchange Rate Service, "Foreign Currency Units per 1 Canadian Dollar," 1948–2014, http://fx.sauder.ubc.ca/.

38 Harry Waisglass and Andrew Hogan, *A Submission to the Atlantic Development Board on the Prospects for Nova Scotia's Steel Industry* (28 March 1966): 11; It should be noted that a company-sponsored report in 1966 challenged viability of New England markets; see Tom Webb, "The Dosco Crisis: Some Political Aspects of a Regional Economic Problem" (Master's thesis, Carleton University, 1972), 36.

39 R.B. Elver, "Competitive Position of Dosco as a Steel Producer," prepared for the Royal Commission on Coal, 1959, Sydney Steel Corporation, Box 44, Natural Resources Canada Fonds, RG 21, LAC.

40 Dominion Steel and Coal Company, "Munitions: Korea," 1952–1953, Nova Scotia Steel and Coal, Trenton Works, Hawker Siddeley Collection, F-17, Dalhousie University Archives.

41 Address by L.A. Forsyth, President of Dosco, to the Maritime Provinces Board of Trade, 1951, Nova Scotia Steel and Coal, Trenton Works, Hawker Siddeley Collection, K-74, Dalhousie University Archives.

42 Richard E. Craves, Grant L. Leuber, Robert W. Baguley, John M. Curtis, and Raymond Lubitz, *Capital Transfers and Economic Policy: Canada, 1951–1962* (Cambridge, MA: Harvard University Press, 1971), 183.

43 Dosco Annual Report, 1954, Corporate Records, 1990-215-001, File 1, Halifax Industries Limited Fonds, NSARM.

44 Address to Annual Meeting of Shareholders, 7 May 1954, Corporate
    Records, Halifax Industries Limited Fonds, File 1, NSARM; Donald Kerr,
    "The Geography of the Canadian Iron and Steel Industry," *Economic
    Geography* 35, 2 (April 1959): 154.
45 "Dosco Net at Record for 1957," *Montreal Gazette*, 3 April 1958.
46 Peter C. Newman, "Lionel Forsyth," *Atlantic Advocate* (January 1960): 63–4.
47 Annual Address to Shareholders, June 1957, Nova Scotia Steel and Coal,
    Trenton Works, Hawker Siddeley Collection, K-43, Dalhousie University
    Archives.
48 "Hawker Siddeley Switches Emphasis to General Industry," *New Scientist*
    3, 60 (9 January 1958): 31.
49 A.V. Roe dumped these Algoma shares following the acquisition of Dosco.
    See McDowall, *Steel at the Sault*, 234.
50 Hawker Siddeley Canada, 1963, Orenda Engines Division, T-3419,
    Department of Labour Fonds, RG 27, LAC.
51 Crawford Gordon to C.B. Lang, 7 August 1957, Sydney Local 1064
    Correspondence and Reports, USWA Fonds, LAC.
52 R.M. Baiden, "A.V. Roe's Bid for Dosco Control," *Saturday Night*, 14
    September 1967, 7–33, G-17, W.G. Allen Fonds, MS 2–96, Dalhousie
    University Archives.
53 Gordon to Lang, 7 August 1957.
54 Notes, August 1957, G-17, W.G. Allen Fonds, Dalhousie University
    Archives.
55 R.A. Jodrey and F.H. Sobey to Dosco Shareholders, 30 August 1957,
    Sydney Local 1064 Correspondence and Reports, USWA Fonds, LAC.
56 "A.V. Roe in Control of Dosco Shares," *Saint John's Daily News*, 16 October
    1957.
57 Dofasco installed North America's first basic oxygen furnace in 1954.
    Daniel Madar, *Big Steel: Technology, Trade, and Survival in a Global Market*
    (Vancouver: University of British Columbia Press, 2009), 24.
58 W.S. MacNutt, "The Atlantic Revolution," *Atlantic Advocate* (1957): 11–13.
59 Margaret Conrad, "The 1950s: The Decade of Development," in *The
    Atlantic Provinces in Confederation*, ed. E.R. Forbes and D.A. Muise (Toronto:
    University of Toronto Press, 1993), 386.
60 Margaret Conrad, *George Nowlan: Maritime Conservative in National Politics*
    (Toronto: University of Toronto Press, 1986), 237–8.
61 Libbie Park and Frank Park, *Anatomy of Big Business* (Toronto: James,
    Lewis, and Samuel, 1973), 109.
62 Palmiro Campagna, *Storms of Controversy: The Secret Arrow Files Revealed*
    (Toronto: Stoddart, 1992), 93–5.
63 Stewart, *Arrow through the Heart*, 152.
64 Elver, "Competitive Position of Dosco as a Steel Producer," 15.

65 I.C. Rand, *Report on the Royal Commission on Coal, August 1960* (Ottawa: Roger Duhamel, 1960), 23–4.
66 Arthur D. Little Inc., *The Future of Steel-Making in Sydney: Report to the Government of Nova Scotia* (Cambridge, MA: Arthur D. Little, 1960), 28.
67 Waisglass and Hogan, *A Submission to the Atlantic Development Board*, 2.
68 Daniel MacFarlane, *Negotiating a River: Canada, the US, and the Creation of the St. Lawrence Seaway* (Vancouver: University of British Columbia Press, 2014), 51.
69 "Britain; Economics," Labor clippings files, 1941–1968, HCLA 1941, Box 7, USWA Fonds, Eberly Family Special Collections Library, Pennsylvania State University (PSU), State College, PA.
70 James S. Gordon, "Shipping Regulation and the Federal Maritime Commission, Pt. 1," *University of Chicago Law Review* 37, 1 (Autumn 1969): 142–5.
71 Marjorie Earl, "How Roy Dobson Pushed Us into the Jet Age," *Maclean's*, 20 July 1957.
72 Dosco, report for the five month fiscal period ending December 31, 1960, Corporate Records, File 2, Halifax Industries Limited Fonds, NSARM.
73 Dosco Annual Reports, 1962, Corporate Records, File 3, Halifax Industries Limited Fonds, NSARM.
74 Palmiro Campagna, *Requiem for a Giant: A.V. Roe and the Avro Arrow* (Toronto: Dundurn Group, 2003), 157–8.
75 A.V. Roe Canada Annual Report, 1961, Corporate Records, File 3, Halifax Industries Limited Fonds, NSARM.
76 "A.V. Roe Canada President," *Flight* (31 August 1961): 276.
77 "The Board of Directors announces that effective immediately the group of company's operating as A.V. Roe Canada Limited will now be known as Hawker Siddeley Canada Ltd.," *Ottawa Journal*, 3 May 1962.
78 Hawker Siddeley Canada, report on operations, 30 April 1964, Corporate Records, File 4, Halifax Industries Limited Fonds, NSARM.
79 "Major Market Areas Eyed in Dosco Expansion Plans," *Montreal Gazette*, 14 February 1963; "Dosco's New Flat-Rolled Mill Will Reduce Sheet Steel Costs to Industries in Quebec," *Montreal Gazette*, 9 February 1966; As early as 1964, the Quebec government expressed interest in the possibility of purchasing the Contrecoeur operation. "Takeover Hint Lifts Shares of Dominion," *New York Times*, 21 August 1964.
80 Hawker Siddeley Canada Annual Report, 1965, Corporate Records, File 4, Halifax Industries Limited Fonds, NSARM.
81 Hawker Siddeley Canada Limited, Annual Report, 1965.
82 Weir, "The Wabana Ore Miners of Bell Island," 31–2.
83 Memorandum: Transfer Sydney Wire Drawing Machine, 23 March 1966, Bras d'Or Collection, 0915, Cape Breton University Library.

84 Waisglass and Hogan, *A Submission to the Atlantic Development Board*, 10.
85 Hawker Siddeley Canada Annual Report, 1967, Corporate Records, File 4, Halifax Industries Limited Fonds, NSARM.
86 Marc Renaud, "Quebec's New Middle Class in Search of Social Hegemony: Causes and Political Consequences," in *The Challenge of Modernity: A Reader on Post-Confederation Canada* ed. Ian McKay (Toronto: McGraw-Hill Ryerson, 1992), 348.
87 Pierre Fortin, "Quebec's Quiet Revolution, 50 Years Later," *Inroads* 29 (Summer/Fall 2011): 91.
88 Albert Cholette, *Le fer du Nouveau-Québec et la saga de la sidérugie: la faillite d'un rêve* (Saint-Nicholas: Les Presses de l'Université Laval, 2000), 1.
89 Hawker Siddeley Canada Annual Report, 1967.

2. Radical Reds and Responsible Unionism

1 Raymond Williams, *The Long Revolution* (London: Chatto & Windus, 1961), 63.
2 Jefferson Cowie and Joseph Heathcott, "Introduction," *Beyond the Ruins: The Meanings of Deindustrialization*, ed. Jefferson Cowie and Joseph Heathcott (Ithaca, NY: Cornell University Press, 2003), 14; Steven High and David W. Lewis, *Corporate Wasteland: The Landscape and Memory of Deindustrialization* (Toronto: Between the Lines, 2007), 94; See also Tim Strangleman, "'Smokestack Nostalgia,' 'Ruin Porn,' or Working Class Obituary: The Role and Meaning of Deindustrial Representation," *International Labor and Working-Class History* 84 (2013): 23–37.
3 David Byrne, "Industrial Culture in a Post-Industrial World," *City* 6, 3 (2002): 287.
4 Raymond Williams and Michael Orrom, *A Preface to Film* (London: Film Drama, 1954), 21.
5 Williams, *The Long Revolution*, 64–5.
6 Raymond Williams, *Marxism and Literature* (Oxford: Oxford University Press, 1977), 129.
7 Ibid., 122.
8 David Frank, "Tradition and Culture in the Cape Breton Mining Community in the Early Twentieth Century," in *Cape Breton at 200 Essays in Honour of the Island's Bicentennial, 1785–1985*, ed. Kenneth Donovan (Sydney, NS: UCCB Press, 1985), 203–18.
9 David Frank, "The Industrial Folk Song in Cape Breton," *Canadian Folklore Canadien* 8, 1–2 (1986): 22.
10 David Frank and Donald MacGillivray, introduction to *Echoes from Labor's War: Industrial Cape Breton in the 1920s*, by Dawn Fraser (Toronto: New Hogtown Press, 1976), 20–1.

11 Michelle Filice, "Rita Joe," *Dictionary of Canadian Biography*. https://www
.thecanadianencyclopedia.ca/en/article/rita-joe.

12 "From Breadlines to Battlefields," *Steelworker and Miner*, 17 August 1940;
"Work-Poetry of Slim McInnis," *Cape Breton Magazine* 64 (August 1993):
48–53; Donald MacGillivray, "The Industrial Verse of Slim McInnis,"
Labour/Le Travail 28 (Fall 1991): 271–83.

13 "The Steel Strike," *Steelworker and Miner*, 27 July 1946.

14 Frank, "The Industrial Folk Song in Cape Breton," 39; Nell Campbell,
"Plain Ol' Miner Boy," audio file, http://www.beatoninstitutemusic.ca
/mining/plain-ole-miner-boy.html, John C. O'Donnell Tape Collection,
Beaton Institute Archives (BI), Sydney, NS.

15 Eric Hobsbawm, *The Age of Extremes: The Short Twentieth Century, 1914–
1991* (London: Abacus, 1994), 257.

16 Williams, *Marxism and Literature*, 82.

17 Gordie Gosse, interview with author, 19 April 2016.

18 David Frank, *J.B. McLachlan: A Biography* (Toronto: James Lorimer, 1999),
303; Donald MacGillivray, "Military Aid to the Civil Power: The Cape
Breton Experience in the 1920s," *Acadiensis* 3, 2 (Spring 1974): 56.

19 Douglas Cruickshank and Gregory S. Kealey, "Strikes in Canada,
1891–1950: I. Analysis," *Labour/Le Travail* 20 (Fall 1987): 117; Laurel Sefton
MacDowell, "The 1943 Steel Strike against Wartime Wage Controls,"
Labour/Le Travail 10 (Autumn 1982): 67.

20 Taylor Hollander, "Making Reform Happen: The Passage of Canada's
Collective-Bargaining Policy, 1943–1944," *Journal of Policy History* 13, 3
(2001): 313–14.

21 Judy Fudge and Eric Tucker, *Labour before the Law: The Regulation of Workers'
Collective Action in Canada, 1900–1948* (Oxford: Oxford University Press,
2001), 273

22 See Aaron McCrorie, "PC 1003: Labour, Capital, and the State," in
Labour Gains, Labour Pains, 15–38, and Anne Forrest, "Securing the Male
Breadwinner: A Feminist Interpretation of PC 1003," *Relations Industrielles/
Industrial Relations* 52, 1 (Winter 1997): 91–113.

23 Peter McInnis, *Harnessing Labour Confrontation: Shaping the Postwar
Settlement in Canada: 1943–1950* (Toronto: University of Toronto Press,
2002), 6–7.

24 The unionization of the Sydney steelworkers has been explored elsewhere.
See: George MacEachern, *George MacEachern: An Autobiography*, ed. David
Frank and Donald MacGillivray (Sydney, NS: UCCB Press, 1987), and
"Organizing Sydney's Steelworkers in the 1930s," in *We Stood Together:
First-Hand Accounts of Dramatic Events in Canada's Labour Past*, ed. Gloria
Montero (Toronto: James Lorimer, 1979), 47–68; Frank, *J.B. McLachlan*;
Craig Heron, *Working in Steel: The Early Years in Canada, 1883–1935*

(Toronto: McClelland and Stewart, 1988); Ron Crawley, "What Kind of Unionism? Struggles among Sydney Steel Workers in the SWOC Years, 1936–1942," *Labour/Le Travail* 39 (Spring 1997): 99–123.

25 "Taylor and Lewis Had Secret Talks," *New York Times*, 3 March 1988; Richard A. Lauderbaugh, "Business, Labor, and Foreign Policy: U.S. Steel, the International Steel Cartel, and the Recognition of the Steel Workers Organizing Committee," *Politics and Society* 6, 4 (December 1976): 433–57.

26 Craig Heron and Robert Storey, "Work and Struggle in the Canadian Steel Industry, 1900–1950," in *On the Job: Confronting the Labour Process in Canada*, ed. Craig Heron and Robert Storey (Kingston and Montreal: McGill-Queen's University Press, 1986), 230.

27 Robert Storey, "Unionization versus Corporate Welfare: The 'Dofasco Way,'" *Labour/Le Travail* 12 (Autumn 1983): 7–42, and "The Struggle to Organize Stelco and Dofasco," *Relations industrielles/Industrial Relations* 42, 2 (1987): 366–85. See also William Kilbourne, *The Elements Combined: A History of the Steel Company of Canada* (Toronto: Clarke, Irwin, 1960); *Baptism of a Union: Stelco Strike of 1946*, ed. Wayne Roberts (Hamilton: McMaster University, 1981).

28 Craig Heron, "The Mill: A Worker's Memoir from 1945–1948," *Labour/Le Travail* 43 (Spring 1999): 172.

29 Storey, "Unionization versus Corporate Welfare: The 'Dofasco Way,'" 7.

30 Heron and Storey, "Work and Struggle in the Canadian Steel Industry, 1900–1950," 233.

31 Following the cessation of the strike, the differential was put to the National War Labour Board for adjudication.

32 "Steelworkers Vote 5–1 to Return to Work," *Sydney Post Record*, 3 October 1946.

33 Ron Crawley, "Conflict within the Union: Struggles among Sydney Steel Workers, 1936–1972" (PhD dissertation, Carleton University, 1995), 160.

34 Tim Buck, *Yours in the Struggle: Reminiscences of Tim Buck*, ed. William Beeching and Phyllis Clarke (Toronto: NC Press, 1977), 329.

35 Roddie Rodd, "Rhyming Roundup," *Steelworker and Miner*, 24 August 1946.

36 Memorandum, National War Labour Board on Dosco and USWA, Local 1064, 26 November 1946, Box 120, A1 viii e.) File 1, Dominion Steel and Coal Company Papers, MG 14, 26, BI.

37 E.B. Jolliffe to J.C. Nicholson, 8 October 1946, Correspondence, briefs, and reports, 80–157–1187, D. 3, United Steelworkers of America, MG 19, 7, BI.

38 Craig Heron, *The Canadian Labour Movement: A Short History* (Toronto: James Lorimer, 1989), 89; John Hinshaw, *Steel and Steelworkers: Race and Class Struggle in Twentieth-Century Pittsburgh* (Albany, NY: SUNY Press, 2002).

39 "Bulwarks," *Steelworker and Miner*, 17 April 1948.

40 "11 Pieces of Silver," *Steelworker and Miner*, 1 May 1948.

41 For further discussion of the CSU strike, see Jim Green, *Against the Tide: The Story of the Canadian Seamen's Union* (Toronto: Progress Books, 1986); William Kaplan, *Everything That Floats: Pat Sullivan, Hal Banks, and the Seamen's Unions of Canada* (Toronto: University of Toronto Press, 1987); Craig Heron, "Communists, Gangsters, and Canadian Sailors," *Labour/Le Travail* 24 (Fall 1989): 231–7.

42 Crawley, "Conflict within the Union," 204.

43 MacEachern, *George MacEachern*, 135–6.

44 Walter Pickles, interview by Michael Earle, 15 May 1990, Steel Project, MG 14, 206, Box 6, File 65, transcript, BI.

45 Wally MacKinnon told Michael Earle that he did not believe the story of Corbett's trip to Ottawa. See Wally MacKinnon, interview by Michael Earle, 11 April 1990, Steel Project, Box 5, File 40, transcript, BI; "Anson's Allies in Steel Union Engineer Sell Out of Seamen at 'Fixed,' Stormy Meeting!" *Steelworker and Miner*, 28 May 1949.

46 Ira Katznelson, "The 'Bourgeois' Dimension: A Provocation about Institutions, Politics, and the Future of Labour History," *International Journal of Labour and Working-Class History* 46 (Fall 1994): 26–7.

47 Sidney Mifflen, minority report to the Regional War Labour Board for Nova Scotia, 17 October 1946, Box 120, A1 viii e.) File 11–12, Dosco Papers, BI; Wage Rates, 1944–45, 1946–1947, Box 12, B i. b) Files 11–12, Dosco Papers, BI; Bryan C. Williams, "Collective Bargaining and Wage Equalization in Canada's Iron and Steel Industry," *Relations industrielles/ Industrial Relations* 26, 2 (1971): 317–19.

48 "Supplemental Agreement to 6 February 1947," and Dosco – Local 1064 contract, 1 May 1948," Box 119, A1 viii b.) Files 1–2, Dosco Papers, BI.

49 Dosco – Local 1064 contract, 5 July 1949, Box 119, A1 viii b.) File 3, Dosco Papers, BI; Crawley, "Conflict within the Union," 188.

50 Wally MacKinnon, interview by Michael Earle, 11 April 1990.

51 Crawley, "Conflict within the Union," 218.

52 Dosco – Local 1064 contact, 1950–1952, Box 119, A1 viii. b.) File 5, Dosco Papers, BI.

53 Stelco – Local 1005 contract, 1952, Box 4, File 1, United Steelworkers of America: Local 1005 (Hamilton, Ontario), Thomas McClure sous-fonds, 1928–1976, RC0300, McMaster University Archives and Research Collections, Hamilton, ON; L.A. Forsyth to C.H. Millard, Sydney Local 1064 Correspondence and Reports, C-13112, United Steelworkers of America Fonds, MG 28 i268, Library and Archives Canada (LAC), Ottawa, ON.

54 "Job Classification Analysis by Occupation" and "Wage Administrative Agreement, 1954," Box 134, Files 27–8, Dosco Papers, BI; Williams, "Collective Bargaining," 325.

55 Crawley, "Conflict within the Union," 262.

56 No relation between Mickey Campbell and John Campbell.

57 John Campbell, interview with author, 6 September 2014.

58 Bernie Britten, interview with author, 2 September 2014.

59 Mickey Campbell, interview with author, 1 September 2014.

60 Tim Strangleman, "The Nostalgia of Organizations and the Organization of Nostalgia: Past and Present in the Contemporary Railway Industry," *Sociology* 33, 4 (November 1999): 727; Steven High, "Beyond Aesthetics: Visibility and Invisibility in the Aftermath of Deindustrialization," *International Labor and Working-Class History Journal* 84 (Fall 2013): 140–53.

61 Jackie Clarke, "Closing Moulinex: Thoughts on the Visibility and Invisibility of Industrial Labour in Contemporary France," *Modern and Contemporary France* 19, 4 (2011): 443–58.

62 Ian McKay, *The Quest of the Folk: Antimodernism and Cultural Selection in Twentieth Century Nova Scotia* (Montreal and Kingston: McGill-Queen's University Press, 1994); Meaghan Beaton and Del Muise, "The Canso Causeway: Tartan Tourism, Industrial Development and the Promise of Progress for Cape Breton," *Acadiensis* 37, 2 (Summer 2008): 39–69.

63 Wendy Bergfeldt-Munro, "Tuned-In: Radio, Ritual and Resistance: Cape Breton's Traditional Music, 1973–1998" (Master's thesis, Athabasca University, 2015), 25–28.

64 "Dumping the Slag," c. 1950, Lloyd McInnis Fonds, unaccessioned, 2015-010, Box 3, File: CJCB Radio, BI.

65 *Sydney Steel Museum website*, "Sounds of Silence – The End of an Era," entry by Syd S. Slaven, http://www.sydneysteelmuseum.com/history/end_era.htm.

66 "Untitled Entry," c. 1950, Lloyd McInnis Fonds, 2015-010, Box 3, File: CJCB Radio, BI.

67 "Spring in Sydney," c. 1950, Lloyd McInnis Fonds, 2015-010, Box 3, File: CJCB Radio, BI.

68 *Maritime Labour Herald*, February 3, 1923. Quoted in Frank, *J.B. McLachlan*, 294.

69 Williams, *Marxism and Literature*, 131.

70 Crawley, "Conflict within the Union," 170.

71 Harry J. Waisglass to G.I. Smith, 25 June 1964, General Correspondence, C-13112, USWA Fonds, LAC.

72 Alexander Proudfoot Company, "Dominion Steel and Coal Corporation, Ltd. Operating Procedures," 1962, Box 145, B1.i k.) File 2, Dosco Papers, BI.

73 Otis Cossit, interview by Michael Earle, 12 June 1990, Steel Project, Box 5, File 9, transcript, BI.

74 Walter Clarke, interview by Diane Chisholm, 4 July 1990, Steel Project, Box 5, File 7, transcript, BI.

75 Memorandum: Work Stoppages, 1961–1964, Box 13 B. i. c.) File 2, Dosco Papers, BI.

76 Review of Strikes since 1957, Box 14. B. i. c.) File 75, Dosco Papers, BI.

77 "Walkout Staged at Steel Plant," *Cape Breton Post*, 11 October 1961.

78 "750 involved in plant walkout," *Cape Breton Post*, 24 January 1962; "Mill Employees Walk off Job," *Cape Breton Post*, 13 March 1962.

79 Draft report of the Committee on Unauthorized Strike Activity," First Accrual, Box 134, File 12, United Steelworkers of America District 6 (Toronto, Ont.) Fonds, McMaster University Archives and Research Collections.

80 Bryan Palmer, *Canada's 1960s: The Ironies of Identity in a Rebellious Era* (Toronto: University of Toronto Press, 2009), 223.

81 Ibid., 217.

82 Ian Milligan, *Rebel Youth: 1960s Labour Unrest, Young Workers, and New Leftists in English Canada* (Vancouver: University of British Columbia Press, 2014), 46.

83 Palmer, *Canada's 1960s*, 227.

84 Rod and Bar Mill Seniority List, 1964, Box 125, File 23, Dosco Papers, BI.

85 F.E. Curry, Rod and Bar Mills, 3 September 1963, Box 14. B. i. c.) File 75, Dosco Papers, BI.

86 Rod and Bar Mill Seniority List, 1964, Dosco Papers, BI.

87 Ryan's tenure as president was short-lived. Merner returned to the presidency in 1964 after Ryan failed to achieve majority support for the 1963 contract.

88 Roy Flood to William Mahoney, 1963, Sydney Local 1064 Correspondence and Reports, USWA Fonds, LAC.

89 William Mahoney to Ben O'Neill, 1963, Sydney Local 1064 Correspondence and Reports, USWA Fonds, LAC; Henry Harm, a the regional director of the CLC, also identified resurging radicalism within 1064 by 1965. Henry Harm to C.A. Scotton, 9 October 1965, Atlantic Region: Sydney and District, 1961–1967, Volume 488, File 27, Canadian Labour Congress Fonds, MG 28 i103, LAC

90 Palmer, *Canada's 1960s*, 221.

91 Sydney Works Personnel Statistics, Box 7, B. i. a.) File 1, Dosco Papers, BI.

92 Ibid.

3. It Brought Us Joy, It Brought Us Tears

1 "Ottawa Meeting Casts Gloom over Future of Sydney Mill," *Chronicle Herald*, 13 October 1967.

2 Peter C. Newman, *The Canadian Establishment*, vol. 1: *The Old Order* (Toronto: McClelland and Stewart, 1975), 447; for further discussion of

the Drury family and their involvement with Maritimes industry, see: A.J.P. Taylor, *Beaverbrook* (New York: Simon and Schuster, 1972), 24–8, and Dimitry Anastakis, "Building a 'New Nova Scotia': State Intervention, The Auto Industry, and the Case of Volvo in Halifax, 1963–1998," *Acadiensis* 34, 1 (Autumn 2004): 3–30.

3 Charles MacDonald, interview with author, 3 March 2015.

4 Voluntary Economic Planning Board, *Sydney Steelmaking Study* (Halifax: Queen's Printers, 1968). Dosco executives and the Atlantic Development Board also played a significant role in researching and publishing this report. "Steel Report Is Released: Sydney Plant Will Remain Basic Producer," *Cape Breton Post*, 3 October 1967.

5 Dosco Meeting Minutes, 13 October 1967, Premier's Correspondence, Volume 39, File 11, Office of the Premier Fonds, RG 100, Nova Scotia Archives and Records Management (NSARM), Halifax, NS.

6 Emmert offers differing accounts of exactly when Premier Smith was informed of the decision to close the plant. In his testimony before the legislature, Emmert mentions that he informed the premier on 12 October. Later in the same session, he clarifies that he had only mentioned that the subject of conversation would be the Sydney steel mill. Nova Scotia, *Debates and Proceedings of the Nova Scotia House of Assembly*, 5 December 1967, 172–78.

7 "Closing of Dosco Stuns Cape Breton," *Brandon Sun*, 14 October 1967.

8 J.N. Kelley – Hawker Siddeley Canada Press Release, 13 October 1967, Premier's Correspondence, Volume 39, File 11, Office of the Premier Fonds, NSARM; The stated reason for announcing the decision on Friday evening was to avoid an impact on stock prices. In the words of Arthur Pattillo, senior council to Dosco: "[It was] so that there would be an opportunity for the week end, for people not to become hysterical and perhaps go into the market, and try to make money or upend things." Nova Scotia, *Debates and Proceedings of the Nova Scotia House of Assembly*, 5 December 1967, 150.

9 Nova Scotia, *Debates and Proceedings of the Nova Scotia House of Assembly*, 5 December 1967: 4.

10 The earliest reference to "Black Friday" that I have identified is in a *Cape Breton Post* article that uses the term as though it is already in common usage. See "Called Black Friday," *Cape Breton Post*, 17 October 1967.

11 Adrian Murphy, interview with author, 1 September 2014.

12 Fabian Smith, interview with author, 7 September 2014.

13 Mickey Campbell, interview with author, 1 September 2014.

14 Steven High, *Industrial Sunset: The Making of North America's Rust Belt: 1969–1984* (Toronto: University of Toronto Press, 2003), 53.

15 "Street Reaction," *Cape Breton Post*, 14 October 1967.

16 Staughton Lynd, *The Fight against Shutdowns: Youngstown's Steel Mill Closings* (San Pedro: Singlejack Books, 1982), 4.

17 Roy George, *The Life and Times of Industrial Estates Limited* (Halifax: Dalhousie University Institute of Public Affairs, 1974), 7.

18 Peter Clancy, "Concerted Action on the Periphery? Voluntary Economic Planning in 'The New Nova Scotia,'" *Acadiensis* 26, 2 (Spring 1997): 8.

19 Clancy, "Concerted Action on the Periphery?," 9.

20 Ed Haliburton, *My Years with Stanfield* (Windsor, NS: Lancelot Press, 1972), 93.

21 Andrew Thiesen, "G.I. Smith and Economic Development in Nova Scotia" (Master's thesis, Saint Mary's University, 1995), 100–1.

22 Anastakis, "Building a New Nova Scotia," 8.

23 James P. Bickerton, *Nova Scotia, Ottawa, and the Politics of Regional Development* (Toronto: University of Toronto Press, 1990), 171.

24 When the election was over, the PC party took forty of the forty-six available seats in Nova Scotia. The Liberals sat in the legislature with a mere six seats, while the NDP were unable to hold a single seat. Richard Clippingdale, *Robert Stanfield's Canada: Perspectives of the Best Prime Minister We Never Had* (Kingston, ON: Queen's University School of Policy Studies, 2008); Geoffrey Stevens, *Stanfield* (Toronto: McClelland and Stewart, 1973), 138.

25 P.E. Bryden, *A Justifiable Obsession: Conservative Ontario's Relationship with Ottawa* (Toronto: University of Toronto Press, 2013), 153; for a fuller discussion of Stanfield's campaign for national leadership, see Stevens, *Stanfield*, 172–80.

26 "Premier Smith Irked: 'An Incredible Change of Attitude,'" *Cape Breton Post*, 14 October 1967.

27 G.I. Smith, handwritten note, Premier's Correspondence, Volume 39, File 10, Office of the Premier Fonds, NSARM.

28 "Plant Nationalization Possibility – MacEachen; Says Cape Breton Development Corporation Has Wide Powers," *Cape Breton Post*, 17 October 1967.

29 J.R. Donald, *The Cape Breton Coal Problem* (Ottawa: Queen's Printer, 1966), 52.

30 Donald, *The Cape Breton Coal Problem*, 34–5.

31 Bickerton, *Nova Scotia, Ottawa, and the Politics of Regional Underdevelopment*, 200.

32 Allan Tupper, "Public Enterprise as Social Welfare: The Case of the Cape Breton Development Corporation," *Canadian Public Policy/Analyse de Politiques* 4, 4 (Autumn 1978): 530–46.

33 Lester Pearson to G.I. Smith, 8 November 1967, Premier's Correspondence, Volume 39, File 3, Office of the Premier Fonds, NSARM.

34 "Provincial Government Acts in the Sydney Steel Crisis; Offers to 'Buy Time,'" *Cape Breton Post*, 17 October 1967.

35 Memorandum, 19 October 1967, Michael V. Knight Correspondence, Volume 7, File 6, Office of Economic Development Fonds, RG 30, NSARM.

36 G.I. Smith to T.J. Emmert, draft letter, 24 October 1967, Premier's Correspondence, Volume 39, File 9, Office of the Premier Fonds, NSARM.

37 G.I. Smith to Touche, Ross, Bailey and Smart, 31 October 1967, Premier's Correspondence, Volume 39, File 9, Office of the Premier Fonds, NSARM.

38 "Auditors Work on Dosco Records," *Cape Breton Post*, 31 October 1967; "Premier Smith in Talks with Stelco, Algoma," *Cape Breton Post*, 7 November 1967.

39 Allan J. MacEachen, address to Atlantic Ports Day Dinner, 7 December 1967, Allan J. MacEachen papers, MG 9, 1, Beaton Institute Archives (BI), Sydney, NS.

40 "Provincial Government to Operate Steel Mill," *Cape Breton Post*, 16 November 1967.

41 Nova Scotia, *Debates and Proceedings of the Nova Scotia House of Assembly*, 1 December 1967, 56–61; "Steel Agreement Will Be Signed Today: Government Will Take Over on Jan. 1," *Cape Breton Post*, 22 November 1967.

42 Nova Scotia, *Debates and Proceedings of the Nova Scotia House of Assembly*, 1 December 1967, 63; See also Joan Bishop, "Sydney Steel: Public Ownership and the Welfare State, 1967–1975," in *The Island: New Perspectives on Cape Breton History, 1713–1990*, ed. Ken Donovan (Fredericton: Acadiensis Press, 1990), 169.

43 "Dosco, Sysco Talks Are Scheduled," *Cape Breton Post*, 1 January 1968.

44 Judith Stein, *Running Steel, Running America: Race, Economic Policy, and the Decline of Liberalism* (Chapel Hill, NC: UNC Press, 1998), 214.

45 Stein, *Running Steel*, 214.

46 Jefferson Cowie, *Capital Moves: RCA's Seventy Year Quest for Cheap Labour* (Ithaca, NY: Cornell University Press, 1999), 188.

47 Tim Strangleman, *Work Identity at the End of the Line: Privatization and Culture Change in the U.K. Rail Industry* (Basingstoke, UK: Palgrave MacMillan, 2004).

48 High, *Industrial Sunset*, 172–6.

49 Ibid., 191.

50 Dimitry Anastakis, *Autonomous State: The Struggle for a Canadian Car Industry from OPEC to Free Trade* (Toronto: University of Toronto Press, 2013), 353.

51 Andrew Perchard and Jim Phillips, "Transgressing the Moral Economy: Wheelerism and the Management of the Nationalised Coal Industry in Scotland," *Contemporary British History* 25, 3 (2011): 400.

52 E.P. Thompson, "The Moral Economy of the English Crowd in the Eighteenth Century," *Past and Present* 50 (February 1971): 79.

53 Various articles in the local newspaper the day after Black Friday used language indicative of a violation of the moral economy. The company was "farcical," accused one writer, while others called the decision "the biggest double-cross in Cape Breton history," a "terrible hoax," and a "cruel and callous decision." See *Cape Breton Post*, 14 October 1967.

54 Nova Scotia Information Service, press release, 3 October 1967, Dosco National Committee, n.d., 1957–1969, C-13107, United Steelworkers of America Fonds, MG28 i268, Library and Archives Canada (LAC), Ottawa, ON.

55 Nova Scotia, *Debates and Proceedings of the Nova Scotia House of Assembly*, 5 December 1967, 153.

56 "By Clergymen, Local Control Is Advocated," *Cape Breton Post*, 16 October 1967.

57 Andrew Hogan, *Teach-In: The Sydney Steel Crisis* (Halifax: King's University, 1967), 2–3.

58 "Students Demonstrate," *Cape Breton Post*, 18 October 1967; Andy Parnaby, "Growing Up Even More Uncertain: Children and Youth Confront Industrial Ruin in Sydney, Nova Scotia, 1967," in *The Deindustrialized World: Confronting Ruination in Post-Industrial Places*, ed. Steven High, Lachlan MacKinnon, and Andrew Perchard (Vancouver: University of British Columbia Press, 2017).

59 Helena to Lester Pearson, 5 November 1967, PMO Correspondence, 1965–1968, Volume 46, File 217.31, Lester B. Pearson Fonds, MG 26-N4, LAC.

60 Support was also offered by the Nova Scotia Teachers' Union, the Sydney Garage Workers' Union, the Cape Breton Real Estate Board, and the Canadian Brotherhood of Railway, Transport and General Workers. See "U.M.W. Backs Steelworkers," *Cape Breton Post*, 18 October 1967.

61 "Like a Nagging Pain, Wife Says," *Cape Breton Post*, 18 October 1967.

62 William Mahoney, 25 October 1967, Nova Scotia Correspondence and Reports, C-13112, USWA Fonds, LAC.

63 Nova Scotia, Debates and Proceedings of the Nova Scotia House of Assembly, 1 December 1967.

64 "Parade of Concern for Sydney Steel, A Conversation with Fr. William Roach about the 1967 March," *Cape Breton's Magazine* 58 (1991): 41.

65 "Parade of Concern Plans: Expect 20,000," *Cape Breton Post*, 15 November 1967.

66 "Parade of Concern for Sydney Steel," *Cape Breton's Magazine*, 51.

67 "Talks to Resume Today," *Cape Breton Post*, 20 November 1967.

68 "CBC Radio, "Parade of Concern," Audio-Visual holdings, T-0069, Side 1, 00:26:50, BI.

69 Ibid., 00:33:13.
70 CBC Radio, "Parade of Concern," Audio-Visual holdings, T-0069, Side 2, 00:01: 10, BI.
71 T.W. Acheson, "The National Policy and the Industrialization of the Maritimes, 1880–1910," *Acadiensis* 1, 2 (Spring 1972): 28.
72 "Parade of Concern Is Huge Success," *Cape Breton Post*, 20 November 1967.
73 No relation to author.
74 CJCB – Parade of Concern, 19 November 1967, MP3 audio file, Audio-Visual holdings, T-70, BI.
75 "Parade of Concern for Sydney Steel," *Cape Breton's Magazine*, 50.
76 Leon Colford, interview by Michael Earle, 18 September 1990, Steel Project, MG 14, 206, Box 6, File 12, transcript, BI.
77 Russell Cameron, interview by Michael Earle, 7 February 1990, Steel Project, Box 5, File 5, transcript, BI.
78 Alistair Thomson, *Anzac Memories: Living with the Legend* (2013 repr.; Oxford: Oxford University Press, 1994), 11–12.
79 Pamela Sugiman, "'Life Is Sweet': Vulnerability and Composure in the Wartime Narratives of Japanese Canadians," *Journal of Canadian Studies* 43, 1 (Winter 2009): 203.
80 Elizabeth Faue, "Community, Class, and Comparison in Labour History and Local History," *Labour History* 78 (May 2000): 156.
81 "J.N. A Disgruntled Cape Bretoner," 1 November 1967, Premier's Correspondence, Volume 39, File 8, Office of the Premier Fonds, NSARM.
82 Kathryn Marie Dudley, *The End of the Line: Lost Jobs, New Lives in Postindustrial America* (Chicago: University of Chicago Press, 1994), 26.
83 Lucy Taksa, "Like a Bicycle, Forever Teetering between Indvidualism and Collectivism: Considering Community in Relation to Labour History," *Labour History* 78 (May 2000): 10.
84 "Street Reaction," *Cape Breton Post*, 14 October 1967; "Unreasonable and Wrong," *Cape Breton Post*, 18 October 1967.
85 "Like a Nagging Pain, Wife Says," *Cape Breton Post*, 18 October 1967.
86 Doreen Massey, "Places and Their Pasts," *History Workshop Journal* 39 (1995): 188.
87 Joy Parr, *The Gender of Breadwinners: Women, Men, and Change in Two Industrial Towns, 1880–1950* (Toronto: University of Toronto Press, 1990), 8; For another Canadian discussion of changes in place-identity prompted by deindustrialization, see Steven High, "Placing the Displaced Worker: Narrating Place in Deindustrializing Sturgeon Falls, Ontario," in *Placing Memory and Remembering Place in Canada*, ed. James Opp and John C. Walsh (Vancouver and Toronto: University of British Columbia Press, 2010), 159–86.
88 Steven High, "Deindustrialization on the Industrial Frontier: The Rise and Fall of Mill Colonialism in Northern Ontario," in *The Deindustrialized*

World: Confronting Ruination in Post-Industrial Places, ed. Steven High, Lachlan MacKinnon, and Andrew Perchard (Vancouver: University of British Columbia Press, 2017).

89 William C. Wicken, *The Colonization of Mi'kmaw Memory and History, 1794–1928: The King v. Gabriel Syliboy* (Toronto: University of Toronto Press, 2012), 214.

90 Wicken, *The Colonization of Mi'kmaw Memory and History*, 226.

91 "We Were There," *Cape Breton Post*, 20 November 1967.

92 See Ian McKay, review of Steven High, *Industrial Sunset: The Making of North America's Rust Belt, 1969–1984*, H-Canada, H-Net Revews (April 2005), http://www.h-net.org/reviews/showrev.php?id=10458.

93 "Dosco, Sysco Talks Are Scheduled," *Cape Breton Post*, 1 January 1968.

4. Decades in Transition

1 Garfield Ross, interview by Michael Earle, 19 March 1990, Steel Project MG 14, 206, Box 6, File 70, transcript, Beaton Institute Archives (BI), Sydney, NS.

2 Voluntary Economic Planning Board, *Sydney Steelmaking Study* (Halifax: Queen's Printers, 1968).

3 Arthur McKee and Company of Canada, "Preliminary Review of Operations, Sydney Steel Corporation, Sydney, Nova Scotia," 1968, Box 21, B(i) k File 4, Dominion Steel and Coal Company Papers, MG 14, 26, BI.

4 Sydney Steel Corporation, "Notice: To All Department Heads," 19 August 1968, Box 117, File 13, Dosco Papers, BI.

5 Technical description of Sydney Steel Works, c. 1960, Box 32, File 12, Dosco Papers, BI.

6 Clarence Butler, interview by Michael Earle, 13 February 1990, Steel Project, Box 6, File 2, transcript, BI.

7 John Campbell, interview with author, 6 September 2014.

8 Elizabeth Beaton, "Slag Houses in a Steel City," *Material Culture Review* 44 (Fall 1996): 64–78.

9 The No. 1 blast furnace had a hearth diameter of 20′6″, while the No. 3 furnace is listed as 21′6 ″. See Technical description of Sydney Steel Works, BI.

10 R.B. Cameron, organizational charts, 1969, Box 114, File 1, Dosco Papers, BI.

11 Adrian Murphy, interview with author, 1 September 2014.

12 Introducing Sydney Steel Corporation to the Engineering Student (1968) and Sydney Railroad Rails, (1968), Box 32, Dosco Papers, BI.

13 Voluntary Economic Planning Board, *Sydney Steelmaking Study* (Halifax: Queen's Printers, 1968); John Campbell, interview with author, 6 September 2014.

14 Mickey Campbell and Adrian Murphy, interview with author, 1 September 2014.

15　Ibid.

16　R.B. Cameron, organizational charts, 1969; Sydney Steel Corporation, "Steelmaking at Sydney," 1968, Box 32, File 12, Dosco Papers, BI.

17　Voluntary Economic Planning Board, *Sydney Steelmaking Study* (Halifax: Queen's Printers, 1968).

18　Owen Bonnell, interview by Michael Earle, 28 March 1990, Steel Project, Box 5, File 2, transcript, BI.

19　R.B. Cameron, organizational charts, 1969.

20　David Ervin, interview with author, 8 August 2013.

21　John Campbell, interview with author, 6 September 2014.

22　Sysco Submission to the Parliamentary Committee on Regional Transportation, 1967: 2, Box 86, File 2, Dosco Papers, BI.

23　R.B. Cameron, "Speech to the Empire Club of Canada," *The Empire Club of Canada Addresses* (Toronto: 1970), 423–32.

24　Fabian Smith, interview with author, 7 September 2014.

25　"Work is Resumed at Steel Plant," *Cape Breton Post*, 12 March 1969.

26　Ibid.

27　Joan Bishop, "Sydney Steel: Public Ownership and the Welfare State, 1967–1975," in *The Island: New Perspectives on Cape Breton history 1713–1990*, ed. Kenneth Donovan (Fredericton and Sydney: Acadiensis Press and UCCB Press, 1990), 171.

28　"Plant's Nail Mill to Close Oct. 31," *Cape Breton Post*, 12 August 1969.

29　Bishop, "Sydney Steel," 171.

30　"Wire, Nail Mill Will Close Today," *Cape Breton Post*, 31 October 1969.

31　"Wildcat Strike Hits Steel Plant," *Cape Breton Post*, 30 October 1969.

32　"Wildcat Strike: Furnaces to Be Banked?" *Cape Breton Post*, 31 October 1969.

33　"Between the Lines: Brinkmanship," *Cape Breton Post*, 1 November 1969.

34　Bob Russell, *More with Less: Reorganization in the Canadian Mining Industry* (Toronto: University of Toronto Press, 1999), 14.

35　Eric Tucker, "Should Wagnerism Have No Dominion?" *Just Labour: A Canadian Journal of Work and Society* 21 (Spring 2014): 3–4.

36　"Co-operative Wage Study Manual for Job Description, Classification and Wage Administration," 6 May 1957, Box 133, File 15, Dosco Papers, BI.

37　Robert Storey, "The Struggle for Job Ownership in the Canadian Steel Industry: An Historical Analysis," *Labour/Le Travail* 33 (Spring 1994): 86.

38　See Craig Heron and Robert Storey, "On the Job in Canada," in *On the Job: Confronting the Labour Process in Canada*, ed. Craig Heron and Robert Storey (Montreal and Kingston: McGill-Queen's University Press, 1986), 19.

39　John Kirk and Christine Wall, *Work and Identity: Historical and Cultural Contexts* (London: Palgrave-Macmillan, 2011), 7.

40　Braverman, *Labor and Monopoly Capital*, 443.

41 Craig Heron, *Working in Steel: The Early Years in Canada, 1883–1935* (Toronto: McClelland and Stewart, 1988), 54.

42 Ibid., 56–7.

43 Charles Anderson, interview by Michael Earle, 18 May 1990, Steel Project, Box 5, File 1, transcript, BI.

44 Adrian Murphy, interview with author, 1 September 2014.

45 Stephen Ackroyd and Paul Thompson, *Organizational Misbehaviour* (London: Sage, 1999), 49.

46 "Modernization Planned in Two Phases; No Major Government Aid," *Cape Breton Post*, 20 February 1970.

47 D.W.R. Haysom to the General Manager, V.O.E.S.T. Linz Austria, 11 October 1968, Box 114, File 1, Dosco Papers, BI; see also Federal Government Involvement with Sysco, 1978, Cape Breton Island – Sydney Steel Corporation, Vol. 5370, File 4052-03-05 pt. 3, Department of Finance Fonds, RG 19, Library and Archives Canada (LAC), Ottawa, ON.

48 Bishop, "Sydney Steel," 176.

49 Ibid. 176–7.

50 A federal loan guarantee authority of $70 million was put into place in 1973 when the Coke Ovens Department was transferred back into the control of Sysco from Devco. See Robillard Report on Sydney Steel, 1977, Cape Breton Island – Sydney Steel Corporation, Department of Finance Fonds, LAC.

51 Sysco adjustment program, 1978, Cape Breton Island – Sydney Steel Corporation, Department of Finance Fonds, LAC.

52 R.P. Nicholson, Sysco Operations, 1973, Box 32, Dosco Papers, MG 14, 26, BI.

53 Derek Haysom and William Wells, inventors, "Method of Operating an Open Hearth Furnace," Sydney, Nova Scotia, Canada, Assignee: Sydney Steel Corporation, Filed: Oct. 30, 1972, App. No.: 301,809, http://www.google.ca/patents/US3859078.

54 Bishop, "Sydney Steel," 180.

55 Harry Collins, interview by Michael Earle, 5 February 1990, Steel Project, Box 5, File 8, transcript, BI.

56 "Bar Mill to Close This Summer: Low Productivity Chief Reason," *Cape Breton Post*, 13 June 1972.

57 "Disappointing Decision," *Cape Breton Post*, 14 July 1972; "Steelworkers' Stage Walkout: Protest Plan to Close Bar Mill," *Cape Breton Post*, 15 July 1972. The number of plant employees does not include those working at the coke ovens, which was still under Devco control at the time of the walkout. Winston Ruck was elected as Union president in the summer of 1970.

58 "Resume Full Production at Steel Plant Today," *Cape Breton Post*, 19 June 1972.

59 Ron Crawley, "Conflict within the Union: Struggles among Sydney Steel Workers, 1936–1972" (PhD dissertation, Carleton University, 1995), 328.

60 "Union Blames Government for Three-Week Old Strike," *Cape Breton Post*, 10 October 1972.

61 "Sydney Residents to March Today as They Did in 1967," *Cape Breton Post*, 13 October 1972.

62 "Steelworkers Approve Contract; Men Ready Plant for Production," *Cape Breton Post*, 23 October 1972; Crawley, "Conflict within the Union," 329.

63 Economic Development Division, *CANSTEL*, EDD – Regional Development, Atlantic Canstel Study, Volume 6190, File 1, July 1974, Department of Finance Fonds, LAC.

64 Steel Company of Canada, *CANSTEL Preliminary Report*, 1974, Bras d'Or Collection, 1251, Cape Breton University Library, Sydney, NS; Steel Company of Canada, *Canstel Project: Site Selection Report*, April 1974, Bras d'Or Collection, 2805, Cape Breton University Library.

65 Cansteel Corporation, Annual Report, 31 March 1976, Bras d'Or Collection, 2067, Cape Breton University Library.

66 Analysis of closure options 'A,' 'B,' and 'C' 1976, Sydney Steel Corporation Records, Box 1992-229-002, Files 18–20, Office of Economic Development Fonds, Nova Scotia Archives and Records Management (NSARM), Halifax, NS.

67 Robillard Report on Sydney Steel, 1977, Cape Breton Island – Sydney Steel Corporation, Department of Finance Fonds, LAC.

68 'New Life at Sydney Steel," *Ottawa Journal*, 23 August 1977.

69 DREE Briefing File, "Sydney Steel Corporation Post-Private Sector Era," August 1978, Cape Breton Island – Sydney Steel Corporation, Department of Finance Fonds, LAC.

70 "Kent Sees Increased Sales in Coming Year," *Chronicle Herald*, 30 December 1977; Nova Scotia Department of Development, "Problems Related to the Sydney Steel Corporation," 11 September 1979, Sysco Records, Box 1992-229-003, File 48, Office of Economic Development Fonds, NSARM.

71 Department of Development, "Problems Related to Sydney Steel," 6.

72 Storey, "The Struggle for Job Ownership in the Canadian Steel Industry," 91.

73 Trevor Bain, *Banking the Furnace: Restructuring of the Steel Indutry in Eight Countries* (Kalamazoo, MI: Upjohn Press, 1992), 2.

74 "Sysco Production Up; Losses Cut," *Cape Breton Post*, 21 December 1979.

75 "Buchanan Says Sysco Layoffs Unfortunate, Regrettable; Sydney Mayor Seeks Answers," *Cape Breton Post*, 26 July 1980; "Layoffs Discouraging – Ruck," *Cape Breton Post*, 26 July 1980.

76 "A Heavy Blow," *Cape Breton Post*, 28 July 1980.

77 Charles MacDonald, Letter to the Editor, *Cape Breton Post*, 5 August 1980.

78 "Steelworkers Union Given Support at Emotional Two-Hour Rally," *Cape Breton* Post, 20 August 1980.

79 "Workers Agree Sysco Has Problems But 'She Won't Close,'" *Cape Breton Post*, 23 August 1980.

80 "Appointments to Top Sysco Posts Announced by Premier," *Cape Breton Post*, 3 September 1980.

81 "Sysco Chairman Welcomes Signing of Agreement; 'Now We Can Start with Plant's Modernization," *Cape Breton Post*, 3 June 1981.

82 Sysco, DREE, N.S. Department of Development, confidential – proposed Sysco business plan," 6 October 1980, Sysco Records, Box 1992-229-003, File 49, Office of Economic Development Fonds, NSARM.

83 David Harvey, *The Condition of Postmodernity: An Enquiry into the Origins of Cultural Change* (Oxford: Basil Blackwell, 1989), 147.

84 Stevenson and Kellogg, "Sysco Management Information Systems Analysis Study," 27 April 1979, Sysco Records, Box 1992-229-001, File 1, Office of Economic Development Fonds, NSARM.

85 Storey, "The Struggle for Job Ownership in the Canadian Steel Industry," 93.

86 "Strike Starts; Sysco on Shaky Ground," *Cape Breton Post*, 28 April 1982.

87 "Union President Says Steelworkers Can't Give Anymore in Wage Demands," *Cape Breton Post*, 28 April 1982.

88 "1,270 Union Layoffs Effective Sunday," *Cape Breton Post*, 8 May 1982.

89 "1,402 Plant Workers Register for UIC Benefits on Tuesday," *Cape Breton Post*, 10 May 1982.

90 Allen J. MacEachen to Otto Lang, 23 November 1977, Department of Transport Minister's Correspondence, Volume 3907, File 2-11-41, Department of Transport Fonds, RG 12, LAC.

91 "CN Rail Order 'Great News' Says MacLellan," *Cape Breton Post*, 12 June 1982.

92 "Operations to Resume over Next Two Weeks," *Cape Breton Post*, 3 August 1982; "Grezel Returns to Plant Work," *Cape Breton Post*, 4 August 1982.

93 "Plant Close Down Plan Scrapped; Rail Order Obtained by Premier," *Cape Breton Post*, 12 February 1983.

94 "Sysco Shaves Operating Losses despite Depressed Steel Markets," *Cape Breton Post*, 21 May 1983.

95 "Phasedown at Sysco Set For Late July," *Cape Breton Post*, 21 May 1983. Summer phase-downs became a regular occurrence over the next years at Sysco.

96 "Sysco's Decision to Suspend Coke-Making under Heavy Fire," *Cape Breton Post*, 18 August 1983; "Coke Ovens Will Re-Open: Premier," 6 November 1985.

97 A gas-cleaning plant was also added to the site in 1984.

98 Sydney Steel Corporation, "A Description of the Facilities and Operations of Sydney Steel Corporation," November 1985, Box 32, File 7, Dosco Papers, BI.

99 "Sysco, Tar Pond Projects Announced," *Cape Breton Post*, 28 December 1985.

100 "Sysco President Optimistic, Union Boss Relieved with Plant Modernization Plan," *Cape Breton Post*, 28 December 1985.

101 "MacLean Has Mixed Feelings over SYSCO Modernization Plan," *Cape Breton Post*, 31 December 1985; Hatch Associates, "Sysco Phase II Study," 1983, Sysco Records, Box 1992-244-002, File 106, Office of Economic Development Fonds, NSARM; Philip Peapell to James D. McNiven, 20 October 1983, Sysco Records, Box 1991-244-002, File 107, NSARM.

102 Adrian Murphy, interview with author, 1 September 2014.

103 "Electric Arc Furnace," *Cape Breton Post*, 6 January 1986.

104 "Greg Kerr Slammed over Sysco Comment," *Cape Breton Post*, 4 October 1986.

105 Manning MacDonald, interview with author, 27 July 2015; "Sysco's Survival 'Essential' Says Mayor," *Cape Breton* Post, 19 November 1986.

106 Tippins Inc., Sysco modernization plans, 15 September 1987, Box 159, File (i) v 1, Dosco Papers, BI.

107 Fumio Tomizawa and Edward C. Howard, "Arc Furnace Productivity in the 1980's," *Iron and Steel Engineer* 62, 5 (May 1985): 34–37.

108 Dravo Automation Sciences Inc., "Tippins Incorporated – Automation System for Sydney Steel," February 1988, Box 159, E1.iv.b.) File 1, Dosco Papers, BI.

109 "Steelworkers Strike," *Cape Breton Post*, February 1, 1988.

110 Collective agreements between Sysco and USWA Local 1064: 1974–76, 1976–78, 1979–81, 1981–83, Box 120, Files 14–18, Dosco Papers, BI.

111 "Management Needs Union Help in Maintaining Coke Battery," *Cape Breton Post*, 3 February 1988.

112 "Heavy Voter Turnout Wants Back to Work," *Cape Breton Post*, 17 March 1988.

113 Don Macpherson, interview by Michael Earle, 20 June 1990.

114 Cameron took over from interim premier Roger Bacon in February 1991, after Buchanan left for a position in the Canadian senate.

115 "Black Friday Again at Sysco," *Cape Breton Post*, 1 January 1989.

116 George Hess, "Getting Sydney Steel Back on Track," *Iron Age* (December 1991): 16.

117 Donald Cameron, "The Privatization of Sydney Steel," 24 January 1992, Progressive Conservative Party Records, John Leefe Papers, MG 2, 1701, NSARM.

118 Final Report: Skills Adjustment Study Sydney Steel, Submitted to Labour Canada Technology Impact Program, 30 September 1991, Box 3, File 1, Steel Project, BI.

119 Final Report: Skills Adjustment Study, Steel Project, BI.

120 Michael Redmond, "Casting Its Future," *Atlantic Business* (May/June 1989), 8.

121 Barry Sonmor, "Publisher's Statement: Steel!" *Trade: Cape Breton's Business Magazine* (December 1989), 2.

122 "Sysco Gearing Up for Full Production," *Cape Breton Post*, 10 January 1990.

123 Dave Ervin, interview with author, 8 August 2013.

124 Final Report: Skills Adjustment Study, Steel Project, BI.

125 John Murphy, interview with author, September 2015.

126 Bennett Harrison, *Lean and Mean: Why Large Corporations Continue to Dominate the Global Economy* (New York: Guilford Press, 1997), 258–9.

127 Yuko Aoyama and Manuel Castells, "An Empirical Assessment of the Informational Society: Employment and Occupational Structures of G-7 Countries, 1920–2000," *International Labour Review* 141, 1–2 (Spring 2000): 123–59.

128 Leslie MacCuish, interview by Michael Earle, 6 April 1990, Steel Project, Box 6, File 38, transcript, BI.

129 John Murphy, interview by Michael Earle, 10 January 1990, Steel Project, Box 7, File 57, transcript, BI.

130 Barry Brocklehurst, interview by Diane Chisholm, 5 November 1990, Steel Project, Box 6, File 2, transcript, BI.

131 Duncan Gallie, "Skills, Job Control, and the Quality of Work: The Evidence from Britain," *The Economic and Social Review* 43, 3 (Autumn 2012): 334.

132 Tommy McCarron and Gerry McCarron, interview with author, 7 August 2013.

5. Labour Environmentalism

1 Don MacPherson, "What Will It Take to Shake Complacency over Plight of Former Coke Workers?" *Chronicle Herald*, 29 April 1989.

2 Joe Legge, interview with author, 1 September 2014.

3 "*Making Steel*," directed by Elizabeth Beaton (Sydney, NS: Beaton Institute Archives and the National Film Board of Canada, 1992), DVD; "*Heart of Steel*," directed by Peter Giffen (Sydney, NS: Public Works and Government Services Canada, 2012), DVD.

4 Maude Barlow and Elizabeth May, *Frederick Street: Life and Death on Canada's Love Canal* (Toronto: Harper Collins, 2000); Lorraine Deveaux,

interview with author, 9 December 2014; Tommy and Gerry McCarron, interview with author, 7 August 2013.

5 M. Katz and R.D. McKay, *Report on Dustfall Studies at Sydney, N.S.: Analysis and Distribution of Dustfall in the Sydney Area during the Period February 1958 through September 1959* (Ottawa: Department of National Health and Welfare Canada, 1959); M. Katz, H.P. Sanderson, and R.D. McKay, *Evaluation of Air Pollution Levels in Relation to Steel Manufacturing and Coal Combustion in Sydney, Nova Scotia* (Ottawa: Department of National Health and Welfare Canada, 1965).

6 E.J. Kilotat and H.J. Wilson, *An Evaluation of Air Pollution Levels in Sydney, Nova Scotia* (Ottawa: Department of National Health Directorate, Air Pollution Control Division, 1970).

7 J. William Lloyd, Frank E. Lundin, Jr, Carol K. Redmond, and Patricia B. Geiser, "Long Term Mortality Study of Steelworkers: IV Mortality by Work Area," *Journal of Occupational Medicine* 12, 5 (1970): 157.

8 G.M. Davies, "A Mortality Study of Coke Oven Workers in two South Wales Integrated Steelworks," *British Journal of Industrial Medicine* 34 (1977): 291–7; J.P. Bertrand et al., "Mortality Due to Respiratory Cancers in the Coke Oven Plants of the Lorraine Coalmining Industry (Houlliérs du Bassin du Lorraine)," *British Journal of Industrial Medicine* 44, 8 (1987): 559–65.

9 Robert Storey, "Social Assistance or a Worker's Right? Workmen's Compensation and the Struggle of Injured Workers in Ontario, 1970–1985," *Studies in Political Economy* 78 (2006): 67–91.

10 Laurel Sefton MacDowell, "The Elliot Lake Uranium Miners' Battle to Gain Occupational Health and Safety Improvements, 1950–1980," *Labour/Le Travail* 69 (Spring 2012): 91–118.

11 Robert Storey, "From the Environment to the Workplace ... And Back Again? Occupational Health and Safety Activism in Ontario, 1970s–2000," *Canadian Review of Sociology/Revue canadienne de sociologie* 41, 4 (2004): 425.

12 "Star Profile, Dan Hannan, Cokeworker," *Philadelphia Star*, 8 September 1977.

13 Dan Hannan, testimony to the Advisory Standards Committee, OSHA, 4 March 1975, Safety and Health Department Records, HCLA 1966, Box 23, United Steelworkers of America Fonds, Eberly Family Special Collections Library, Pennsylvania State University (PSU), State College, PA.

14 David McCaffrey, *OSHA and the Politics of Health Regulation* (New York: Plenum Press, 1982), 90.

15 John A. Lennie, request, 24 August 1976, District 6 correspondence – coke ovens, Box 17, Health and Safety Department Records, USWA Fonds, Eberly Family Special Collections Library, PSU.

16 WCB Ontario, Summary of information, Claim #D10349210, 25 May 1976, District 6 correspondence, Health and Safety Department Records, USWA Fonds, Eberly Family Special Collections Library, PSU.

17 Response to John Lennie, June 1976, District 6 correspondence – coke ovens, Box 17, Health and Safety Department Records, USWA Fonds, Eberly Family Special Collections Library, PSU.

18 "The Killer Coke Ovens," *Spectator*, 15 January 1977; "Coke Oven Death Alarm Ignored," *Spectator*, 15 January 1977.

19 "Coke Ovens and Cancer," *Cape Breton Post*, 5 August 1976.

20 *Report of the Sydney Respiratory Health Survey* (Ottawa: Minister of National Health and Welfare, 1977), 50–1.

21 Dave MacLeod, 26 February 1979, Box 3, Files 7–8, Steel Project, MG, 206, Beaton Institute Archives (BI), Sydney, NS.

22 Dan Yakimchuk, interview by Michael Earle, 20 April 1990, Steel Project, Box 5, File 7, transcript, BI.

23 Lawrence P. Hildebrand, *Environmental Quality in Sydney and Northeast Industrial Cape Breton, Nova Scotia* (Ottawa: Environment Canada, 1982).

24 This report also notes that the Sydney coke ovens were producing at only 50 per cent of total capability during the period of study, and so actual levels of PAH production were likely even higher than those reported. L. Atwell et al., *Ambient Air Polynuclear Aromatic Hydrocarbons Study, Sydney, Nova Scotia* (Ottawa: Environment Canada, 1984).

25 J.R. Hickman, *Health Hazards due to Coke Emissions* (Ottawa: Health and Welfare Canada, 30 August 1985).

26 Supreme Court of Nova Scotia, "Notice of Defense, Hfx. No. 218010" (20 March 2013).

27 "More Study Needed: Industry Links to Cancer Rates Not Established, Says Lavigne," *Cape Breton Post*, 22 May 1985.

28 "Sysco Ignoring Studies; Will Reopen Coke Oven," *Cape Breton Post*, 4 November 1985.

29 "Lack of Evidence Cited in Support of Coke Restart," *Cape Breton Post*, 6 November 1985.

30 Fred James, interview with author, 16 August 2013.

31 Charles MacDonald, interview with author, 3 March 2015; David Ervin, interview with author, 8 August 2013; Fabian Smith, interview with author, 7 September 2014.

32 Dan Yakimchuk, interview by Michael Earle, 20 April 1990.

33 Charles MacDonald, interview with author, 3 March 2014.

34 Don MacPherson, interview by Michael Earle, January 1990, Steel Project, T-2590, transcript, BI.

35 Steven High, Placing the Displaced Worker: Narrating Place in Deindustrializing Sturgeon Falls, Ontario," in *Placing Memory and Remembering Place in Canada*, ed. James Opp and John C. Walsh (Vancouver: University of British Columbia Press, 2010), 173.

36 Arthur McIvor, "Deindustrialization Embodied: Work, Health and Disability in the U.K. since c. 1950," in *The Deindustrialized World: Confronting Ruination*

in Post-Industrial Places, ed. Steven High, Lachlan MacKinnon, and Andrew Perchard (Vancouver: University of British Columbia Press, 2017).

37 David Harvey, "The Body as Accumulation Strategy," *Environment and Planning D: Society and Space* 16, 4 (August 1998): 401–21.

38 Robert Storey, "Pessimism of the Intellect, Optimism of the Will: Engaging with the 'Testimony' of Injured Workers," in *Beyond Testimony and Trauma: Oral History in the Aftermath of Mass Violence*, ed. Steven High (Vancouver: University of British Columbia Press, 2015), 57.

39 Blair Lewis, interview by Diane Chisholm, 6 March 1990, Steel Project, Box 5, File 33, transcript, BI; Joe Keller, interview by Michael Earle, 16 May 1990, Steel Project, Box 5, File 29, transcript, BI; William Ferguson, interview by Michael Earle, 22 February 1990, Steel Project, Box 5, File 18, transcript, BI.

40 Joe Legge, interview with author, 1 September 2014.

41 "Sysco, Tar Pond Projects Announced," *Cape Breton Post*, 28 December 1985; "Sysco President Optimistic, Union Boss Relieved with Plant Modernization Plan," *Cape Breton Post*, 28 December 1985; "MacLean Has Mixed Feelings over SYSCO Modernization Plan," *Cape Breton Post*, 31 December 1985.

42 "Tar Pond Clean Up to Begin Immediately," *Cape Breton Post*, 2 July 1986.

43 "Early Retirement Program Urged for Sysco Workers," *Cape Breton Post*, 27 September 1986

44 "Workers Assured of Tar Ponds Jobs and Universal Mill," *Cape Breton Post*, 26 July 1986.

45 "Covering Up Death at Sysco," *Canadian Tribune*, 1 May 1989; Don MacPherson, interview by Michael Earle, 20 June 1990, Steel Project, Box 5, File 43, transcript, BI.

46 The department had operated under the federal government's Cape Breton Development Corporation (Devco) between the years 1968 and 1974, and employees working in the department at this time were not going to receive Sysco seniority for these years. R.B. Cameron to Gerald Blackmore, 23 February 1968, Box 117, File 13, Dominion Steel and Coal Company Papers, BI; For the terms of this arrangement, see Robillard Report on Sydney Steel, 1977, Cape Breton Island – Sydney Steel Corporation, Volume 5370, File 4052-03-05 pt. 3, Department of Finance Fonds, RG 19, Library and Archives Canada (LAC), Ottawa, ON.

47 Don MacPherson, interview by Michael Earle, 20 June 1990; "Public Campaign, Private Grief: Steelworkers' Battle for Coke Ovens Workers," *Steelabour* 53, 2 (1990): 22–3.

48 Arthur McIvor, "Economic Violence, Occupational Disability, and Death: Oral Narratives of the Impact of Asbestos-Related Diseases in Britain," in *Beyond Testimony and Trauma: Oral History in the Aftermath of Mass Violence*,

ed. Steven High (Vancouver: University of British Columbia Press, 2015), e-book.

49 W.J. Penney to Workers Compensation Board of Nova Scotia, 14 November 1986, Box 3, Files 7–8, Steel Project, BI.

50 R.J. Allen, to Paul McEwan, 10 November 1987, Box 3, Files 7–8, Steel Project, BI.

51 David Dingwall to Ernie Boutilier, 7 December 1987, Box 3, Files 7–8, Steel Project, BI.

52 Ernie Boutilier to Dave Dingwall, 23 December 1987, Box 3, Files 7–8, Steel Project, BI.

53 Charles MacDonald, interview with author, 3 March 2015.

54 Memorandum, John O'Brien, Workers' Compensation Board of Nova Scotia, 21 April 1988, Box 3, Files 7–8, Steel Project, BI.

55 Harvey MacLeod to William MacNeil, 14 June 1990, Box 3, Files 7–8, Steel Project, BI; Don MacPherson, interview by Michael Earle, 20 June 1990; Charles MacDonald, interview with author, 3 March 2015.

56 Occupation, Health and Safety Committee, Local 1064, "Coke Ovens Workers and Retired Employees Who Have Died during the Past 25 Years," 16 September 1988, Box 3, Files 7–8, Steel Project, BI.

57 Don MacPherson to Tom MacMillan, 3 October 1988, Box 3, Files 7–8 Steel Project, BI.

58 Ed Broadbent to Don MacPherson, 14 February 1989; Alexa McDonough to Don MacPherson, 8 July 1988. Jake Epp to Don MacPherson, 17 January 1989, Box 3, Files 7–8, Steel Project, BI.

59 "Workers March on House," *Chronicle Herald*, 17 March 1989.

60 "Covering Up Death at Sysco," *Canadian Tribune*, 1 May 1989.

61 Don MacPherson to Marion Ferguson, 17 July 1989, Box 3, Files 7–8, Steel Project, BI.

62 "Minister Is Committed to 'Fair' Compensation System," *Cape Breton Post*, 20 July 1989.

63 "Widows' Benefits 'Good Omen' for Coke Ovens Workers," *Cape Breton Post*, 18 November 1989.

64 "Sysco Widows Compensated," *Chronicle Herald*, 2 January 1990.

65 "Sysco Widows' Compensation Not Precedent – Board Official," *Chronicle Herald*, 3 January 1990.

66 "Sysco Log Jam No Longer Stopping WCB," *Cape Breton Post*, 15 March 1990.

67 "Sysco's Ovens Workers Get Second Chance," *Cape Breton Post*, 11 April 1990.

68 "Coke Ovens Crusader Hails Province's Stand," *Cape Breton Post*, 11 April 1990.

69 Joe Keller, interview by Michael Earle, 16 May 1990.

70 Nancy Robb, "Were Jobs More Important Than Health in Sydney?" *Canadian Medical Association Journal* 152, 6 (15 March 1995): 919–23.

71 Arthur McIvor, *Working Lives: Work in Britain Since 1945* (London: Palgrave MacMillan, 2013), 166.

72 Chad Montrie, *A People's History of Environmentalism in the United States* (New York: Continuum, 2011).

73 Andrew Hurley, *Environmental Inequalities: Class, Race, and Industrial Pollution in Gary, Indiana* (Chapel Hill: University of North Carolina Press, 1995).

74 Robert D. Bullard, "Environmental Justice in the Twenty-First Century," in *The Quest for Environmental Justice: Human Rights and the Politics of Pollution*, ed. Robert D. Bullard (San Francisco: Sierra Club Books, 2005), 19–42.

75 Olga Pomar, "Toxic Racism on the New Jersey Waterfront," in *The Quest for Environmental Justice: Human Rights and the Politics of Pollution*, ed. Robert D. Bullard (San Francisco: Sierra Club Books, 2005), 125–41; Dorceta E. Taylor, *Toxic Communities: Environmental Racism, Industrial Pollution, and Residential Mobility* (New York: New York University Press, 2014).

76 Joan Martinez-Alier, *The Environmentalism of the Poor: A Study of Ecological Conflicts and Valuation* (Northampton, MA: Edward Elgar Publishing, 2002).

77 Isabelle Anguelovski and Joan Martinez-Alier, "The 'Environmentalism of the Poor' Revisited: Territory and Place in Disconnected Global Struggles," *Ecological Economics* 102 (June 2014): 167–76.

78 Deborah McGregor, "Honouring Our Relations: An Anishnaabe Perspective on Environmental Justice"; Bonita Lawrence, "Reclaiming Ktaqamkuk: Land and Mi'kmaq Identity in Newfoundland"; Pat O'Reilly and Peter Cole, "Coyote and Raven Talk about Environmental Justice," in *Speaking for Ourselves: Environmental Justice in Canada*, ed. Julian Agyeman, Peter Cole, Randolph Haluza-DeLay, and Pat O'Reilly (Vancouver: University of British Columbia Press, 2009).

79 S. Harris Ali, "The Political Economy of Environmental Inequality: The Social Distribution of Risk as an Environmental Injustice," in *Speaking for Ourselves: Environmental Justice in Canada*, ed. Julian Agyeman, Peter Cole, Randolph Haluza-DeLay, and Pat O'Reilly (Vancouver: University of British Columbia Press, 2009), 104.

6. Bury It, Burn It, Truck It Away

1 Photo in Maude Barlow and Elizabeth May, *Frederick Street: Life and Death on Canada's Love Canal* (Toronto: Harper Collins, 2000), 132–3.

2 "Pier Residents Expect Goo Results Today," *Cape Breton Post*, 7 May 1999.

3 "Families Forced from Homes," *Cape Breton Post*, 14 May 1999.

4 "Province Moves Three More Families out of Pier Homes," *Cape Breton Post*, 15 May 1999; Thomas H. Fletcher, *From Love Canal to Environmental Justice: The Politics of Hazardous Waste on the Canada-U.S. Border* (Peterborough, ON: Broadview Press, 2003), 16.

5 Katrin MacPhee, "Canadian Working-Class Environmentalism, 1965–1985," *Labour/Le Travail* 74 (Fall 2014): 129.

6 Barlow and May, *Frederick Street*, 18–9.

7 Debbie Ouellette, email message to author, 21 June 2016.

8 G.R. Sirota, J.F. Uthe, D.G. Robinson, and C.J. Musial, "Polycyclic Aromatic Hydrocarbons in American Lobster (Homarus americanus) and Blue Mussels (Mytilus edulis) Collected in Sydney Harbour, Sydney, Nova Scotia, Canada," *Canadian Manuscript Report of Fisheries and Aquatic Sciences* 1758 (1984).

9 J.H. Vandermeulen, "PAH and Heavy Metal Pollution of the Sydney Estuary: Summary and Review of Studies to 1987," *Canadian Technical Report of Hydrography and Ocean Sciences* 108 (May 1989): 1.

10 Acres Consulting Services Limited, *Sydney Tar Pond Remediation: Phase I Report: Final*, 4 May 1984, Bras d'Or Collection, 6283, Cape Breton University Library, Sydney, NS.

11 Acres Consulting Services Limited, *Sydney Tar Pond Study: Final Project Report, Volume I*, June 1985, Bras d'Or Collection, 5709, Cape Breton University Library.

12 "Sysco, Tar Ponds Projects Announced," *Cape Breton* Post, 28 December 1985.

13 "Agreement Signed to Eliminate Region's Worst Toxic Waste Site," *Cape Breton Post*, 8 November 1986.

14 Ian C. Travers, "Sydney Tar Ponds: A Case Study," presented to Hazmat Canada Conference, Toronto, Ontario, 9–11 September 1987, Bras d'Or Collection, 6292, Cape Breton University Library.

15 Geoff W. Boraston, "Revolving Fluidized Bed Technology for the Treatment of Hazardous Materials," *Abstract Proceedings: Second Forum on Innovative Hazardous Waste Treatment Technologies: Domestic and International* (Philadelphia: U.S. Environmental Protection Agency, 15–17 May 1990), 14.

16 Ocean Chem Ltd, *Examination of Dredged Material Disposal Alternatives Sydney, N.S. Final Report (Dartmouth, N.S.)*, 1984, Bras d'Or Collection, 6340, Cape Breton University Library.

17 Laurel Sefton MacDowell, *An Environmental History of Canada* (Vancouver: University of British Columbia Press, 2012), 195–6.

18 JWEL-IT, *Report on PCB Delineation and Remedial Options for the Muggah Creek Containment Project*, 31 May 1996, Bras d'Or Collection, 5158, Cape Breton University Library.

19 Don MacPherson, interview by Michael Earle, January 1990, Steel Project, MG 14, 206, T-2590, transcript, Beaton Institute Archives (BI), Sydney, NS.

20 Some steelworkers would use the PCB-containing fluid as a curative remedy for arthritis and joint pain. This came up in several interviews.

21 Charles MacDonald, interview by Michael Earle, 9 January 1990, Steel Project, Box 6, File 39, transcript, BI.

22 Leon Colford, interview by Michael Earle, 18 September 1990, Steel Project, Box 6, File 12, transcript, BI.

23 Richard Newman, "From Love's Canal to Love Canal: Reckoning With the Environmental Legacy of an Industrial Dream," in *Beyond the Ruins: The Meanings of* Deindustrialization, ed. Jefferson Cowie and Joseph Heathcott (Ithaca, NY: Cornell University Press, 2003): 127.

24 Sefton MacDowell, *An Environmental History of Canada*, 255; Suroopa Mukherjee, *Surviving Bhopal: Dancing Bodies, Written Texts and Oral Testimonials of Women in the Wake of an Industrial Disaster* (New York: Palgrave Macmillan, 2010), 62.

25 Travers, "Sydney Tar Ponds: A Case Study," 3; "Articles of Agreement for Project Management of the Sydney Tar Ponds Clean up Program," 1987, Bras d'Or Collection, 6286, Cape Breton University Library.

26 Newman, "From Love's Canal to Love Canal," 129.

27 Bill Graham, interview by Michael Earle, 12 September 1990, Steel Project, Box 6, File 24, transcript, BI.

28 Sydney Tar Pond Clean Up Inc., "Annual Report," 1991–1992, Bras d'Or Collection, 5022, Cape Breton University Library.

29 "Tar Ponds Hot Spots Far above Acceptable," *Cape Breton Post*, 14 October 1992.

30 Acres International Limited, *Sydney Tar Ponds Clean Up, PCB Contamination, Interim Report*, October 1992, Bras d'Or Collection, 5999, Cape Breton University Library.

31 Dave Ervin, interview with author, 8 August 2013; ACT! For a Healthy Sydney, *Final Report: Survey of Community Opinions of Health Needs*, 1997, Bras d'Or Collection, 6197, Cape Breton University Library.

32 Barlow and May, *Frederick Street*, 99; "Breathing Poison in Cape Breton," *National Post*, 30 September 1999; "Obituary – Donald Deleskie," *Cape Breton Post*, 2 June 2008.

33 Hajnol Molnar-Szakacs, "An Investigation of Adolescents Perspectives on Belonging to the Community and the Influence of Data Collection Methods on Information" (Master's thesis, Dalhousie University, 1999), 9–10; Sheila Copps to Don MacPherson, 21 Dec 1995, Volume 1329, File 134994, Department of the Environment Fonds, RG 108-A, Library and Archives Canada (LAC), Ottawa, ON; Judith Guernsey, proposal – "Adverse Health Outcomes, Sydney," 25 February 1997, Sydney Tar Ponds

Briefing File, Volume 121, File 7, Lowell Murray Fonds, R14121-19-3-E, LAC.

34 R.V. Anderson, *Sydney Tar Ponds Report: Review of the Sydney Tar Ponds Sediment Remediation System*, July 1994, Bras d'Or Collection, 6262, Cape Breton University Library.

35 Ron Nicholson, report on emissions at Sydney coke ovens, 7 November 1995, Departmental Correspondence, Volume 1339, File 136035, Department of the Environment Fonds, LAC.

36 Nova Scotia, *Debates and Proceedings of the Nova Scotia House of Assembly*, 10 January1996, http://nslegislature.ca/index.php/proceedings/hansard/C60/56_3_81/.

37 "Tar Ponds Burial Slagged," *Chronicle Herald*, 16 January 1996.

38 Kas Roussey, "Tar Ponds Cleanup Plan Unpopular with Sydney Residents," *The National*, CBC, 15 January 1996, http://www.cbc.ca/archives/entry/tar-ponds-cleanup-plan-unpopular-with-sydney-residents.

39 "Local Politicians Kept in the Dark about Details," *Chronicle Herald*, 16 January 1996.

40 "N.S. Orders Assessment of Tar Ponds," *Chronicle Herald*, 17 January 1996; Barlow and May, *Frederick Street*, 109.

41 Sierra Club Joins Debate," *Cape Breton Post*, 16 April 1996.

42 Andrew Hurley, "From Factory Town to Metropolitan Junkyard: Postindustrial Transitions on the Urban Periphery," *Environmental History* 21, 1 (2016): 15.

43 Catherine Corrigal-Brown and Mabel Ho, "How the State Shapes Social Movements: An Examination of the Environmental Movement in Canada," in *Protest and Politics: The Promise of Social Movement Societies*, ed. Howard Ramos and Kathleen Rodgers (Vancouver: University of British Columbia Press, 2015), 105–6.

44 "Tar Ponds Toured," *Cape Breton Post*, 13 August 1996; Ron Deleskie and Don Deleskie were twin brothers.

45 Greg MacLeod, "Let Cape Bretoners Do It," *Cape Breton Post*, 13 August 1996.

46 "Tar Ponds Burial Plan on Ice," *Chronicle Herald*, 13 August 1996.

47 Joint Action Group (JAG), "Key Milestones," 1996, in the author's possession; Annual Report, 24 October 1998, JAGA, 2003-011, Box 1, File 1, JAG Project, BI; Tar ponds related funding, 2008–012. Box 13, File 5, Department of Transportation and Public Works Fonds, Nova Scotia Archives and Records Management (NSARM), Halifax, NS.

48 "JAG Governance Model," 4 December 1996, GOVW, 2003-011, Box 2, File 1, JAG Project, BI.

49 "Tempers Flare while JAG Members Meet," *Cape Breton Post*, 15 January 1997; Minutes, 14 January 1997, EDGR, Box 1, File 2, JAG Project, BI.

50 Environment Canada, news release, 30 January 1997, in the author's possession.

51 Manning MacDonald, interview with author, 27 July 2015.

52 Dave Ervin, interview with author, 8 August 2013.

53 Chad Montrie, *Making a Living: Work and the Environment in the United States* (Chapel Hill: University of North Carolina Press, 2008); Andrew Hurley, *Environmental Inequalities: Class, Race, and Industrial Pollution in Gary, Indiana* (Chapel Hill: University of North Carolina Press, 1995); Mark McLaughlin, "Green Shoots: Aerial Insecticide Spraying and the Growth of Environmental Consciousness in New Brunswick, 1952–1973," *Acadiensis* 40, 1 (2011): 3–23.

54 Deleskie Meeting with Government, 19 April 2000, 2008-012, Box 13, File 5, Department of Transportation and Public Works Fonds, NSARM.

55 Memorandum of Understanding among the Government of Canada, the Government of the Province of Nova Scotia, the Cape Breton Regional Municipality, and the Joint Action Group for Environmental Clean up of the Muggah Creek Watershed Association (JAG), 29 July 1998, JAGA, Collection 2003-011, Box 1, File 18, JAG Project, BI. Italics in original.

56 Health Working Group, 25 February 1997, Sydney Tar Ponds Briefing File, Volume 121, File 7, Lowell Murray Fonds, LAC.

57 Health Risk Perceptions of Sydney Residents: Risk Communication of Sydney Tar Ponds, May 1999, HSWG, 2003-011, Box 4, File 19, JAG Project, BI.

58 Steven High, "Mapping Memories of Displacement: Oral History, Memoryscapes and Mobile Methodologies," in *Place, Writing, and Voice in Oral History*, ed. Shelley Trower (New York: Palgrave Macmillan: 2011), 217–31.

59 Others were denied the opportunity to move out of the neighbourhood. During the Frederick Street evacuations, Anne Ross, a woman who lived on nearby Laurier Street, was told that "conclusive evidence does not link what is going on at her property to the coke ovens property"; see Lawrence MacDonald to Clive Oldreive, 2008-012, Box 13, File 5, Department of Transportation and Public Works Fonds, NSARM.

60 Mimi Sheller and John Urry, "The New Mobilities Program," *Environment and Planning A* 38 (2006): 207–36; Jane Ricketts Hein, James Evans, and Phil Jones, "Mobile Methodologies: Theory, Technology and Practice," *Geography Compass* 2–5 (2008): 1266–85.

61 Sheller and Urry, "The New Mobilities Program," 218.

62 Debbie Ouellette, interview with author, 20 June 2016.

63 Ibid.

64 "Move Us or We'll Sue, Says Sydney Resident," *Chronicle Herald*, 8 July 1998.

65 Cantox Environmental Inc., *Human Health Risk Assessment of Frederick Street Area: Final Report*, 11 August 1998, Bras d'Or Collection, 6218: 3, Cape Breton University Library.

66 Ibid.

67 Debbie Ouellette, email message to author, 20 June 2016.

68 "Cancer Risk Acute in Sydney," *Cape Breton* Post, 21 October 1998; Guernsey's Research Was Published in 2000, see Judith Guernsey, Ron Dewar, Swarna Weerasinghe, Susan Kirkland, and Paul Veugelers, "Incidence of Cancer in Sydney and Cape Breton County, Nova Scotia 1979–1997," *Canadian Journal of Public Health* 91, 4 (July–August 2000): 282–92.

69 Juanita and Rick McKenzie, email requesting seat on JAG roundtable, RTBL 2003–011, Box 10, File 114, JAG Project, BI.

70 Debbie Ouellette, interview with author, 20 June 2016.

71 Ibid.

72 Nova Scotia Department of Transportation and Public Works, news release, "Province Offers to Purchase Homes on Frederick Street and Curry's Lane," 28 May 1999, in author's possession.

73 Barry McCallum to Debbie Ouellette, Secretariat Correspondence, December 2001, RTBL 2003–011, Box 10, File 123, JAG Project, BI.

74 Juanita McKenzie, interview with author, 20 June 2016.

75 Barbara Epstein, "The Environmental Justice/Toxics Movement: Politics of Race and Gender," *Capitalism Nature Socialism* 8, 3 (September 1997): 63–87.

76 Phil Brown and Faith I.T. Ferguson, "Making a Big Stink: Women's Work, Women's Relationships, and Toxic Waste Activism," *Gender and Society* 9, 2 (April 1995): 146.

77 Ronnie Johnston and Arthur McIvor, "Dangerous Work, Hard Men, and Broken Bodies: Masculinity in the Clydeside Heavy Industries, c. 1930–1970s," *Labour History Review* 69, 2 (2004): 136; Craig Heron, "Boys Will Be Boys: Working-Class Masculinities in the Age of Mass Production," *International Labor and Working-Class History* 69 (2006): 6–34.

78 Michael Stewart Foley, *Front Porch Politics: The Forgotten Heyday of American Activism in the 1970s and 1980s* (New York: Hill and Wang, 2013).

79 Phil Brown, "Popular Epidemiology and Toxic Waste Contamination: Lay and Professional Ways of Knowing," *Journal of Health and Social Behavior* 33 (September 1992): 267–81; see also Jennifer Thompson, "Toxic Residents: Health and Citizenship at Love Canal," *Journal of Social History* Advance Access (2015): 1–20, http://jsh.oxfordjournals.org/content/early/2015/12/18/jsh.shv105.full.

80 Celine Krauss, "Challenging Power: Toxic Waste Protests and the Politicization of White, Working-Class Women," in *Community Activism*

and Feminist Politics: Organizing across Race, Class, and Gender, ed. Nancy Naples (New York: Routledge, 1998), 140.

81 Juanita McKenzie, interview with author, 20 June 2016.

82 Ibid.

83 Harry Waisglass and Andrew Hogan, *A Submission to the Atlantic Development Board on the Prospects for Nova Scotia's Steel Industry* (28 March 1966).

84 Juanita McKenzie, interview with author, 20 June 2016.

85 *Sydney Tar Ponds Agency website*, "Memorandum of Agreement between the Government of Canada and the Government of Nova Scotia, respecting Remediation of the Sydney Tar Ponds and Coke Ovens Sites," 12 May 2004, http://www.tarpondscleanup.ca/index.php?sid=3&cid=9&pid=126 &lang=e.

7. From Dependence to Enterprise

1 Recording Secretary's Minute Book, Local 1064, 6 April 1999: 172, in the author's possession.

2 John Hamm, interview with author, 29 July 2015.

3 "Tories 'Hammer' province," *Cape Breton Post*, 28 July 1999.

4 "Cape Bretoners Elect Seven Liberals, Two Tories, Two NDP," *Cape Breton Post*, 28 July 1999.

5 Nova Scotia House of Assembly, for immediate release, "Hamm Urges Premier to Close Sysco," 23 March 1999, in the author's possession.

6 "It's Over," *The Daily News*, 23 March 1999.

7 Parker Barss Donham, "On Your Mark ..." *The Daily News*, 12 May 1999.

8 Don MacDonald, "Psst! Have You Heard about the Election?" *Chronicle Herald*, 21 May 1999.

9 Manning MacDonald, "Private Sector Family Sysco's Key," *Cape Breton Post*, 26 May 1999.

10 "Result of Election Worrisome – or Maybe It Doesn't Matter," *Cape Breton Post*, 20 July 1999.

11 Fred James, interview with author, 16 August 2013.

12 Manning MacDonald, interview with author, 27 July 2015.

13 Daniel Bell, *The Coming of Post-Industrial Society* (New York: Basic Books, 1999), 14–16.

14 Frank Webster, *Theories of the Information Society*, 4th ed. (New York: Routledge, 2014), 46

15 Greta R. Krippner, *Capitalizing on Crisis: The Political Origins of the Rise of Finance* (Cambridge, MA: Harvard University Press, 2011), 138.

16 David Harvey, *A Brief History of Neoliberalism* (Oxford: Oxford University Press, 2005), 3.

17 Dieter Plehwe, Bernhard Walpen, and Gisela Neunhöffer, "Introduction: Reconsidering Neoliberal Hegemony," in *Neoliberal Hegemony: A Global Critique,* ed. Dieter Plehwe, Bernhard Walpen, and Gisela Neunhöffer (London: Routledge, 2006), 1–2.

18 Ira Hakarvy and Harmon Zuckerman, report, *Eds and Meds: Cities' Hidden Assets,* The Brookings Institution (Washington, DC: Center on Urban and Metropolitan Policy, 1999), 3–5.

19 Guian McKee, *Health Care Policy as Urban Policy: Hospitals and Community Development in the Post-industrial City* (San Francisco: Federal Reserve Bank of San Francisco, 2010), http://www.frbsf.org/community-development /files/working_paper_2010_10_healthcare_policy_as_urban_policy.pdf; Carolyn Adams, "The Meds and Eds. in Urban Economic Development," *Journal of Urban Affairs* 25, 5 (2003): 572–3; Roger D. Simon and Brian Allnutt, "Philadelphia, 1982–2007: Toward the Postindustrial City," *Pennsylvania Magazine of History and Biography* 131, 4 (October 2007): 395.

20 Christine Walley, *Exit Zero: Family and Class in Post-Industrial Chicago* (Chicago: University of Chicago Press, 2013), 113–15

21 Fuyuki Kurasaw, "Which Barbarians at the Gates? From the Culture Wars to Market Orthodoxy in the North American Academy," *Canadian Review of Sociology and Anthropology* 39, 3 (2002): 336.

22 Robert Morgan, *Perseverance: The Story of Cape Breton's University College, 1952–2002* (Sydney: UCCB Press, 2004), 28; James D. Cameron, *For the People: A History of St. Francis Xavier University* (Montreal and Kingston: McGill-Queen's University Press, 1996), 283; Moses Coady to C.H. Millard, 3 June 1953, Volume 17, United Steelworkers of America Fonds, MG 28 i268 Library and Archives Canada (LAC), Ottawa, ON.

23 Moses Coady to Malcolm MacLellan, 16 January 1962, "Xavier Scrapbook, 1951–1960," 20, Beaton Institute Archives (BI) Sydney, NS.

24 A. Hogan, L.B. Sears, J. McLaughlin, and J. Day, resolution re: mine closure, 1961, St. F.X. Extension Department, C.12 (b): 1, Education and Educators, MG 11, 7, BI.

25 Ed Murphy to Dr. D.F. Campbell, resolution re: mine closure, 1961, St. F.X. Extension Department, Education and Educators, BI.

26 "Student Accommodations 'Woefully Inadequate,'" *Chronicle Herald,* 13 July 1972.

27 Morgan, *Perseverance,* 56.

28 "Coming Out Fighting over Devco University," 25 May 1974, College of Cape Breton Scrapbook, 1960–1977, BI.

29 "Academic Manipulators Insulting People's Intelligence," *Chronicle Herald,* 12 July 1974.

30 Memorandum, 4 November 1986, OLGS. A.C.O.A. – Sydney Steel Corporation (SYSCO) / General (1986–1987), Volume 92, File 21, Lowell

Murray Fonds, R14121-19-3-E, LAC. The Liberals had also previously considered "putting an end to the idea that Canada owes Sydney a living." See Memorandum, Department of Finance, 3 August 1978, Cape Breton Island – Sydney Steel Corporation, Volume 5370, File 4052-03-5 pt. 3, Department of Finance Fonds, RG 19, LAC.

31 Donald Savoie, *Regional Economic Development: Canada's Search for Solutions* (Toronto: University of Toronto Press, 1986), 127.

32 Communication Strategy, 21 January 1993, OLGS Federal-Provincial Relations Ad. Hoc Committee on Steel Industry, Part 1, Volume 139, File 3, Lowell Murray Fonds, LAC.

33 Department of Finance, *A New Direction for Canada: An Agenda for Economic Renewal* (Ottawa, 1984), 39–40; See also Annual Report on the Industrial and Regional Development Program, 1986–1987, 13 June 1986, Records of Minister of Industrial Expansion, Sinclair Stevens, 1994–95/065 File 101-1, Department of Regional Economic Expansion Fonds, RG 124, LAC.

34 David Milne, *Tug of War: Ottawa and the Provinces under Trudeau and Mulroney* (Toronto: James Lorimer, 1986), 225–6.

35 James Bickerton, "Old Wine in New Bottles? Federal Development Agencies in Cape Breton, 1984–1989" (Saint John's: Atlantic Provinces Political Studies Association, 1990): 185.

36 Although Sysco subsidies were "non-viable," federal bureaucrats also recognized that the circumstances surrounding the corporation were politically fraught. See Lyle Russell to H.M. McGee, 30 May 1985, Regional Industrial Expansion – Programs for Export Market Development (PEMD) – Sydney Steel Corporation, Volume 255, File 7997-A-40321, Department of Regional Economic Expansion Fonds, LAC.

37 Cabinet Memorandum, 1987, Cape Breton Island – Sydney Steel Corporation, Volume 5370, File 4052-03-5 pt. 3, Department of Finance Fonds, LAC.

38 Jeanne Sauvé, Speech from the Throne, 30 September 1986, https://www.poltext.org/en/part-1-electronic-political-texts/canadian-throne-speeches.

39 Atlantic Canada Opportunities Agency (ACOA), *Report of the Enterprise Cape Breton Assessment Team: From Dependence to Enterprise* (Moncton, February 1991), 8, Bras d'Or Collection, 5087, Cape Breton University Library, Sydney, NS; Bickerton, "Old Wine in New Bottles," 188.

40 Deloitte and Touche, *Enterprise Cape Breton Corporation and University College of Cape Breton: Report on Evaluation of Technology Industry Development Program* (February 1994).

41 Paul Patterson and Susan Biagi, *The Loom of Change: Weaving a New Economy on Cape Breton Island* (Sydney: University College of Cape Breton Press, 2003), 12.

42 Jon Van Til, *Growing Civil Society: From Nonprofit Sector to Third Space* (Bloomington: Indiana University Press, 2000), 156.

43 Patterson and Biagi, *The Loom of Change*, 37.

44 E.R. Forbes, *Challenging the Regional Stereotype: Essays on the 20th Century Maritimes* (Fredericton: Acadiensis Press, 1989), 11–12.

45 The Nova Scotia Commission on Building a New Economy, *Now or Never: An Urgent Call to Action for Nova Scotians* (February 2014), vii, http:// onens.ca/commission-report/.

46 Voluntary Planning, *Our Province, Our Future, Our Choice: A Consultation Paper for Nova Scotia Economic Strategy* (Halifax, 1991), 3–5.

47 Voluntary Planning, *Our Province, Our Future, Our Choice*, 16–17.

48 ACOA, *Report of the Enterprise Cape Breton Assessment Team*, 119.

49 Patterson and Biagi, *The Loom of Change*, 37.

50 Harvey, *A Brief History of Neoliberalism*, 54.

51 *Atlantic Institute for Market Studies website*, "Annual Reports, 1996/1997– 2009/2010, http://www.aims.ca/en/home/aboutus/annualreport.aspx.

52 Brian Lee Crowley, *The Self, the Individual and the Community: Liberalism in the Political Thought of F.A. Hayek and Sidney and Beatrice Webb* (Oxford: Clarendon Press, 1987); Brian Lee Crowley, *The Road to Equity: Gender, Ethnicity, and Language* (Toronto: Stoddart, 1994); Brian Lee Crowley, *Taking Ownership: Property Rights and Fishery Management on the Atlantic Coast* (Halifax: Atlantic Institute for Market Studies, 1996).

53 Jacqueline Scott, *Doing Business with the Devil: Land, Sovereignty, and Corporate Partnerships in Membertou Inc.* (Halifax: Atlantic Institute for Market Studies, 2004), vi.

54 Patterson and Biagi, *The Loom of Change*, 71.

55 John Hamm, interview with author, 29 July 2015.

56 NovaKnowledge, *Knowledge Economy Report Card* (Halifax: Nova Knowledge, 1999), 4.

57 Salaries for these non-union call centre positions averaged approximately $26,000 per year. "Province to Train Workers for Bank," *Cape Breton Post*, 25 October 1999.

58 Sydney Steel Corporation, press release: New Management Takes Over, 31 July 1998, in the author's possession.

59 Gerry McCarron, Sheldon Andrews, and George MacNeil, interview with author, 5 August 2015.

60 Manning MacDonald, interview with author, 27 July 2015.

61 Minute Book, Local 1064, 21 December 1999, 9–10.

62 Mary Williams Walsh, "U.S. Moves to Seize Pension Fund in Dispute with Renco," *New York Times*, 3 February 2006.

63 Minute Book, Local 1064, 4 January 2000, 14–15.

64 Minute Book, Local 1064, 18 January 2000, 17–18.

65 Steelworkers' Develop Plan," *Cape Breton Post*, 5 February 2000.

66 Brian MacDonald, "It's Time for Hamm to Deliver for the Steelworkers," *Cape Breton Post*, 21 February 2000.

67 Minute Book, Local 1064, 21 March 2000, 47–8.

68 Ibid.

69 John Hamm, interview with author, 29 July 2015.

70 "Sysco Pension Plans," *Cape Breton Post*, 5 May 2000.

71 John Kingston to Gordon Balser, 1 February 2000, in the author's possession.

72 Local 1064, "On Our Own Terms: Sysco Progress Report," May 2000; Bill McNeil, "North American Metals Offers Jobs and Security," *Cape Breton Post*, 13 May 2000; The union began a public relations campaign pushing for the NAM deal, though the executive remarked that they would have to avoid any association with work stoppages. They decided upon a pamphlet campaign and a series of letters to the editor of the *Post* and the Halifax *Chronicle Herald*. Minute Book, Local 1064, 16 May 2000, 76–7.

73 "Final Sysco Order Rolled," *Cape Breton Post*, 23 May 2000.

74 Dave Nalepa and Gerry McCarron, interview with author, 8 December 2015.

75 Hugh MacKenzie, "Loss of Sysco Rail Mill Would Be Very Costly and Can't Be Justified," *Cape Breton Post*, 10 June 2000. The author of this letter was the director of research at the national office of the USWA; Teresa MacNeil, interview with author, 18 December 2015.

76 Minute Book, Local 1064, 6 June 2000, 81.

77 "Duferco Has Sysco Plan," *Cape Breton Post*, 23 June 2000.

78 Joel MacLean and Gerry McCarron, interview with author, 29 April 2016.

79 "Steelworkers Shut Sysco Down with Pension Protest," *Cape Breton Post*, 3 August 2000.

80 "Steelworkers Crash Party," *Cape Breton Post*, 11 September 2000.

81 Bill McNeil, interview with author, 18 August 2015; see also "Agreement between Province of Nova Scotia and United Steelworkers of America and Its Locals 1064, 6537, and 1064–2," 14 May 2001, in the author's possession.

82 Duferco Farrell Corp and USWA 1064, "Contract Appendix A: Wages," in the author's possession.

83 Dave Nalepa and Gerry McCarron, interview with author, 8 December 2015.

84 John Hamm, interview with author, 29 July 2015

85 Steel Era Ends," *Cape Breton Post*, 19 January 2001.

86 Organization for Economic Co-operation and Development, *Outlook for the Steel Market in 2001 in Countries Participating in the OECD Steel* Committee (22 March 2001), http://www.oecd.org/officialdocuments/publicdisplayd ocumentpdf/?cote=PAC/COM/NEWS%282001%2927&docLanguage=En.

87 "Demolition and Liquidation of Sysco to Begin This Summer," *Globe and Mail*, 6 June 2001.

88 Perry Anderson, "Renewals," *New Left Review* 1 (January–February 2000): 1–20.

89 Pierre Bourdieu, "The Essence of Neoliberalism," *Le Monde Diplomatique* (December 1998), https://mondediplo.com/1998/12/08bourdieu.

90 Jackie Clarke, "Closing Moulinex: Thoughts on the Visibility and Invisibility of Industrial Labour in Contemporary France," *Modern and Contemporary France*, 19, 4 (2011): 449.

91 Charles MacDonald, interview with author, 3 March 2015.

92 Fred James, interview with author, 16 August 2013.

93 Bill McNeil, interview with author, 18 August 2015; edited for clarification at the request of Bill McNeil, 10 January 2019.

94 Karl Marx, *The 18th Brumaire of Louis Bonaparte* (1852; repr. New York: Cosmo Classics, 2008), 1.

95 Such restructuring was globally reinforced through the passage of free trade agreements such as NAFTA and GATT; see Peter Burnham, "Capital, Crisis and the International State System," in *Global Capital, National State and the Politics of Money*, ed. Werner Bonefield and John Holloway (London: Palgrave MacMillan, 1995), 92–4.

96 John Hamm, interview with author, 29 July 2015.

97 Philip Mirowski, "Postface: Defining Neoliberalism," in *The Road from Mont Pelerin: The Making of the Neoliberal Thought Collective*, ed. Philip Mirowski and Dieter Plehwe (Cambridge, MA: Harvard University Press, 2009), 417, 436.

98 Noam Chomsky and David Barsamian, *The Common Good* (Berkeley, CA: Odonian Press, 1998), 43.

99 Oliver Schöller and Olaf Groh-Samburg, "The Education of Neoliberalism," in *Neoliberal Hegemony: A Critique*, ed. Dieter Plehwe, Bernhard Walpen and Gisela Neunhöffer (London: Routledge, 2006), 171–3.

100 Cape Breton County Economic Development, *Strategic Economic Action Plan*, 12 August 1994, Bras d'Or Collection, 5066, Cape Breton University Library.

101 Hans-Jürgen Bieling, "Neoliberalism and Communitarianism: Social Conditions, Discourses, and polItics," in *Neoliberal Hegemony: A Global Critique*, ed. Dieter Plehwe, Bernhard Walpen and Gisela Neunhöffer (London: Routledge, 2006), 207.

102 "Feds Cut Enterprise Cape Breton Corporation," *Chronicle Herald*, 19 March 2014; "Liberal Law Limiting Public-Sector Union Wages Passes Third Reading," *Chronicle Herald*, 18 December 2015.

103 John Ibbitson, "How the Maritimes Became the Incredible Shrinking Region," *Globe and Mail*, 20 March 2015.

104 Ibid.

8. Making History from Sydney Steel

1 Fred James, interview with author, 17 August 2013.
2 "Sydney Steel Demolition Has Started, What's Next?" *CBC*, 23 July 2001.
3 "Falling Steel Beam Kills Former Sysco Worker," *CBC*, 24 September 2004.
4 Tera Camus, "Sysco Stacks Dust in the Wind," *Chronicle Herald*, 31 August 2001.
5 "$1.48 Million Future-Use Design Contract Awarded," *Sydney Tar Ponds Agency*, 23 November 2011, in author's possession.
6 "Park Called Open Hearth to Grace Tar Ponds Site," *Chronicle Herald*, 14 June 2013; Province Approves $1M Loan to Harbourside Commercial Park," *Cape Breton Post*, 6 November 2009.
7 "Heart of Steel Captures Story of Steel Plant," *Cape Breton Post*, 29 January 2012.
8 James Rhodes, "Youngstown's 'Ghost'? Memory, Identity and Deindustrialization," *International Labor and Working-Class History* 84 (Fall 2013): 74.
9 *Public Works and Government Services Canada website*, 30 August 2013, "Stronger Than Steel Celebration Pays Tribute to Sydney's Past, Present and Future," http://news.gc.ca/web/article-en.do?nid=768179.
10 *Government of Nova Scotia website*, Sydney Tar Ponds Agency Press Release, 14 June 2013, "Open Hearth Park Selected as Name of Reclaimed Tar Ponds Site," http://novascotia.ca/news/release/?id=20130614002.
11 Jani Vuolteenaho and Lawrence D. Berg, "Towards Critical Toponymies," in *Critical Toponymies: The Contested Politics of Place Naming*, ed. Lawrence D. Berg and Jani Vuolteenaho (London: Ashgate, 2009), 7.
12 Toby Butler, "Memoryscape: How Audio Walks Can Deepen Our Sense of Place by Integrating Art, Oral History, and Cultural Geography," *Geography Compass* 1, 3 (2007): 365
13 Fabian Smith, interview with author, 7 September 2014.
14 James Duane Marchand, Comment on The Sydney Park Project Facebook page, 12 April 2013 (3:46 p.m.), accessed 5 August 2016, https://www.facebook.com/OpenHearthPark.
15 Michelle Gardiner, Comment on The Sydney Park Project Facebook page, 14 April 2013 (2:26 p.m.), accessed 5 August 2016, https://www.facebook.com/OpenHearthPark..
16 Shane Paul et al., Comment on "Contest to Name Park on Former Tar Ponds Site to Begin," *Cape Breton Post*, 24 March 2013, http://www.capebretonpost.com/News/Local/2013-03-24/article-3206468/Contest-to-name-park-on-former-tar-ponds-site-set-to-begin/1.
17 Debbie Ouellette, interview with author, 20 June 2016.

18 Katelyn McPherson, "Sydney Park Project: Phoenix Park," in the author's possession.
19 "Sydney Park Project: Piley Poqtamkiaq Park," in the author's possession.
20 "S.P.A.R.C.K. Park – Harbourview Montessori," Vimeo Video, 1:13, posted by Mike Targett, 2013, https://vimeo.com/67180047.
21 "Sydney Park Project: History Heroes Park," in the author's possession.
22 "Rants and Raves," *Cape Breton Post*, 16 June 2013.
23 Lucy Taksa, "Labor History and Public History in Australia: Allies or Uneasy Bedfellows?" *International Labor and Working-Class History* 76 (2009): 99.
24 Doreen Massey, *Space, Place, and Gender* (Cambridge, UK: Polity Press, 1994), 122–3.
25 "A Man of Steel: Gordon Kennedy's Biggest Challenge," *Victoria Standard* 3, 5 (August-September 2013).
26 For a full examination of this monument, see Lachlan MacKinnon, "Reading a Labour Landmark in Sydney, Nova Scotia," *Labour/Le Travail* 72 (Fall 2013): 101–28.
27 Sherry Lee Linkon, *The Half Life of Deindustrialization: Working-Class Writing about Economic Restructuring* (Ann Arbor: University of Michigan Press, 2018).
28 *Heart of Steel*, directed by Peter Giffin (Canada: Public Works and Government Services Canada, 2012), DVD, 00:01:30.
29 "Heart of Steel Enshrines Part of Cape Breton," *Chronicle Herald*, 3 February 2012.
30 *Heart of Steel*, 00:02:58.
31 Ron Crawley, "Class Conflict and the Establishment of the Sydney Steel Industry, 1899–1904," in *The Island: New Perspectives on Cape Breton history*, ed. Ken Donovan (Fredericton and Sydney: Acadiensis and University College of Cape Breton Press, 1990), 152.
32 *Heart of Steel*, 00:09:55.
33 John Murphy, interview by Michael Earle, 10 January 1990, Steel Project, MG 14, 206, Box 7, File 57, transcript, Beaton Institute Archives (BI), Sydney, NS.
34 Dan Yakimchuk, interview by Michael Earle, 20 April 1990, Steel Project, Box 5, File 7, transcript, BI.
35 Elizabeth Beaton, "Making Steel: Understanding the Lived Experience," *Scienta Canadiensis: Canadian Journal of the History of Science, Technology, and Medicine* 15, 1 (1991): 63.
36 Gerry McCarron, Alana MacNeil, and George MacNeil, interview with author, 29 April 2016.
37 Jefferson Cowie and Joseph Heathcott, "Introduction: The Meanings of Deindustrialization," in *Beyond the Ruins: The Meanings of*

Deindustrialization, ed. Jefferson Cowie and Joseph Heathcott (Ithaca, NY: Cornell University Press, 2003), 15.

38 *Heart of Steel*, 00:26:50

39 Ibid., 00:29:05.

40 Ibid., 00:40:21.

41 Steven High, "Placing the Displaced Worker: Narrating Place in Deindustrializing Sturgeon Falls, Ontario," *Placing Memory and Remembering Place in Canada*, ed. James Opp and John C. Walsh (Vancouver: University of British Columbia Press, 2010), 163.

42 In March 2013, the unemployment rate for industrial Cape Breton stood at 17.5 per cent. "CBRM to Province: Your Turn," *Chronicle Herald*, 28 March 2013.

43 "Report Says Arsenic Levels in Sydney Neighbourhood Unsafe, *Chronicle Herald*, 17 July 2001.

44 Sherry Lee Linkon, "Narrating Past and Future: Deindustrialized Landscapes as Resources," *International Labor and Working-Class History* 84 (Fall 2013): 40.

45 Kent Curtis, "Greening Anaconda: EPA, ARCO, and the Politics of Space," in *Beyond the Ruins: The Meanings of Deindustrialization*, ed. Jefferson Cowie and Joseph Heathcott (Ithaca, NY: Cornell University Press, 2003), 91–111.

46 *Heart of Steel*, 00:40:15.

47 Linkon, "Narrating Past and Future," 39.

48 Medavie Health Foundation, "Youth at Risk Feasibility Study: Options for Youth in the Cape Breton Regional Health Authority," 30 June 2012, http://medaviehealthfoundation.ca/.

49 "EI Benefits Extended to Resource Dependent Regions," *Globe and Mail*, 22 March 2016.

50 Linkon, "Narrating the Past and Future," 53.

51 Tim Strangleman, James Rhodes, Sherry Linkon, "Introduction to Crumbling Cultures: Deindustrialization, Class, and Memory," *International Labor and Working-Class History* 84 (Fall 2013), 8.

52 John Kirk, Sylvie Contrepois, and Steve Jeffreys, "Approaching Regional and Identity Change in Europe," in *Changing Work and Community Identities in European Regions: Perspectives on the Past and Present*, ed. John Kirk, Sylvie Contrepois, and Steve Jeffreys (New York: Palgrave McMillan, 2012), 14.

53 Sydney Steel Museum website, www.sydneysteelmuseum.com/.

Conclusion

1 Gerry McCarron and Dave Nalepa, interview with author, 8 December 2015.

2 Cathy Stanton, "Keeping 'the Industrial': New Solidarities in Post-Industrial Places," in *The Deindustrialized World: Confronting Ruination in*

Post-Industrial Places, ed. Steven High, Lachlan MacKinnon, and Andrew Perchard (Vancouver: University of British Columbia Press, 2017), 158

3 Ibid., 168

4 Andrew Hurley, "The Transformation of Industrial Suburbs since World War Two," in *The Deindustrialized World: Confronting Ruination in Post-Industrial Places*, ed. Steven High, Lachlan MacKinnon, and Andrew Perchard (Vancouver: University of British Columbia Press, 2017), 223.

5 John Cooper Clarke, *Anthologia* (Sony Records, 2015), CD.

6 Stanton, "Keeping 'the Industrial,'" 167.

7 Hurley, "The Transformation of Industrial Suburbs since World War Two."

8 *Morien Resource Corp. website*, "Donkin Project," http://morienres.com/donkin-project/.

9 Ian McKay, *The Quest of the Folk: Antimodernism and Cultural Selection in Twentieth-Century Nova Scotia* (Montreal and Kingston: McGill-Queen's University Press, 1994); Ian McKay and Robin Bates, *In the Province of History: The Making of the Public Past in Twentieth-Century Nova Scotia* (Montreal and Kingston: McGill-Queen's University Press, 2010).

10 "Union Leader Briefly Puts Donkin Mine Owner in Spotlight," *Cape Breton Post*, 11 June 2016.

11 *Port of Sydney website*, "Positioned for Success, 2016 Business Prospectus," http://www.sydneyport.ca/portofsydney/port-of-sydney-prospectus/.

12 "Novaporte – Sydney, Nova Scotia," Youtube Video, 2:37, posted by 4582 n11, 19 May 2016, https://www.youtube.com/watch?v=xjBdUMUqwxg.

13 "The Steel Boom Comes to Sydney, 1899," *Cape Breton's Magazine* 39 (1985): 33.

14 Jefferson Cowie, *The Great Exception: The New Deal and the Limits of American Politics* (Princeton: Princeton University Press, 2016), 9.

15 Tim Strangleman, "Deindustrialization and the Historical Sociological Imagination: Making Sense of Work and Industrial Change," *Sociology* 50, 1 (2016): 1–17.

16 Sven Beckert et al., "Interchange: The History of Capitalism," *Journal of American History* 101, 2 (September 2014): 506.

Bibliography

Archival Sources and Special Collections

Beaton Institute Archives

Allan J. MacEachen Papers. MG 9, 1.
Dominion Steel and Coal Company Papers. MG 14, 26.
Education and Educators. MG 11, 7.
Joint Action Group Papers. Unaccessioned.
Lloyd McInnis Fonds. Unaccessioned.
Steel Project Papers. MG 14, 206.

Dalhousie University Archives

Nova Scotia Steel and Coal, Trenton Works, Hawker Siddeley Collection.
    MS-4-106.
W.G. Allen Fonds. MS-2-96.

Eberly Family Special Collection Library, Pennsylvania State University Archives

United Steelworkers of America Records.

Library and Archives Canada

Canadian Labour Congress Fonds. MG 28 i103.
Department of the Environment Fonds. RG 108-A.
Department of Finance Fonds. RG 19.
Department of Labour Fonds. RG 27.
Department of Reconstruction and Supply Fonds. RG 28-A.

Department of Regional Economic Expansion Fonds. RG 124.
Department of Transport Fonds. RG 12.
Lester B. Pearson Fonds. MG 26-N4.
Lowell Murray Fonds. R14121–19–3-E.
Natural Resources Canada Fonds. RG 21.
United Steelworkers of America Fonds. MG 28 i268.

McMaster University Archives and Research Collections

United Steelworkers of America:
Local 1005 (Hamilton, Ontario), Thomas McClure sous-fonds. RC0300.

Nova Scotia Archives and Records Management

Angus L. Macdonald Fonds. MG 2. Volume 1297.
Department of Transportation and Public Works Fonds. 2006-003; 2008-012.
Halifax Industries Ltd. Fonds. 1990-215-001.
John Leefe Fonds. MG 2. Volume 1701.
Office of Economic Development Fonds. RG 30.
Office of the Premier Fonds. RG 100.

Interviews

Interviews by Author (2013–2016)

Beaton, Elizabeth. 10 August 2013.
Britten, Bernie. 2 September 2014.
Campbell, John. 6 September 2014.
Campbell, Mickey and Adrian Murphy. 1 September 2014.
Ervin, Dave. 8 August 2013.
Deveaux, Lorraine. 9 December 2014.
Gosse, Gordie. 19 April 2016.
Hamm, John. 29 July 2015.
James, Fred. 16 August 2013.
Legge, Joe. 1 September 2014.
MacDonald, Charles. 3 March 2015.
MacDonald, Manning. 27 July 2015.
MacGillivray, Donald. 22 January 2016.
MacLeod, Greg. 16 December 2015.
MacNeil, Teresa. 18 December 2015.
McCarron, Gerry, Alana MacNeil, and George MacNeil. 29 April 2016.
McCarron, Gerry, and Dave Nalepa. 8 December 2015.

McCarron, Gerry, and Joel MacLean. 29 April 2016.
McCarron, Gerry, Sheldon Andrews, and George MacNeil. 5 August 2015.
McCarron, Gerry, and Tommy McCarron. 7 August 2013.
McKenzie, Juanita. 20 June 2016.
McNeil, Bill. 18 August 2015.
Murphy, John. September 2015.
Ouellette, Debbie. 20 June 2016.
Smith, Fabian. 7 September 2014.
Stewart, Scott. 21 December 2015.

Steel Project Interviews (1990)

Anderson, Charles. Interview by Michael Earle. 18 May 1990.
Bonnell, Owen. Interview by Michael Earle. 28 March 1990.
Brocklehurst, Barry. Interview by Diane Chisholm. 5 November 1990.
Butler, Clarence. Interview by Michael Earle. 13 February 1990.
Cameron, Russell. Interview by Michael Earle. 7 February 1990.
Clarke, Walter. Interview by Diane Chisholm. 4 July 1990.
Colford, Leon. Interview by Michael Earle. 18 September 1990.
Collins, Harry. Interview by Michael Earle. 5 February 1990.
Cossit, Otis. Interview by Michael Earle. 12 June 1990.
Ferguson, William. Interview by Michael Earle. 22 February 1990.
Graham, Bill. Interview by Michael Earle. 12 September 1990.
Keller, Joe. Interview by Michael Earle. 16 May 1990.
Lewis, Blair. Interview by Diane Chisholm. 6 March 1990.
MacCuish, Leslie. Interview by Michael Earle. 6 April 1990.
MacDonald, Charles. Interview by Michael Earle. 9 January 1990.
MacKinnon, Wally. Interview by Michael Earle. 11 April 1990.
MacPherson, Don. Interview by Michael Earle. January 1990.
MacPherson, Don. Interview by Michael Earle. 20 June 1990.
Murphy, John. Interview by Michael Earle. 10 January 1990.
Parris, Eddie. Interview by Diane Chisholm. 5 October 1990.
Pickles, Walter. Interview by Michael Earle. 15 May 1990.
Ross, Garfield. Interview by Michael Earle. 19 March 1990.
Sylvester, Romeo. Interview by Diane Chisholm. 12 March 1990.
Yakimchuk, Dan. Interview by Michael Earle. 20 April 1990.

Newspapers

Brandon Sun (Brandon, ON; 1967)
Canadian Tribune (Calgary, AB; 1989)
Cape Breton Post (Sydney, NS; 1956–2016)

Chronicle Herald (Halifax, NS; 1967–2016)
Daily News (Truro, NS; 1999)
Globe and Mail (Toronto, ON; 2001–2016)
Indianapolis Business Journal (Indianapolis, IN; 2016)
Montreal Gazette (Montreal, QC; 1953–1966)
Maritime Labour Herald (Glace Bay, NS; 1923)
National Post (Toronto, ON; 1999)
New York Times (New York, NY; 1964–2006)
Ottawa Journal (Ottawa, ON; 1962–1977)
Philadelphia Star (Philadelphia, PA; 1977)
Saint John's Daily News (Saint John's, NL; 1957)
Spectator (Hamilton, ON; 1977)
Steelworker and Miner (Glace Bay, NS; 1940–1949)
Sydney Post Record (Sydney, NS; 1933–1956)
Victoria Standard (Victoria, BC; 2013)

Newsletters and Magazines

Atlantic Advocate (1957)
Atlantic Business (1989)
Cape Breton's Magazine (1976–1993)
Cape Breton's Business Magazine (1989)
Iron Age (1991)
Iron and Steel Engineer (1985)
Maclean's (1957)
Flight (1961)
New Scientist (1958)
Steelabour (1967–1990)
Steelabor: Canadian Edition (1974)

Films, Audio, and Video

4582 n11. "Novaporte – Sydney, Nova Scotia." YouTube Video. 2:37. 19 May
    2016. https://www.youtube.com/watch?v=xjBdUMUqwxg.
Brunner, Joe. "Carrier Air Conditioner (part of United Technologies) Moving
    1,400 Jobs to Mexico." YouTube Video. 3:31. 11 February 2016. https://www
    .youtube.com/watch?v=Y3ttxGMQOrY.
Cooper Clarke, John. *Anthologia*. CD. Sony Records, 2015.
Heart of Steel. DVD. Directed by Peter Giffen. Sydney, NS: Public Works and
    Government Services Canada, 2012.
Last Shift: The Story of a Mill Town. DVD. Directed by Tony Tremblay and Ellen
    Rose. Fredericton, NB: A Golden Girl Production, 2011.

Making Steel. DVD. Directed by Elizabeth Beaton. Sydney, NS: Beaton Institute
  Archives and the National Film Board of Canada, 1992.
Roussey, Kas. "Tar Ponds Cleanup Plan Unpopular with Sydney Residents."
  The National. CBC Television. January 15, 1996. http://www.cbc.ca/archives
  /entry/tar-ponds-cleanup-plan-unpopular-with-sydney-residents.

Published Primary Sources

Acres Consulting Services Limited. *Sydney Tar Pond Remediation: Phase I
  Report: Final.* 4 May 1984.
– *Sydney Tar Pond Study: Final Project Report, Volume I.* June 1985.
Acres International Limited. *Sydney Tar Ponds Clean up, PCB Contamination,
  Interim Report.* October 1992.
ACT! For a Healthy Sydney. *Final Report: Survey Of Community Opinions of
  Health Needs.* 1997.
Anderson, R.V. *Sydney Tar Ponds Report: Review of the Sydney Tar Ponds
  Sediment Remediation System.* July 1994.
Arthur D. Little Inc. *The Future of Steel-Making in Sydney: Report to Government
  of Nova Scotia.* Cambridge, MA: Arthur D. Little, 1960.
Arthur G. McKee & Company. *Report on Steel Industry, Royal Commission on
  Provincial Development and Rehabilitation.* Halifax: King's Printer, 1944.
Atlantic Canada Opportunities Agency. *Report of the Enterprise Cape Breton
  Assessment Team: From Dependence to Enterprise.* Moncton: 1991.
Atwell, L., P. Hennigar, J.H. Kozak, M. Morin, and C.P. Oldreive. *Ambient
  Air Polynuclear Aromatic Hydrocarbons Study, Sydney, Nova Scotia.* Ottawa:
  Environment Canada, 1984.
Cameron, R.B. "Speech to the Empire Club of Canada." In *The Empire Club of
  Canada Addresses.* Toronto: 1970.
Cantox Environmental Inc. *Human Health Risk Assessment of Frederick Street
  Area: Final Report,* 11 August 1998.
Cape Breton County Economic Development. *Strategic Economic Action Plan.*
  12 August 1994
Carroll, William F. *Report of the Commissioner on Trenton Steel Works, 1943.*
  Halifax: King's Printer, 1944.
Carroll, William F., Angus J. Morrison, and C.C. McLaurin. *Report of the Royal
  Commission on Coal, 1946.* Ottawa: King's Printer, 1947.
Deloitte and Touche. *Enterprise Cape Breton Corporation and University College
  of Cape Breton: Report on Evaluation of Technology Industry Development
  Program.* February 1994.
Department of Finance. *A New Direction for Canada: An Agenda for Economic
  Renewal.* Ottawa: Queen's Printer, 1984.
Donald, J.R. *The Cape Breton Coal Problem.* Ottawa: Queen's Printer, 1966.

Elver, R.B. *Economic Character and Change in the Canadian Steel Industry since 1945.* Ottawa: Queen's Printer, 1969.

Firestone, O.J. *Encouragement to Industrial Expansion in Canada: Operation of Special Depreciation Provisions, 10 April 1944–31 March 1949.* Ottawa: King's Printer, 1948.

Hickman, J.R. *Health Hazards Due to Coke Emissions.* Ottawa: Health and Welfare Canada, 1985.

Hildebrand, Lawrence P. *Environmental Quality in Sydney and Northeast Industrial Cape Breton, Nova Scotia.* Ottawa: Environment Canada, 1982.

Hogan, Andrew. *Teach-In: The Sydney Steel Crisis.* Halifax: King's University, 1967.

JWEL-IT. *Report on PCB Delineation and Remedial Options for the Muggah Creek Containment Project.* 31 May 1996.

Katz, M., and R.D. McKay. *Report on Dustfall Studies at Sydney, N.S.: Analysis and Distribution of Dustfall in the Sydney Area during the Period February 1958 through September 1959.* Ottawa: Department of National Health and Welfare Canada, 1959.

Katz, M., H.P. Sanderson, and R.D. McKay. *Evaluation of Air Pollution Levels in Relation to Steel Manufacturing and Coal Combustion in Sydney, Nova Scotia.* Ottawa: Department of National Health and Welfare Canada, 1965.

Kilotat, E.J., and H.J. Wilson. *An Evaluation of Air Pollution Levels in Sydney, Nova Scotia.* Ottawa: Department of National Health Directorate, Air Pollution Control Division, 1970.

Medavie Health Foundation. "Youth at Risk Feasibility Study: Options for Youth in the Cape Breton Regional Health Authority." 30 June 2012. http://medaviehealthfoundation.ca/.

Morgan, L.I. *The Canadian Primary Iron and Steel Industry.* Ottawa: Queen's Printer, 1956.

NovaKnowledge. *Knowledge Economy Report Card.* Halifax: Nova Knowledge, 1999.

Nova Scotia, *Debates and Proceedings of the Nova Scotia House of Assembly.*

Ocean Chem Ltd., *Examination of Dredged Material Disposal Alternatives Sydney, N.S. Final Report.* Dartmouth, NS: 1984.

Organization for Economic Co-operation and Development. *Outlook for the Steel Market in 2001 in Countries Participating in the OECD Steel* Committee. 22 March 2001. http://www.oecd.org/officialdocuments/publicdisplaydoc umentpdf/?cote=PAC/COM/NEWS%282001%2927&docLanguage=En.

Rand, I.C. *Report on the Royal Commission on Coal, August 1960.* Ottawa: Roger Duhamel, 1960.

Report of the Sydney Respiratory Health Survey. Ottawa: Minister of National Health and Welfare, 1977.

Shea, F., and D.A. Murray. "Limestones and Dolomites of Nova Scotia – Cape Breton Island, Part 1," *Bulletin, Nova Scotia Department of Mines.* Halifax: Department of Mines, 1969.

Steel Company of Canada. *CANSTEL Preliminary Report.* 1974.

– *Canstel Project: Site Selection Report.* April 1974.

– *Sydney Steelmaking Study.* Halifax: Queen's Printers, 1968.

Voluntary Planning Board. *Our Province, Our Future, Our Choice: A Consultation Paper for Nova Scotia Economic Strategy.* Halifax: 1991.

Waisglass, Harry, and Andrew Hogan. *A Submission to the Atlantic Development Board on the Prospects for Nova Scotia's Steel Industry* (28 March 1966).

Secondary Sources

Acheson, T.W. "The National Policy and the Industrialization of the Maritimes, 1880–1910." *Acadiensis* 1, 2 (Spring 1972): 3–28.

Ackroyd, Stephen, and Paul Thompson. *Organizational Misbehaviour.* London: Sage, 1999.

Adams, Carolyn. "The Meds and Eds. in Urban Economic Development." *Journal of Urban Affairs* 25, 5 (2003): 572–3.

Alderman, Derek H. "A Street Fit for a King: Naming Places and Commemoration in the American South." *Professional Geographer* 52, 2 (2000): 672–84.

Alexander, David. "Economic Growth in the Atlantic Region, 1880–1940." *Acadiensis* 8, 1 (Autumn 1978): 47–76.

Anastakis, Dimitry. *Autonomous State: The Struggle for a Canadian Car Industry from OPEC to Free Trade.* Toronto: University of Toronto Press, 2013.

– "Building a 'New Nova Scotia': State Intervention, The Auto Industry, and the Case of Volvo in Halifax, 1963–1998." *Acadiensis* 34, 1 (Autumn 2004): 3–30.

– "Industrial Sunrise? The Chrysler Bailout, the State, and the Re-industrialization of the Canadian Automotive Sector, 1975–1986." *Urban History Review* 35, 2 (Spring 2007): 37–50.

Anderson, Perry. "Renewals." *New Left Review* 1 (January–February 2000): 1–20.

Anguelovski, Isabelle, and Joan Martinez-Alier. "The 'Environmentalism of the Poor' Revisited: Territory and Place in Disconnected Global Struggles." *Ecological Economics* 102 (June 2014): 167–76.

Aoyama, Yuko, and Manuel Castells. "An Empirical Assessment of the Informational Society: Employment and Occupational Structures of G-7 Countries, 1920–2000." *International Labour Review* 141, 1–2 (Spring 2000): 123–59.

Arnessen, Eric. *Encyclopedia of U.S. Labor and Working-Class History, Volume 1.* New York: Routledge, 2007.

Atlantic Institute for Market Studies. Annual Reports, 1996/1997–2009/2010. http://www.aims.ca/en/home/aboutus/annualreport.aspx.

Aylen, Jonathan. "Plant Size and Efficiency in the Steel Industry: An International Comparison." *National Institute Economic Review* 100, 1 (May 1982): 65–76.

Baptism of a Union: Stelco Strike of 1946, edited by Wayne Roberts. Hamilton: McMaster University, 1981.

Barlow, Maude, and Elizabeth May. *Frederick Street: Life and Death on Canada's Love Canal.* Toronto: HarperCollins, 2000.

Beaton, Elizabeth. "The Beaton Institute's Steel Project." *Archivaria* 27 (Winter 1988–9): 194–8.

– "Making Steel: Understanding the Lived Experience." *Scienta Canadiensis: Canadian Journal of the History of Science, Technology, and Medicine* 15, 1 (1991): 58–72.

– "Slag Houses in a Steel City." *Material Culture Review* 44 (Fall 1996): 64–78.

Beaton, Meaghan, and Del Muise. "The Canso Causeway: Tartan Tourism, Industrial Development and the Promise of Progress for Cape Breton." *Acadiensis* 37, 2 (Summer 2008): 39–69.

Beckert, Sven, Angus Burgin, Peter Hudson, Louis Hyman, Naomi Lamoreaux, Scott Marler, Stephen Mihm, Julia Ott, Philip Scranton, and Elizabeth Shermer. "Interchange: The History of Capitalism." *Journal of American History* 101, 2 (September 2014): 503–36.

Bell, Daniel. *The Coming of Post-Industrial Society.* New York: Basic Books, 1999.

Bergfeldt-Munro, Wendy. "Tuned-In: Radio, Ritual and Resistance: Cape Breton's Traditional Music, 1973–1998." Master's thesis, Athabasca University, 2015.

Bertrand, J.P., N. Chau, A. Patris, J.M. Mur, Q.T. Pham, J.J. Moulin, P. Morviller, G. Auburtin, A. Figueredo, J. Martin. "Mortality due to Respiratory Cancers in the Coke Oven Plants of the Lorraine Coalmining Industry (Houlliérs du Bassin du Lorraine)." *British Journal of Industrial Medicine* 44, 8 (1987): 559–65.

Bickerton, James P. *Nova Scotia, Ottawa, and the Politics of Regional Development.* Toronto: University of Toronto Press, 1990.

– "Old Wine in New Bottles? Federal Development Agencies in Cape Breton, 1984–1989." Saint John's: Atlantic Provinces Political Studies Association, 1990.

Bieling, Hans-Jürgen. "Neoliberalism and Communitarianism: Social Conditions, Discourses, and Politics." In *Neoliberal Hegemony: A Global Critique*, edited by Dieter Plehwe, Bernhard Walpen, and Gisela Neunhöffer, 207–21. London: Routledge, 2006.

Bishop, Joan. "Sydney Steel: Public Ownership and the Welfare State, 1967–1975." In *The Island: New Perspectives on Cape Breton history 1713–1990*, edited by Kenneth Donovan, 165–86. Fredericton and Sydney: Acadiensis Press and UCCB Press, 1990.

Bluestone, Barry, and Bennett Harrison. *The Deindustrialization of America: Plant Closings, Community Abandonment, and the Dismantling of Basic Industry.* New York: Basic Books, 1982.

Bolland, O. Nigel. "Review." *Labour/Le Travail* 39 (Spring 1997): 345.

Boraston, Geoff W. "Revolving Fluidized Bed Technology for the Treatment of Hazardous Materials." *Abstract Proceedings: Second Forum on Innovative Hazardous Waste Treatment Technologies: Domestic and International.* Philadelphia: U.S. Environmental Protection Agency, 15–17 May 1990.

Bourdieu, Pierre. "The Essence of Neoliberalism." *Le Monde Diplomatique* (December 1998): https://mondediplo.com/1998/12/08bourdieu.

Braverman, Harry. *Labor and Monopoly Capital: The Degradation of Work in the Twentieth Century.* New York and London: Monthly Review Press, 1974.

Brown, Phil. "Popular Epidemiology and Toxic Waste Contamination: Lay and Professional Ways of Knowing." *Journal of Health and Social Behavior* 33 (September 1992): 267–81.

Brown, Phil, and Faith I.T. Ferguson. "Making a Big Stink: Women's Work, Women's Relationships, and Toxic Waste Activism," *Gender and Society* 9, 2 (April 1995): 145–72.

Brown, Roger, and James Kulick. "Flashbulb Memories." *Cognition* 5, 1 (1977): 73–99.

Bryden, P.E. *A Justifiable Obsession: Conservative Ontario's Relationship with Ottawa.* Toronto: University of Toronto Press, 2013.

Buck, Tim. *Yours in the Struggle: Reminiscences of Tim Buck,* edited by William Beeching and Phyllis Clarke. Toronto: NC Press, 1977.

Bullard, Robert D. "Environmental Justice in the Twenty-First Century." In *The Quest for Environmental Justice: Human Rights and the Politics of Pollution,* edited by Robert D. Bullard, 19–42. San Francisco: Sierra Club Books, 2005.

Bunker, Stephen G., and Paul Ciccantell. *East Asia and the Global Economy: Japan's Ascent, with Implications for China's Future.* Baltimore: Johns Hopkins University Press, 2007.

Burnham, Peter. "Capital, Crisis and the International State System." In *Global Capital, National State and the Politics of Money,* edited by Werner Bonefield and John Holloway, 92–115. London: Palgrave MacMillan, 1995.

Burril, Gary. *Away: Maritimers in Massachusetts, Ontario, and Alberta: An Oral History of Leaving Home.* Montreal and Kingston: McGill-Queen's University Press, 1992.

Butler, Toby. "Memoryscape: How Audio Walks Can Deepen Our Sense of Place by Integrating Art, Oral History, and Cultural Geography." *Geography Compass* 1, 3 (2007): 360–72.

Byrne, David. "Industrial Culture in a Post-Industrial World: The Case of the North East of England." *City* 6, 3 (2002): 279–89.

Cameron, James D. *For the People: A History of St. Francis Xavier University.* Montreal and Kingston: McGill-Queen's University Press, 1996.

Cameron, James M. *Industrial History of the New Glasgow District.* New Glasgow, NS: Hector Publishing, 1960.

Campagna, Palmiro. *Storms of Controversy: The Secret Arrow Files Revealed.* Toronto: Stoddart, 1992.

– *Requiem for a Giant: A.V. Roe and the Avro Arrow.* Toronto: Dundurn Group, 2003.

Cholette, Albert. *Le fer du Nouveau-Québec et la saga de la sidérugie: la faillite d'un rêve.* Saint-Nicholas: Les Presses de l'Université Laval, 2000.

Chomsky, Noam, and David Barsamian. *The Common Good.* Berkeley, CA: Odonian Press, 1998.

The CIO's Left-Led Unions, edited by Steve Rosswurm. New Brunswick, NJ: Rutgers University Press, 1992.

Clancy, Peter. "Concerted Action on the Periphery? Voluntary Economic Planning in 'The New Nova Scotia.'" *Acadiensis* 26, 2 (Spring 1997): 3–30.

Clarke, Jackie. "Closing Moulinex: Thoughts on the Visibility and Invisibility of Industrial Labour in Contemporary France." *Modern and Contemporary France* 19, 4 (November 2011): 443–58.

Clippingdale, Richard. *Robert Stanfield's Canada: Perspectives of the Best Prime Minister We Never Had.* Kingston, ON: Queen's University School of Policy Studies, 2008.

Conrad, Margaret. "The 1950s: The Decade of Development." In *The Atlantic Provinces in Confederation,* edited by E.R. Forbes and D.A. Muise, 382–420. Toronto: University of Toronto Press, 1993.

– *George Nowlan: Maritime Conservative in National Politics.* Toronto: University of Toronto Press, 1986.

Corrigal-Brown, Catherine and Mabel Ho. "How the State Shapes Social Movements: An Examination of the Environmental Movement in Canada." In *Protest and Politics: The Promise of Social Movement Societies,* edited by Howard Ramos and Kathleen Rodgers, 101–17. Vancouver: University of British Columbia Press, 2015.

Coupland, Bethan. "Remembering Blaenoven: What Can Group Interviews Tell Us about 'Collective Memory'?" *Oral History Review* 42, 2 (2015): 277–99.

Covert, Frank Manning. *50 Years in the Practice of Law,* edited by Barry Cahill. Montreal and Kingston: McGill-Queen's University Press, 2005.

Cowie, Jefferson. *Capital Moves: RCA's Seventy-Year Quest for Cheap Labour.* Ithaca, NY: Cornell University Press, 1999.

– *The Great Exception: The New Deal and the Limits of American Politics.* Princeton, NJ: Princeton University Press, 2016.

Cowie, Jefferson, and Joseph Heathcott. "Introduction: The Meanings of Deindustrialization." In *Beyond the Ruins: The Meanings of Deindustrialization,* edited by Jefferson Cowie and Joseph Heathcott, 1–18. Ithaca, NY: Cornell University Press, 2003.

Craves, Richard E., Grant L. Leuber, Robert W. Baguley, John M. Curtis, and Raymond Lubitz. *Capital Transfers and Economic Policy: Canada, 1951–1962.* Cambridge, MA: Harvard University Press, 1971.

Crawley, Ron. "Class Conflict and the Establishment of the Sydney Steel Industry, 1899–1904." In *The Island: New Perspectives on Cape Breton History, 1713–1990,* edited by Kenneth Donovan, 145–64. Fredericton and Sydney: Acadiensis and UCCB Press, 1990.

– "Conflict within the Union: Struggles among Sydney Steel Workers, 1936–1972." PhD dissertation, Carleton University, 1995.

– "What Kind of Unionism? Struggles among Sydney Steel Workers in the SWOC Years, 1936–1942." *Labour/Le Travail* 39 (Spring 1997): 99–123.

Crowley, Brian Lee. *The Road to Equity: Gender, Ethnicity, and Language.* Toronto: Stoddart, 1994.

– *The Self, the Individual and the Community: Liberalism in the Political Thought of F.A. Hayek and Sidney and Beatrice Webb.* Oxford: Clarendon Press, 1987.

– *Taking Ownership: Property Rights and Fishery Management on the Atlantic Coast.* Halifax: Atlantic Institute for Market Studies, 1996.

Cruickshank, Douglas, and Gregory S. Kealey. "Strikes in Canada, 1891–1950: I. Analysis." *Labour/Le Travail* 20 (Fall 1987): 85–145.

Curtis, Kent. "Greening Anaconda: EPA, ARCO, and the Politics of Space." In *Beyond the Ruins: The Meanings of Deindustrialization,* edited by Jefferson Cowie and Joseph Heathcott, 91–111. Ithaca, NY: Cornell University Press, 2003.

Davies, G.M. "A Mortality Study of Coke Oven Workers in Two South Wales Integrated Steelworks." *British Journal of Industrial Medicine* 34 (1977): 291–7.

Dawson, Michael. "Victoria Debates Its Post-Industrial Reality: Tourism, Deindustrialization and Store Hour Regulations, 1900–1958." *Urban History Review* 35, 2 (Spring 2007): 14–24.

Dudley, Kathryn Marie. *The End of the Line: Lost Jobs, New Lives in Postindustrial America.* Chicago: University of Chicago Press, 1994.

Epstein, Barbara. "The Environmental Justice/Toxics Movement: Politics of Race and Gender." *Capitalism Nature Socialism* 8, 3 (September 1997): 63–87.

Fahrni, Magda, and Robert Rutherdale, "Introduction." In *Creating Postwar Canada: Community, Diversity, and Dissent, 1945–1975,* edited by Magda Fahrni and Robert Rutherdale, 1–22. Vancouver: UBC Press, 2008.

Farber, David. *Everybody Ought to Be Rich: The Life and Times of John J. Raskob, Capitalist*. Oxford: Oxford University Press, 2013.

Faue, Elizabeth. "Community, Class, and Comparison in Labour History and Local History." *Labour History* 78 (May 2000): 155–62.

Fink, Leon. "Intellectuals versus 'Workers': Academic Requirements and the Creation of Labour History." In *In Search of the Working Class: Essays in American Labor History and Political Culture*, edited by Leon Fink, 201–35. Urbana and Chicago: University of Illinois Press, 1994.

– ed. *Workers across the Americas: The Transnational Turn in Labour History*. Oxford: Oxford University Press, 2011.

Fletcher, Thomas H. *From Love Canal to Environmental Justice: The Politics of Hazardous Waste on the Canada-U.S. Border*. Peterborough, ON: Broadview Press, 2003.

Foley, Michael Stewart. *Front Porch Politics: The Forgotten Heyday of American Activism in the 1970s and 1980s*. New York: Hill and Wang, 2013.

Forbes, E.R. "Consolidating Disparity: The Maritimes and the Industrialization of Canada during the Second World War." In *Challenging the Regional Stereotype: Essays on the 20th Century Maritimes*, edited by E.R. Forbes, 172–99. Fredericton, NB: Acadiensis Press, 1989.

– *The Maritime Rights Movement, 1919–1927: A Study in Canadian Regionalism*. Montreal and Kingston: McGill-Queen's University Press, 1979.

Forrest, Anne. "Securing the Male Breadwinner: A Feminist Interpretation of PC 1003." *Relations Industrielles/Industrial Relations* 52, 1 (Winter 1997): 91–113.

Fortin, Pierre. "Quebec's Quiet Revolution, 50 Years Later." *Inroads* 29 (Summer/Fall 2011): 90–9.

Frank, David. "The Cape Breton Coal Industry and the Rise and Fall of the British Empire Steel Corporation." *Acadiensis* 7, 1 (Spring 1977): 3–34.

– "The Industrial Folk Song in Cape Breton." *Canadian Folklore Canadien* 8, 1–2 (1986): 21–42.

– *J.B. McLachlan: A Biography*. Toronto: James Lorimer, 1999.

– "Tradition and Culture in the Cape Breton Mining Community in the Early Twentieth Century." In *Cape Breton at 200: Essays in Honour of the Island's Bicentennial, 1785–1985*, edited by Kenneth Donovan, 203–18. Sydney, NS: UCCB Press, 1985.

Frank, David, and Donald MacGillivray. Introduction to *Echoes from Labor's War: Industrial Cape Breton in the 1920s*, by Dawn Fraser. Toronto: New Hogtown Press, 1976.

Frisch, Michael. *A Shared Authority: Essays on the Craft and Meaning of Oral and Public History*. Albany, NY: SUNY Press, 1990.

– "Three Dimensions and More: Oral History beyond the Paradoxes of Method." In *Handbook of Emergent Methods*, edited by Sharlene Nagy Hesse-Biber and Patricia Leavy, 228–38. New York: Guildford Press, 2008.

Frost, James D. "The 'Nationalization' of the Bank of Nova Scotia, 1880–1910." *Acadiensis* 12, 1 (Autumn 1982): 3–38.

Fudge, Judy, and Eric Tucker. *Labour before the Law: The Regulation of Workers' Collective Action in Canada, 1900–1948.* Oxford: Oxford University Press, 2001.

Gallie, Duncan. "Skills, Job Control, and the Quality of Work: The Evidence from Britain." *The Economic and Social Review* 43, 3 (Autumn 2012): 325–41.

George, Roy. *The Life and Times of Industrial Estates Limited.* Halifax: Dalhousie University Institute of Public Affairs, 1974.

Goode, Richard. "Accelerated Depreciation Allowances as a Stimulus to Investment." *Quarterly Journal of Economics* 69, 2 (May 1955): 191–220.

Gordon, James S. "Shipping Regulation and the Federal Maritime Commission, Pt. 1." *University of Chicago Law Review* 37, 1 (Autumn 1969): 90–158.

Government of Nova Scotia. http://novascotia.ca/news/release/?id=20130 614002.

Guernsey, Judith, Ron Dewar, Swarna Weerasinghe, Susan Kirkland, and Paul Veugelers. "Incidence of Cancer in Sydney and Cape Breton County, Nova Scotia 1979–1997," *Canadian Journal of Public Health* 91, 4 (July–August 2000): 282–92.

Green, Jim. *Against the Tide: The Story of the Canadian Seamen's Union.* Toronto: Progress Books, 1986.

Hak, Gordon. *Capital and Labour in the British Columbia Forest Industry, 1934–1974.* Vancouver: University of British Columbia Press, 2007.

Hakarvy, Ira, and Harmon Zuckerman. *Eds and Meds: Cities' Hidden Assets.* Washington, DC: Center on Urban and Metropolitan Policy, 1999.

Haley, Brendan. "From Staples Trap to Carbon Trap: Canada's Peculiar Form of Carbon Lock In." *Studies in Political Economy* 88, 1 (2011): 97–132.

Haliburton, Ed. *My Years with Stanfield.* Windsor, NS: Lancelot Press, 1972.

Harrison, Bennett. *Lean and Mean: Why Large Corporations Continue to Dominate the Global Economy.* New York: Guilford Press, 1997.

Harvey, David. "The Body as Accumulation Strategy." *Environment and Planning D: Society and Space* 16, 4 (August 1998): 401–21.

– *A Brief History of Neoliberalism.* Oxford: Oxford University Press, 2005.

– *The Condition of Postmodernity: An Enquiry into the Origins of Cultural Change.* Oxford: Basil Blackwell, 1989.

– "The Urban Process under Capitalism: A Framework for Analysis." *International Journal of Urban and Regional Research* 2 (March–December 1978): 101–31.

Harvey, E. Roy. *Sydney, Nova Scotia: An Urban Study.* Toronto: Clarke, Irwin: 1971.

Hayter, Roger, and Trevor Barnes. "Innis' Staples Theory, Exports, and Recession: British Columbia, 1981–1986." *Economic Geography* 66 (1990): 156–73.

Hayter, Roger, Trevor Barnes, and Michael Bradshaw. "Relocating Resource
    Peripheries to the Core of Economic Geography's Theorizing: Rationale
    and Agenda." *Area* 35, 1 (2003): 15–23.
Hein, Jane Ricketts, James Evans, and Phil Jones. "Mobile Methodologies:
    Theory, Technology and Practice." *Geography Compass* 2–5 (2008): 1266–85.
Heron, Craig. "Boys Will Be Boys: Working-Class Masculinities in the Age of
    Mass Production." *International Labor and Working-Class History* 69 (2006):
    6–34.
– *The Canadian Labour Movement.* Toronto: James Lorimer, 1989.
– "Communists, Gangsters, and Canadian Sailors." *Labour/Le Travail* 24 (Fall
    1989): 231–7.
– "The Great War and Nova Scotia Steelworkers." *Acadiensis* 16, 2 (Spring
    1987): 3–34.
– *Lunch Bucket Lives: Remaking the Workers' City.* Toronto: Between the Lines,
    2015.
– "The Mill: A Worker's Memoir from 1945–1948." *Labour/Le Travail* 43 (Spring
    1999): 171–94.
– *Working in Steel: The Early Years in Canada, 1883–1935.* Toronto: McClelland
    and Stewart, 1988.
Heron, Craig, and Robert Storey. "Work and Struggle in the Canadian Steel
    Industry, 1900–1950." In *On the Job: Confronting the Labour Process in Canada*,
    edited by Craig Heron and Robert Storey, 210–44. Montreal and Kingston:
    McGill-Queen's University Press, 1986.
High, Steven. "Beyond Aesthetics: Visibility and Invisibility in the Aftermath
    of Deindustrialization." *International Labor and Working-Class History* 84
    (Fall 2013): 140–153.
– "Deindustrialization on the Industrial Frontier: The Rise and Fall of
    Mill Colonialism in Northern Ontario." In *The Deindustrialized World:
    Confronting Ruination in Post-Industrial Places*, edited by Steven High,
    Lachlan MacKinnon, and Andrew Perchard. Vancouver: University of
    British Columbia Press, 2017.
– "'I'll Wrap the F*#@ Canadian Flag around Me': A Nationalist Response to
    Plant Shutdowns, 1969–1984." *Journal of the Canadian Historical Association*
    12, 1 (2001): 199–225.
– *Industrial Sunset: The Making of North America's Rust Belt, 1969–1984.* Toronto:
    University of Toronto Press, 2003.
– "Introduction." *Urban History Review* 35, 2 (Spring 2007): 2–13.
– "Mapping Memories of Displacement: Oral History, Memoryscapes and
    Mobile Methodologies." In *Place, Writing, and Voice in Oral History*, edited
    by Shelley Trower, 217–31. New York: Palgrave Macmillan: 2011.
– *Oral History at the Crossroads: Sharing Life Stories of Survival and Displacement.*
    Vancouver: University of British Columbia Press, 2014.

– "Placing the Displaced Worker: Narrating Place in Deindustrializing Sturgeon Falls, Ontario." In *Placing Memory and Remembering Place in Canada*, edited by James Opp and John C. Walsh, 159–86. Vancouver and Toronto: University of British Columbia Press, 2010.

– "Sharing Authority in the Writing of Canadian History: The Case of Oral History." In *Contesting Clio's Craft: New Directions and Debates in Canadian History*, edited by Christopher Dummitt and Michael Dawson, 20–46. London: University of London, 2008.

– "'The Wounds of Class': A Historiographical Reflection on the Study of Deindustrialization, 1973–2013." *History Compass* 11, 11 (November 2013): 994–1007.

High, Steven, and David Lewis. *Corporate Wasteland: The Landscape and Memory of Deindustrialization*. Ithaca, NY: Cornell University Press, 2007.

High, Steven, and David Sworn. "After the Interview: The Interpretive Challenges of Oral History Video Indexing." *Digital Studies/Le champ numérique* 1, 2 (2009). http://www.digitalstudies.org/ojs/index.php /digital_studies/article/view/173/215.

High, Steven, Stacey Zembrzycki, and Jessica Mills. "Telling Our Stories/ Animating Our Past: A Status Report on Oral History and New Media." *Canadian Journal of Communications* 37, 3 (2012): 1–22.

Hinshaw, John. *Steel and Steelworkers: Race and Class Struggle in Twentieth-Century Pittsburgh*. Albany, NY: SUNY Press, 2002.

Hobsbawm, Eric. *The Age of Extremes: The Short Twentieth Century, 1914–1991*. London: Abacus, 1994.

– "The Machine Breakers," *Past and Present* 1 (February 1952): 57–70.

Hollander, Taylor. "Making Reform Happen: The Passage of Canada's Collective-Bargaining Policy, 1943–1944." *Journal of Policy History* 13, 3 (2001): 299–328.

Hornsby, Stephen J. *Nineteenth Century Cape Breton: A Historical Geography*. Montreal and Kingston: McGill-Queen's University Press, 1992.

Huk, John. *Strangers in the Land: The Ukrainian Presence in Cape Breton*. Sydney: City Printers, 1986.

Hurley, Andrew. *Environmental Inequalities: Class, Race, and Industrial Pollution in Gary, Indiana*. Chapel Hill: University of North Carolina Press, 1995.

– "From Factory Town to Metropolitan Junkyard: Postindustrial Transitions on the Urban Periphery." *Environmental History* 21, 1 (2016): 3–29.

– "The Transformation of Industrial Suburbs since World War Two." In *The Deindustrialized World: Confronting Ruination in Post-Industrial Places*, edited by Steven High, Lachlan MacKinnon, and Andrew Perchard. Vancouver: University of British Columbia Press, 2017.

Hurst, William, Randy Buckner, Andrew Budson, Alexandru Cuc, John Gabrieli, Marcia Johnson, Keith Lyle, Cindy Lustig, Mara Mather, Robert

Meksin, Karen Mitchell, Kevin Oschner, Daniel Schacter, Jon Simons, and Chandan Vaidya. "Long-Term Memory for the Terrorist Attack of September 11: Flashbulb Memories, Long Term Memories, and the Factors That Influence Their Retention." *Journal of Experimental Psychology General* 138, 2 (May 2009): 161–76.

Inwood, Kris E. "Local Control, Resources and the Nova Scotia Steel and Coal Company." *Historical Papers* 21, 1 (1986): 254–82.

James, Daniel. *Doña Maria's Story: Life History, Memory, and Political Identity.* Durham, NC: Duke University Press, 2000.

Johnson, Christopher. "Deindustrialization and Globalization." *International Review of Social History* 47 (November 2002): 3–33.

– *The Life and Death of Industrial Languedoc, 1700–1920: The Politics of Deindustrialization.* Oxford: Oxford University Press, 1995.

Johnston, Ronnie, and Arthur McIvor. "Dangerous Work, Hard Men, and Broken Bodies: Masculinity in the Clydeside Heavy Industries, c. 1930–1970s." *Labour History Review* 69, 2 (2004): 135–51.

Kaplan, William. *Everything That Floats: Pat Sullivan, Hal Banks, and the Seamen's Unions of Canada.* Toronto: University of Toronto Press, 1987.

Katznelson, Ira. "The Bourgeois Dimension: A Provocation about Institutions, Politics, and the Future of Labour History." *International Labor and Working-Class History* 46 (1994): 7–32.

Kealey, Gregory S. "1919: The Canadian Labour Revolt." *Labour/Le Travail* 13 (Spring 1984): 11–44.

– "Stanley Bréhaut Ryerson: Canadian Revolutionary Intellectual – Part 1." *Studies in Political Economy* 9 (1982): 7–36.

Kerr, Donald. "The Geography of the Canadian Iron and Steel Industry." *Economic Geography* 35, 2 (April 1959): 151–63.

Kilbourne, William. *The Elements Combined: A History of the Steel Company of Canada.* Toronto: Clarke, Irwin, 1960.

Kirk, John, Sylvie Contrepois, and Steve Jeffries, eds. *Changing Work and Community Identities in European Regions: Perspectives on the Past and Present.* New York: Palgrave Macmillan, 2012.

Kirk, John, and Christine Wall. *Work and Identity: Historical and Cultural Contexts.* London: Palgrave Macmillan, 2011.

Kirk, John, Sylvie Contrepois, and Steve Jeffreys. "Approaching Regional and Identity Change in Europe." In *Changing Work and Community Identities in European Regions: Perspectives on the Past and Present*, edited by John Kirk, Sylvie Contrepois, and Steve Jeffreys, 1–22. New York: Palgrave McMillan, 2012.

Koechl, Marc. "Sailor's Ashore: A Comparative Analysis of Wartime Recreation and Leisure in Halifax and Saint John's." Master's thesis, Memorial University of Newfoundland, 2003.

Krauss, Celine. "Challenging Power: Toxic Waste Protests and the Poltiicization of White, Working-Class Women." In *Community Activism and Feminist Politics: Organizing across Race, Class, and Gender*, edited by Nancy Naples, 129–50. New York: Routledge, 1998.

Krippner, Greta R. *Capitalizing on Crisis: The Political Origins of the Rise of Finance*. Cambridge, MA: Harvard University Press, 2011.

Kurasaw, Fuyuki. "Which Barbarians at the Gates? From the Culture Wars to Market Orthodoxy in the North American Academy." *Canadian Review of Sociology and Anthropology* 39, 3 (2002): 323–47.

Lauderbaugh, Richard A. "Business, Labor, and Foreign Policy: U.S. Steel, the International Steel Cartel, and the Recognition of the Steel Workers Organizing Committee." *Politics and Society* 6, 4 (December 1976): 433–57.

Linkon, Sherry Lee. "Narrating Past and Future: Deindustrialized Landscapes as Resources." *International Labor and Working-Class History* 84 (Fall 2013): 38–54.

Linkon, Sherry Lee, and John Russo. *Steeltown U.S.A.: Work and Memory in Youngstown*. Lawrence: University Press of Kansas, 2003.

Lloyd, J. William, Frank E. Lundin, Jr., Carol K. Redmond, and Patricia B. Geiser. "Long Term Mortality Study of Steelworkers: IV Mortality by Work Area." *Journal of Occupational Medicine* 12, 5 (1970): 151–7.

Lynd, Staughton. *The Fight against Shutdowns: Youngstown's Steel Mill Closings*. San Pedro: Singlejack Books, 1982.

Madar, Daniel. *Big Steel: Technology, Trade, and Survival in a Global Market*. Vancouver: University of British Columbia Press, 2009.

Mah, Alice. *Industrial Ruination, Community, and Place: Landscapes and Legacies of Urban Decline*. Toronto: University of Toronto Press, 2012.

MacDowell, Laurel Sefton. "The 1943 Steel Strike against Wartime Wage Controls." *Labour/Le Travail* 10 (Autumn, 1982): 65–85.

– "The Career of a Canadian Trade Union Leader: C.H. Millard 1937–1946." *Relations industrielles/Industrial Relations* 43, 3 (1988): 609–32.

– "The Elliot Lake Uranium Miners' Battle to Gain Occupational Health and Safety Improvements, 1950–1980." *Labour/Le Travail* 69 (Spring 2012): 91–118.

– *An Environmental History of Canada*. Vancouver: University of British Columbia Press, 2012.

MacEachern, George. *George MacEachern: An Autobiography*, edited by David Frank and Donald MacGillivray. Sydney, NS: UCCB Press, 1987.

– "Organizing Sydney's Steelworkers in the 1930s." In *We Stood Together: First-Hand Accounts of Dramatic Events in Canada's Labour Past*, edited by Gloria Montero, 47–68. Toronto: James Lorimer, 1979.

MacFarlane, Daniel. *Negotiating a River: Canada, the US, and the Creation of the St. Lawrence Seaway*. Vancouver: University of British Columbia Press, 2014.

MacGillivray, Donald. "Henry Melville Whitney Comes to Cape Breton: The
    Saga of a Gilded Age Entrepreneur." *Acadiensis* 9, 1 (Autumn 1979): 44–70.
– "The Industrial Verse of Slim McInnis." *Labour/Le Travail* 28 (Fall 1991):
    271-83
– "Military Aid to the Civil Power: The Cape Breton Experience in the 1920s."
    Acadiensis 3, 2 (Spring 1974): 45–64.
MacKinnon, Lachlan. "Reading a Labour Landmark in Sydney, Nova Scotia."
    Labour/Le Travail 72 (Fall 2013): 101–28.
MacPhee, Katrin. "Canadian Working-Class Environmentalism, 1965–1985."
    Labour/Le Travail 74 (Fall 2014): 123–49.
Martinez-Alier, Joan. *The Environmentalism of the Poor: A Study of Ecological
    Conflicts and Valuation.* Northampton, MA: Edward Elgar Publishing, 2002.
Marx, Karl. *The 18th Brumaire of Louis Bonaparte.* New York: Cosmo Classics,
    2008. First published 1852.
Massey, Doreen. "Places and their Pasts." *History Workshop Journal* 39 (1995):
    182–92.
– *Space, Place, and Gender.* Minneapolis: University of Minnesota Press 1994.
McCaffrey, David. *OSHA and the Politics of Health Regulation.* New York:
    Plenum Press, 1982.
McCrorie, Aaron. "PC 1003: Labour, Capital, and the State." In *Labour Gains,
    Labour Pains: 50 Years of PC 1003,* edited by Cy Gonick, Paul Phillips, and
    Jesse Vorst, 15–38. Winnipeg and Halifax: Society for Socialist Studies and
    Fernwood Publishing, 1995.
McDowell, Duncan. *Steel at the Sault: Francis H. Clergue, Sir James Dunn, and the
    Algoma Steel Corporation, 1901–1956.* Toronto: University of Toronto Press,
    1984.
McInnis, Peter. *Harnessing Labour Confrontation: Shaping the Postwar Settlement
    in Canada: 1943–1950.* Toronto: University of Toronto Press, 2002.
McIvor, Arthur. "Deindustrialization Embodied: Work, Health and Disability
    in the U.K. since c. 1950." In *The Deindustrialized World: Confronting
    Ruination in Post-Industrial Places,* edited by Steven High, Lachlan
    MacKinnon, and Andrew Perchard, 25–45. Vancouver: University of British
    Columbia Press, 2017.
– "Economic Violence, Occupational Disability, and Death: Oral Narratives
    of the Impact of Asbestos-Related Diseases in Britain." In *Beyond Testimony
    and Trauma: Oral History in the Aftermath of Mass Violence,* edited by Steven
    High, 257–84. Vancouver: University of British Columbia Press, 2015.
– *Working Lives: Work in Britain Since 1945.* London: Palgrave MacMillan, 2013.
McKay, Ian. *The Quest of the Folk: Antimodernism and Cultural Selection in
    Twentieth Century Nova Scotia.* Montreal and Kingston: McGill-Queen's
    University Press, 1994.

– "Review of Steven High, *Industrial Sunset: The Making of North America's Rust Belt, 1969–1984*." H-Canada, H-Net Revews (April 2005). http://www.h-net.org/reviews/showrev.php?id=10458.

McKay, Ian, and Robin Bates. *In the Province of History: The Making of the Public Past in Twentieth-Century Nova Scotia*. Montreal and Kingston: McGill-Queen's University Press, 2010.

McKee, Guian. *Health Care Policy as Urban Policy: Hospitals and Community Development in the Post-Industrial City*. San Francisco: Federal Reserve Bank of San Francisco, 2010. http://www.frbsf.org/community-development/files/working_paper_2010_10_healthcare_policy_as_urban_policy.pdf.

McLaughlin, Mark. "Green Shoots: Aerial Insecticide Spraying and the Growth of Environmental Consciousness in New Brunswick, 1952–1973." *Acadiensis* 40, 1 (2011): 3–23.

Migliore, Sam and A. Evo DiPierro. *Italian Lives, Cape Breton Memories*. Sydney: UCCB Press, 1999.

Milligan, Ian. *Rebel Youth: 1960s Labour Unrest, Young Workers, and New Leftists in English Canada*. Vancouver: University of British Columbia Press, 2014.

Milne, David. *Tug of War: Ottawa and the Provinces under Trudeau and Mulroney* Toronto: James Lorimer, 1986.

Mirowski, Philip. "Postface: Defining Neoliberalism." In *The Road from Mont Pelerin: The Making of the Neoliberal Thought Collective*, edited by Philip Mirowski and Dieter Plehwe, 417–56. Cambridge, MA: Harvard University Press, 2009.

Molnar-Szakacs, Hajnol. "An Investigation of Adolescents Perspectives on Belonging to the Community and the Influence of Data Collection Methods on Information." Master's thesis, Dalhousie University, 1999.

Montrie, Chad. *Making a Living: Work and the Environment in the United States*. Chapel Hill: University of North Carolina Press, 2008.

– *A People's History of Environmentalism in the United States*. New York: Continuum, 2011.

Morck, Randall K., Michael Percy, Gloria Y. Tian, and Bernard Yeung. "The Rise and Fall of the Widely Held Firm: A History of Corporate Ownership in Canada." In *A History of Corporate Governance around the World: Family Business Groups to Professional Managers*, edited by Randall K. Morck, 65–148. Chicago: University of Chicago Press, 2005.

Morgan, Robert. *Perseverance: The Story of Cape Breton's University College, 1952–2002*. Sydney, NS: UCCB Press, 2004.

– *Rise Again! The Story of Cape Breton Island from 1900 to Today*. Sydney, NS: Breton Books, 2009.

Morien Resource Corp. "Donkin Project." http://morienres.com/donkin-project/.

Muirhead, Bruce. "Perception and Reality: The GATT's Contribution to the Development of a Bilateral North American Relationship, 1947–1951." *American Review of Canadian Studies* 20, 3 (1990): 279–301.

Mukherjee, Suroopa. *Surviving Bhopal: Dancing Bodies, Written Texts and Oral Testimonials of Women in the Wake of an Industrial Disaster.* New York: Palgrave Macmillan, 2010.

Nerbas, Don. "Adapting to Decline: The Changing Business World of the Bourgeoisie in Saint John, NB, in the 1920s." *Canadian Historical Review* 89, 2 (2008): 151–87.

Newman, Peter C. *The Canadian Establishment*, vol. 1: *The Old Order.* Toronto: McClelland and Stewart, 1975.

Newman, Richard. "From Love's Canal to Love Canal: Reckoning with the Environmental Legacy of an Industrial Dream." In *Beyond the Ruins: The Meanings of* Deindustrialization, edited by Jefferson Cowie and Joseph Heathcott, 112–38. Ithaca, NY: Cornell University Press, 2003.

Norcliffe, Glen. *Global Game, Local Arena: Restructuring in Corner Brook.* Saint John's, NL: Iser, 2005.

Nova Scotia Commission on Building a New Economy. *Now or Never: An Urgent Call to Action for Nova Scotians.* February 2014. http://onens.ca /commission-report/.

Orange, Hilary, ed. *Reanimating Industrial Spaces: Conducting Memory Work in Post-Industrial Societies.* Walnut Creek, CA: Left Coast Press, 2015.

Owram, Doug. "Economic Nationalism." In *Canadian History Post-Confederation*, edited by John Douglas Belshaw. BC Campus: OpenEd, https://opentextbc.ca/postconfederation/.

Palmer, Bryan. *Canada's 1960s: The Ironies of Identity in a Rebellious Era.* Toronto: University of Toronto Press, 2009.

– *Marxism and Historical Practice: Interventions and Appreciations*, vol. 2. Leiden: Brill, 2015.

– *Working Class Experience: Rethinking the History of Canadian Labour, 1800–1991.* Toronto: University of Toronto Press, 1992.

Park, Libbie, and Frank Park. *Anatomy of Big Business.* Toronto: James, Lewis, and Samuel, 1973.

Parnaby, Andy. "Growing Up Even More Uncertain: Children and Youth Confront Industrial Ruin in Sydney, Nova Scotia, 1967." In *The Deindustrialized World: Confronting Ruination in Post-Industrial Places*, edited by Steven High, Lachlan MacKinnon, and Andrew Perchard. Vancouver: University of British Columbia Press, 2017.

Parr, Joy. *The Gender of Breadwinners: Women, Men, and Change in Two Industrial Towns, 1880–1950.* Toronto, University of Toronto Press, 1990.

Patterson, Paul, and Susan Biagi. *The Loom of Change: Weaving a New Economy on Cape Breton Island.* Sydney, NS: University College of Cape Breton Press, 2003.

Perchard, Andrew, and Jim Phillips. "Transgressing the Moral Economy: Wheelerism and the Management of the Nationalised Coal Industry in Scotland." *Contemporary British History* 25, 3 (2011): 387–405.

Pilon, Denis. "Review Essay: The Long Lingering Death of Social Democracy." *Labour/Le Travail* 70 (Fall 2012): 245–60.

Plehwe, Dieter, Bernhard Walpen, and Gisela Neunhöffer. "Introduction: Reconsidering Neoliberal Hegemony." In *Neoliberal Hegemony: A Global Critique*, edited by Dieter Plehwe, Bernhard Walpen, and Gisela Neunhöffer, 1–24. London: Routledge, 2006.

Pomar, Olga. "Toxic Racism on the New Jersey Waterfront." In *The Quest for Environmental Justice: Human Rights and the Politics of Pollution*, edited by Robert D. Bullard, 125–41. San Francisco: Sierra Club Books, 2005.

Portelli, Alessandro. "Oral History as Genre." In *Narrative and Genre*, edited by Mary Chamberlain and Paul Thompson, 23–45. London: Routledge, 1998.

– "What Makes Oral History Different?" In *The Oral History Reader*, edited by Robert Perks and Alistair Thomson, 63–74. London: Routledge, 1998.

Port of Sydney. "Positioned for Success, 2016 Business Prospectus." http://www.sydneyport.ca/portofsydney/port-of-sydney-prospectus/.

Public Works and Government Services Canada. http://news.gc.ca/web/article-en.do?nid=768179.

Reilly, Sharon. "Deindustrialization as Public History: An Exhibition at the Manitoba Museum." *Urban History Review* 35, 2 (Spring 2007): 77–82.

Renaud, Marc. "Quebec's New Middle Class in Search of Social Hegemony: Causes and Political Consequences." In *The Challenge of Modernity: A Reader on Post-Confederation Canada*, edited by Ian McKay, 48–79. Toronto: McGraw-Hill Ryerson, 1992.

Rhodes, James. "Youngstown's 'Ghost'? Memory, Identity and Deindustrialization." *International Labor and Working-Class History* 84 (Fall 2013): 55–77.

Richie, Donald. *Doing Oral History*. 3rd ed. Oxford: Oxford University Press, 2015.

Robb, Nancy. "Were Jobs More Important Than Health in Sydney?" *Canadian Medical Association Journal* 152, 6 (15 March 1995): 919–23.

Ross, Moira. "Dr. Arthur Samuel Kendall, His Life and Times as a Medical Doctor, Politician and Citizen of Cape Breton Island, 1861–1944." Master's thesis, St Mary's University, 1998.

Russell, Bob. "Labour's Magna Carta? Wagnerism in Canada at Fifty." In *Labour Gains, Labour Pains: 50 Years of PC 1003*, edited by Cy Gonick, Paul Phillips, and Jesse Vorst, 382–418. Winnipeg and Halifax: Society for Socialist Studies and Fernwood Publishing, 1995.

– *More with Less: Reorganization in the Canadian Mining Industry*. Toronto: University of Toronto Press, 1999.

Sandberg, L. Anders. "Dependent Development, Labour and the Trenton Steel Works, Nova Scotia, c. 1900–1943." *Labour/Le Travail* 27 (Spring 1991): 127–62.

Sauvé, Jeanne. Speech from the Throne. 30 September 1986. https://www .poltext.org/en/part-1-electronic-political-texts/canadian-throne-speeches.

Savoie, Donald. *Regional Economic Development: Canada's Search for Solutions.* Toronto: University of Toronto Press, 1986.

Schacter, Daniel L. *Searching for Memory: The Brain, the Mind, and the Past.* New York: HarperCollins, 1996.

Schöller, Oliver, and Olaf Groh-Samburg. "The Education of Neoliberalism." In *Neoliberal Hegemony: A Critique*, edited by Dieter Plehwe, Bernhard Walpen, and Gisela Neunhöffer, 171–87. London: Routledge, 2006.

Scott, Jacqueline. *Doing Business with the Devil: Land, Sovereignty, and Corporate Partnerships in Membertou Inc.* Halifax: Atlantic Institute for Market Studies, 2004.

Schumpeter, Joseph. *Capitalism, Socialism, and Democracy.* London: Routledge, 2003. First published 1942 by Harper Perennial.

Sheller, Mimi, and John Urry. "The New Mobilities Program." *Environment and Planning A* 38 (2006): 207–36

Shopes, Linda. "Commentary: Sharing Authority." *Oral History Review* 30, 1 (Winter-Spring 2003): 103–10.

Simon, Roger D., and Brian Allnutt, "Philadelphia, 1982–2007: Toward the Postindustrial City." *Pennsylvania Magazine of History and Biography* 131, 4 (October 2007): 395–444.

Sirota, G.R., J.F. Uthe, D.G. Robinson, and C.J. Musial. "Polycyclic Aromatic Hydrocarbons in American Lobster (Homarus americanus) and Blue Mussels (Mytilus edulis) Collected in Sydney Harbour, Sydney, Nova Scotia, Canada." *Canadian Manuscript Report of Fisheries and Aquatic Sciences* 1758 (1984).

Sitzia, Lorraine. "A Shared Authority: An Impossible Goal?" *Oral History Review* 30, 1 (Winter-Spring 2003): 87–101.

Slim, Hugo, Paul Thompson, Olivia Bennett, and Nigel Cross. "Ways of Listening." In *The Oral History Reader*, edited by Robert Perks and Alistair Thomson, 114–25. London: Routledge, 1998.

Slumkoski, Corey. *Inventing Atlantic Canada: Regionalism and the Maritime Reaction to Newfoundland's Entry into Canadian Confederation.* Toronto: University of Toronto Press, 2011.

Speaking for Ourselves: Environmental Justice in Canada, edited by Julian Agyeman, Peter Cole, Randolph Haluza-DeLay, and Pat O'Reilly. Vancouver: University of British Columbia Press, 2009.

Stanton, Cathy. "Keeping 'the Industrial': New Solidarities in Post-Industrial Places." In *The Deindustrialized World: Confronting Ruination in*

Post-Industrial Places, edited by Steven High, Lachlan MacKinnon, and Andrew Perchard. Vancouver: University of British Columbia Press, 2017.

Stein, Judith. *Running Steel, Running America: Race, Economic Policy, and the Decline of Liberalism*. Chapel Hill: University of North Carolina Press, 1998.

Stevens, Geoffrey. *Stanfield*. Toronto: McClelland and Stewart, 1973.

Stewart, Greig. *Arrow through the Heart: The Life and Times of Crawford Gordon and the Avro Arrow*. Toronto: McGraw-Hill, 1998.

Storey, Robert. "From the Environment to the Workplace ... And Back Again? Occupational Health and Safety Activism in Ontario, 1970s–2000." *Canadian Review of Sociology/Revue canadienne de sociologie* 41, 4 (2004): 419–47.

– "Pessimism of the Intellect, Optimism of the Will: Engaging with the 'Testimony' of Injured Workers." In *Beyond Testimony and Trauma: Oral History in the Aftermath of Mass Violence*, edited by Steven High, 56–87. Vancouver: University of British Columbia Press, 2015.

– "Social Assistance or a Worker's Right? Workmen's Compensation and the Struggle of Injured Workers in Ontario, 1970–1985." *Studies in Political Economy* 78 (2006): 67–91.

– "The Struggle for Job Ownership in the Canadian Steel Industry: An Historical Analysis." *Labour/Le Travail* 33 (Spring 1994): 75–106.

– "The Struggle to Organize Stelco and Dofasco." *Relations industrielles/ Industrial Relations* 42, 2 (1987): 366–85.

– "Unionization versus Corporate Welfare: The 'Dofasco Way.'" *Labour/Le Travail* 12 (Autumn 1983): 7–42.

– "Workers, Unions, and Steel: The Shaping of the Hamilton Working Class, 1935–1948." PhD dissertation, University of Toronto, 1981.

Story, Donald C., and Russell Isinger. "The Origins of the Cancellation of Canada's Avro CF-105 Arrow Fighter Program: A Failure of Strategy." *Journal of Strategic Studies* 30, 6 (2007): 1025–50.

Strangleman, Tim. "Deindustrialization and the Historical Sociological Imagination: Making Sense of Work and Industrial Change." *Sociology* 50, 1 (2016): 1–17.

– "The Nostalgia of Organizations and the Organization of Nostalgia: Past and Present in the Contemporary Railway Industry." *Sociology* 33, 4 (November 1999): 725–46.

– "The Nostalgia for Permanence at Work? The End of Work and Its Commentators." *Sociological Review* 55, 1 (2007): 81–103.

– "'Smokestack Nostalgia,' 'Ruin Porn,' or Working Class Obituary: The Role and Meaning of Deindustrial Representation." *International Labor and Working-Class History* 84 (2013): 23–37.

– *Work Identity at the End of the Line: Privatization and Culture Change in the UK Rail Industry*. Basingstoke, UK: Palgrave MacMillan, 2004.

Strangleman, Tim, James Rhodes, and Sherry Linkon. "Introduction to Crumbling Cultures: Deindustrialization, Class and Memory." *International Labor and Working-Class History* 84 (Fall 2013): 7–22.

Sugiman, Pamela. "'Life Is Sweet': Vulnerability and Composure in the Wartime Narratives of Japanese Canadians." *Journal of Canadian Studies* 43, 1 (Winter 2009): 186–218.

Summerby-Murray, Robert. "Interpreting Personalized Industrial Heritage in the Mining Towns of Cumberland County, Nova Scotia: Landscape Examples from Springhill and River Hebert." *Urban History Review* 35, 2 (Spring 2007): 51–9.

Sydney Steel Museum. www.sydneysteelmuseum.com.

Sydney Tar Ponds Agency. "Memorandum of Agreement between the Government of Canada and the Government of Nova Scotia, respecting Remediation of the Sydney Tar Ponds and Coke Ovens Sites." 12 May 2004. http://www.tarpondscleanup.ca/index.php?sid=3&cid=9&pid=126& lang=e.

Taksa, Lucy. "Labor History and Public History in Australia: Allies or Uneasy Bedfellows?" *International Labor and Working-Class History* 76 (2009): 82–104.

– "Like a Bicycle, Forever Teetering between Indvidualism and Collectivism: Considering Community in Relation to Labour History." *Labour History* 78 (May 2000): 7–32.

Taylor, A.J.P. *Beaverbrook*. New York: Simon and Schuster, 1972.

Taylor, Dorceta E. *Toxic Communities: Environmental Racism, Industrial Pollution, and Residential Mobility*. New York: New York University Press, 2014.

Thiesen, Andrew. "G.I. Smith and Economic Development in Nova Scotia." Master's thesis, Saint Mary's University, 1995.

Thomson, Alistair. *Anzac Memories: Living with the Legend*. Victoria: Monash University Publishing, 2013. First published Oxford University Press, 1994.

– "Four Paradigm Transformations in Oral History." *Oral History Review* 34, 1 (2006): 49–70.

Thompson, E.P. *The Making of the English Working Class*. 2nd ed. New York: Random House, 1976.

– "The Moral Economy of the English Crowd in the Eighteenth Century." *Past and Present* 50 (February 1971): 76–136.

Thompson, Jennifer. "Toxic Residents: Health and Citizenship at Love Canal." *Journal of Social History* Advance Access (2015): 1–20. http://jsh .oxfordjournals.org/content/early/2015/12/18/jsh.shv105.full.

Thompson, Paul. *The Voice of the Past: Oral History*. 3rd ed. London: Oxford University Press, 2000.

Thornton, Patricia A. "The Problem of Out-Migration from Atlantic Canada, 1871–1921: A New Look." *Acadiensis* 15, 1 (Autumn, 1985): 3–34.

Til, Jon Van. *Growing Civil Society: From Nonprofit Sector to Third Space.* Bloomington: Indiana University Press, 2000.

Tonts, Matthew, Kirsten Martinus, Paul Plummer. "Regional Development, Redistribution and the Extraction of Mineral Resources: The Western Australian Goldfields as a Resource Bank." *Applied Geography* 45 (2013): 365–74.

Tucker, Eric. "Should Wagnerism Have No Dominion?" *Just Labour: A Canadian Journal of Work and Society* 21 (Spring 2014): 1–27.

Tupper, Allan. "Public Enterprise as Social Welfare: The Case of the Cape Breton Development Corporation." *Canadian Public Policy/Analyse de Politiques* 4, 4 (Autumn 1978): 530–46.

University of British Columbia Sauder School of Business Pacific Exchange Rate Service. "Foreign Currency Units per 1 Canadian Dollar," 1948–2014. http://fx.sauder.ubc.ca/.

Vandermeulen, J.H. "PAH and Heavy Metal Pollution of the Sydney Estuary: Summary and Review of Studies to 1987." *Canadian Technical Report of Hydrography and Ocean Sciences* 108 (May 1989): 1–48.

Vuolteenaho, Jani, and Lawrence D. Berg. "Towards Critical Toponymies." In *Critical Toponymies: The Contested Politics of Place Naming*, edited by Lawrence D. Berg and Jani Vuolteenaho, 1–18. London: Ashgate, 2009.

Walley, Christine. *Exit Zero: Family and Class in Postindustrial Chicago.* Chicago: University of Chicago Press, 2013.

Warrian, Peter. *The Importance of Steel Manufacturing to Canada: A Research Study.* Toronto: Munk School of Global Affairs, 2010.

Watkins, Mel. "Staples Redux." *Studies in Political Economy* 79 (Spring 2007): 213–26.

– "The Staple Theory Revisited." *Journal of Canadian Studies* 12 (1977): 83–95.

Webb, Tom. "The Dosco Crisis: Some Political Aspects of a Regional Economic Problem." Master's thesis, Carleton University, 1972.

Webster, Frank. *Theories of the Information Society.* 4th ed. New York: Routledge, 2014.

Weir, Gail. "The Wabana Ore Miners of Bell Island, Conception Bay, Newfoundland: Their Occupational Folklife and Oral Folk History." Master's thesis, Memorial University of Newfoundland, 1986.

Wells, Don. "The Impact of the Postwar Compromise on Canadian Unionism: The Formation of an Auto Worker Local in the 1950s." *Labour/Le Travail* 36 (Fall 1995): 147–73.

Wellstead, Adam. "The (Post) Staples Economy and the (Post) Staples State in Historical Perspective." *Canadian Political Science Review* 1, 1 (2007): 8–25.

Wicken, William C. *The Colonization of Mi'kmaw Memory and History, 1794–1928: The King v. Gabriel Syliboy.* Toronto: University of Toronto Press, 2012.

Williams, Bryan C. "Collective Bargaining and Wage Equalization in
    Canada's Iron and Steel Industry." *Relations industrielles/Industrial Relations*
    26, 2 (1971): 308–44.
Williams, Raymond. *The Long Revolution*. London: Chatto & Windus, 1961.
– *Marxism and Literature*. Oxford: Oxford University Press, 1977.
Williams, Raymond, and Michael Orrom. *A Preface to Film*. London: Film
    Drama, 1954.
Winston, Anthony, and Belinda Leach. *Contingent Work, Disrupted Lives:
    Labour and Community in the New Rural Economy*. Toronto: University of
    Toronto Press, 2002.
Yow, Valerie Raleigh. *Recording Oral History: A Guide for the Humanities and
    Social Scientists*. 3rd ed. New York: Rowman and Littlefield, 2015.
Zembrycki, Stacey. *According to Baba: A Collaborative Oral History of Sudbury's
    Ukrainian Community*. Vancouver: University of British Columbia Press,
    2014.

Index

Italic page numbers denote a photo or map. Page numbers followed by *t* denote a table.

Printed and bound by CPI Group (UK) Ltd, Croydon, CR0 4YY

16/04/2025

14658334-0001